2 Prospectors

SOUTHWESTERN WRITERS COLLECTION SERIES

The Wittliff Collections at Texas State University
SAN MARCOS

Steven L. Davis, Editor

Johnny and Sam

1982
Mill Valley
calif.

2

Prospectors

The Letters of
Sam Shepard & Johnny Dark

EDITED BY CHAD HAMMETT

University of Texas Press ⌄⌄ Austin

The Southwestern Writers Collection Series originates from the Wittliff
Collections, a repository of literature, film, music, and southwestern and
Mexican photography established at Texas State University–San Marcos.

Requests for permission to reproduce material
from this work should be sent to:
    Permissions
    University of Texas Press
    P.O. Box 7819
    Austin, TX 78713-7819
    http://utpress.utexas.edu/index.php/rp-form

Design by Lindsay Starr

LIBRARY OF CONGRESS CATALOGING-IN-PUBLICATION DATA
Two prospectors : the letters of Sam Shepard and Johnny Dark /
edited by Chad Hammett
        pages   cm. — (Southwestern Writers Collection Series)
    "The Southwestern Writers Collection Series originates from the Wittliff
Collections, a repository of literature, film, music, and Southwestern and
Mexican photography established at Texas State University/San Marcos."
    Includes index.
    ISBN 978-0-292-76196-4
1. Shepard, Sam, 1943–   Correspondence. 2. Dark, Johnny, 1940–
Correspondence. 3. Dramatists, American—20th century—Correspon-
dence. 4. Authors, American—20th century—Correspondence. I. Ham-
mett, Chad, 1972–   editor. II. Shepard, Sam, 1943–   Correspondence.
Selections. III. Dark, Johnny, 1940–   Correspondence. Selections.
IV. Title: Letters of Sam Shepard and Johnny Dark.
    PS3569.H394Z48 2013
    812'.54—dc23 [B]   2013027664

doi:10.7560/735828

Contents

"So we have two prospectors . . ."

Sam Shepard, taped conversation
with Johnny Dark, early 1980s

Editor's Introduction

Most accounts of Sam Shepard's life tell the same story. A Beckett-inspired young man from California named Samuel Shepard Rogers IV (born November 5, 1943) heads for New York in the 1960s and remakes himself as Sam Shepard, the offbeat, off-Broadway playwright. After a three-year relocation to England in the early 1970s, Shepard returned to the States and shed his one-act rock-and-roll guise, reinventing himself, in one of the most interesting second acts in American life, as Eugene O'Neill's heir by writing masterly family dramas such as *True West* (1980) and the 1979 Pulitzer Prize winner *Buried Child*. His screen career, which began in earnest with a starring role in Terrence Malick's *Days of Heaven* (1978), went on to include appearances in more than forty films and an Academy Award nomination for his portrayal of Chuck Yeager in *The Right Stuff* (1983). His former father-in-law Johnny Dark is rarely more than a footnote in this story, usually mentioned in passing alongside a reference to Shepard's first wife, O-Lan, or in connection with his photographs for *Motel Chronicles*. Dark, though, is much more than a minor character in Shepard's biography. He has been the playwright's confidant and sounding board for both his writing and his personal life. Dark is the closest thing Shepard has to a brother, and the correspondence that covers much of their forty-five-year relationship may be the deepest personal look we will get into Shepard's world, since he has said in a number of interviews that he has no interest in writing a memoir. But this book is more than a behind-the-scenes look into an icon's personal reflections; it is also a tale of friendship, masculinity, addiction, and fidelity, as both men try to overcome their personal shortcomings and feelings of rootlessness.

While Shepard's rise has been told many times before, Johnny Dark's story is noteworthy in its own right. Born on December 29, 1940, Dark was, as he states in a letter, "bought (adopted) in 1942 at about a year old for $6000 the way you buy a puppy." He grew up in Jersey City with the Dark family, and he was expected to take over his father's plastics business. The teenage Johnny, though, like so many of his generation, came across a copy of Jack Kerouac's *On the Road* and in 1958 went off to wander—the Eastern Seaboard, Tangiers, Spain. While back in New York in 1967, he met Scarlett Johnson, the mother of two daughters, Kristy and O-Lan, who was named for a character in Pearl Buck's *The Good Earth*.

Shepard and Dark met in 1967, on Second Avenue and 11th Street in New York. According to Dark, he had seen a play of Shepard's the night before (most likely *Forensic and the Navigators*), and he approached the twenty-four-year-old playwright to ask him just what drug he had been on while writing the play. They chatted for a few minutes, and Dark asked Shepard up for a spaghetti diner.

The following year, Dark and Scarlett moved to California, and by the time the two men met again, in 1970, Shepard had married Dark's step-daughter O-Lan, a young actress, and the two had started a family (Jesse Mojo Shepard was born in 1970). Dark, meanwhile, continued his life of odd jobs (dogcatcher, postal carrier, masseuse, housecleaner, as well as stints in libraries, kennels, and delis), while writing, recording, and archiving his life and the lives of those closest to him. His one published book to date is a set of personal photographs and reminiscences from the photographer Bruce Weber's Little Bear Press, called *People I May Know*.

In the late sixties, after Shepard's experience as a screenwriter on Michelangelo Antonioni's *Zabriskie Point*, he toured as the drummer for the psychedelic folk band the Holy Modal Rounders, and in a conversation that Johnny taped years later, Shepard listed 1968 as "the tail end of the worst time in my life," though "everything started to look up" when he began seeing O-Lan. They married in November 1969, and Jesse arrived in May 1970. After briefly leaving O-Lan (and Jesse) in 1971 to move in with the artist (but not yet) singer Patti Smith at the Chelsea Hotel, Shepard took his family to England for a three-year stay that lasted until 1974. His correspondence with Dark began in 1972, during this period.

One of the initial subjects of the letters, and one revisited through the years, was the participation by both men in "The Work," group meetings based on the teachings of George Ivanovich Gurdjieff. Born in Armenia, Gurdjieff (1866–1949) was a spiritual teacher whose "Fourth Way" (fourth in that it followed the ways of the fakir, the monk, and the yogi) stressed that people's natural state is one of waking sleep, though they can "wake up" through a series of exercises, retreats, dances, and meditations, which are rarely talked about with those not "in The Work." The shared experiences in this group are an important part of the friendship and correspondence between the two men, and as a consequence, many Gurdjieffian Work references and the names of influential group leaders such as Lord Pentland and Basil Tilley pop up throughout the correspondence.

Shepard writes that his involvement in the group was as the "'bad boy' trying to shape up to [his] imagination of the 'Conscious Ones'—the real adults." Dark's reason was more tongue-in-cheek. He joined the work "to be even more wonderful than [he] already thought he was." Neither man found the acolyte's easy truth via Gurdjieff.

In the summer of 1973, the Shepard and Dark families vacationed together at a place Shepard bought in Nova Scotia, and as his letters from England indicate, Shepard hatched a plan for both families to live together in California and "divide the house up evenly between the Darks and Sheps" upon

In August 1973 after a week of driving Scarlett, Kristy, Nana and I arrived in Cumberland Co. (west Advocate) Nova Scotia. Sams new house

his return from England in 1974. Initially, the families rented a Northern California horse ranch called the Flying Y; after the lease was up, in November 1977, they purchased a house on Evergreen Avenue in Mill Valley, where they lived until Shepard left on St. Patrick's Day 1983 to be with the actress Jessica Lange, his co-star in *Frances*. There are few letters from their time as housemates (and most of them were written to and from Shepard's movie sets), but it was in those years that the two men strengthened their friendship (and some of their housemate antics are referred to in subsequent letters). At the tail end of their time together, Dark began to tape some of their conversations, including their attempt to cowrite a play about two pickax-carrying prospectors in red long johns. Though they haven't lived together since 1983, their correspondence has lasted to the present day.

Dark's ties to Shepard need to be explored in order to show the necessity of including so much of his side of the correspondence. In *Rolling Thunder Logbook*, Shepard's account of Bob Dylan's Rolling Thunder Revue in 1975, he introduced the world to his friend and father-in-law on the book's first page, which describes the day he received the call to join Dylan's tour as screenwriter for a proposed film: "Johnny Dark is behind the wheel. The white Chevy Nova is rolling down through San Anselmo, lazy spoiled brat of a California town." Dark has twice interviewed his friend for publication, first in "The 'True West' Interviews" in 1981 for the journal *West Coast Plays* and next in "A Conversation with Sam Shepard about a Very Corny Subject" for *San Francisco* magazine in 1983.

Shepard's *Cruising Paradise* is dedicated to Dark (and to Shepard's son Jesse and their three-person Garcia y Vega club—named after the cigars the two men smoked in the Mill Valley house). One story, "Thin Skin," features a character named J.D. in the midst of a messy breakup that mirrors Dark's relationship with one of his many girlfriends. Elements of this story were recast as the play *Simpatico*. In early drafts of the play, Vinnie, like Dark, once worked in a kennel, and some elements of the play (like Vinnie's pretending to be a detective) echo "Thin Skin." Similarly, the dialogue "The Hero Is in His Kitchen" has a Shepard stand-in named Clayton call the character John from a pay phone after a bad spell with his wife. In a telephone conversation taped by Dark in March 1995, Shepard introduces a reading of this work to his friend by saying, "You'll recognize this."

Shepard's *Day Out of Days* (2010) recounts a trip he took with Dark and their friend the actor Dennis Ludlow, in the four "Highway 152" sections of the book, a trip the two men discuss in the letters. In addition, other stories told in the correspondence find their way into the book, including "India-napolis" (about meeting a former lover forty years after parting) and "Land of the Living" (which recounts a man's heart attack onboard an airplane at thirty thousand feet). The first drafts of many of Shepard's true-to-life stories were vetted initially in a letter to Dark.

It is certainly possible to argue as well for Dark's imprint on what is perhaps the most famous of Shepard's plays. *True West* is a play about broth-ers, and Dark, as both men mention often in the letters, is the nearest thing Shepard has to one. Shepard even goes so far as to sign off a letter to Johnny (using Bob Dylan lyrics) as the "brother you never had." Though Johnny states in one of his letters that Shepard has a tendency to write with the "trademark two sides of [him]self talking to each other," these two "broth-ers," Dark and Shepard, happened to be sharing living quarters when *True West* was written and staged.

Dark's effect on Shepard's work goes beyond serving occasionally as a model for various characters. In a letter of 2008, Shepard makes the claim that while working on *Day Out of Days*, he "went through [his] entire book & changed everything [he]'d written in verse-style back to prose-style," because of a comment by Johnny that he preferred Shepard's "lines un-broken."

And yet the greatest value of Dark's letters may be their insight into Shepard. Only the closest of friends could make comments as Dark does in his letters, for example: "Sam's suffering has always come from trying to be authentic. That's what it seems to me he's always been striving for—authen-tic cowboy, authentic lord of the manor, authentic sportsman etc. and yet always feeling like an impostor, surrounding himself with 'the real ones' but never being able to climb inside their skin. He himself is 'a real one' but he doesn't realize which one that is." In addition, Dark contextualizes his analy-sis. His reference to a letter describing Shepard's move with Jessica Lange to Santa Fe comes with an appropriate literary allusion. Shepard's journey becomes "the further adventures of Huck Finn as written to his friend Tom, in which Huck goes to the American Southwest and begins to get along with himself." Where the private Shepard isn't forthcoming, Dark fills in the gaps.

Volumes of collected correspondence are used primarily for scholarly refer-ence and are rarely read straight through. But since I like stories, my hope is that readers of this volume will discover that the letters have been edited to read like a narrative, even with the gaps that necessarily exist in a forty-year correspondence.

I started with the thousand pages of the complete existing letters between Shepard and Dark (as well as their almost forty hours of taped conversations), and as I pruned the correspondence into book shape, I kept the narrative concept in the foreground, eliminating letters that didn't tease out the compelling story revealed by this correspondence. As well, I cut letters that simply report uninteresting details about train schedules and missed telephone calls. A large number of the letters are from the last ten years, so I kept as many of the early ones as possible. Whenever I made a letter more concise or removed sensitive or extraneous material at the request of the two principals, I indicated that fact with brackets. I used whole letters wherever possible and noted whether letters were typed or handwritten (or both). Though the letters and conversations were edited at times for clarity and consistency, the personalities and spontaneity of the authors have been preserved. When exact dates were not available, I made educated guesses.

Where books or films are mentioned, I added italics and made sure to include any references to Shepard's theater, prose, and film work. Many of these are listed in footnotes (the numbering starts over with each new letter).

As I worked, I realized that it took a great deal of bravery on the part of both men to expose so much of their selves to others. The title for their unfinished cowritten play seemed an apt one for this book also, because in digging through their life choices, shared histories, and file cabinets to produce these documents for sale and publication, they, as Dark states in a letter detailing the process of collecting materials for this book, "in fact HAVE become The Two Prospectors."

Chad Hammett
San Marcos, Texas

Acknowledgments

I have told both Sam and Johnny how grateful I am for their courage in offering their lives up to the reader with such depth and forthrightness. Both men have been instrumental throughout this process, offering advice and kind words as well as notes since the start of this project. I can only hope this work qualifies me for honorary membership in the Lisa Vale Fan Club.

Putting together this book would not have been possible without the constant and careful assistance I received from the founders, archivists, and staff of the Wittliff Collections, housed at Texas State University–San Marcos. Bill and Sally Wittliff, Steve Davis, and Katie Salzmann in particular have my deepest gratitude.

Special thanks goes to my wife, Erica, and my mother, Barbara Hammett. Each knows how much she has helped.

Sam + Johnny.
Nova Scotia
1973

2 Prospectors

Characters

Sam Shepard   BORN NOVEMBER 5, 1943
Renowned playwright and actor

Johnny Dark   BORN DECEMBER 29, 1940
Sam's longtime friend and former housemate

Scarlett (Johnson) Dark   BORN AUGUST 13, 1933; DIED 2010
Johnny's wife (1972–2010), Sam's mother-in-law

O-Lan (Johnson)   BORN MAY 23, 1950
(Shepard) Jones   Actress and composer, Sam's wife (1969–1984),
Johnny's stepdaughter

Jessica Lange   BORN APRIL 20, 1949
Award-winning actress, Long-term relationship
with Sam (1983–   )

Jesse Mojo Shepard   BORN 1970
Sam and O-Lan's son

Hannah Shepard   BORN 1986
Sam's daughter with Jessica Lange

Walker Shepard	BORN 1987 Sam's son with Jessica Lange
Kristy Johnson	BORN 1960 O-Lan's younger sister
Aleksandra (Shura) Baryshnikov	BORN 1981 Lange's daughter with the dancer Mikhail Baryshnikov
Dennis Ludlow	Friend of Sam and Johnny
G. I. Gurdjieff	BORN 1866; DIED 1949 Armenian-born spiritual teacher
Lord Pentland (Henry Sinclair, 2nd Baron Pentland)	BORN 1907; DIED 1984 Gurdjieff Foundation president (1953–1984)
Basil Tilley	Gurdjieff group leader

Cunard RMS Queen Elizabeth 2

Well we've just come back fr
our first re-introduction to "T
W O R K" & I'm feeling m
as a snake. It just caught me
the wrong end of a scale or som
I gotta admit that I, for th
moment, really hate the move
Maybe that's too strong but =
don't dig them a lot. That's
better. First off we had to
into Charing Cross & buy so
dumb ballet shoes at some
fruity ballet store. Then we
to move like little wooden sol
all in lines to some morbid pi
music all in the same rhyth

October 19, 1972—London

[HANDWRITTEN ON RMS *QUEEN ELIZABETH 2* STATIONERY]

Well, we've just come back from our first re-introduction to "the work" &
I'm feeling mean as a snake. It just caught me on the wrong end of a scale or
something.[1] I gotta admit that I, for the moment, really hate the movements.[2]
Maybe that's too strong but I *don't* dig them a lot. That's better. First off we
had to go into Charing Cross & buy some dumb ballet shoes at some fruity
ballet store. Then we had to move like little wooden soldiers all in lines to
some morbid piano music all in the same rhythm being dictated by some fat
little tank of a woman in a long black dress who fancies herself as the rein-
carnation of George Ivanovitch himself. Then we get snubbed by all these
stoney faced English twerps who're all taking themselves so seriously it's
hard to imagine how they get out of bed in the morning. Next, we find out
we gotta go out to Bray on the very day that they're running the Anglo-Irish
challenge cup at White City—the four fastest greyhounds on the planet and
I gotta miss it! Still there's something that keeps me hanging onto all this like
a drowning man. I know that without it I got no chance for anything in life.
Maybe I should become a Catholic like Kathryn Hulme or a fuckup like Cassady.[3] What are the alternatives. Life or Death. Thank you very much. And
now the football scores! I'll try to keep from "wiseacreing" throughout this &
give you the straight lowdown.

It was great to see Mr. Tilley again & he seemed glad to see us, which is
always a relief.[4] There's always that nagging doubt in the back of my mind
that we're going to get scratched from the card for being too crass or something. Lo brought up her favorite question about the position of women in
the WORK again to my chagrin.[5] Mr. Tilley asked us about San Francisco

---

1. "The Work" is a name for the teachings of George Ivanovich Gurdjieff, founder of the Fourth Way; see the editor's introduction.
2. "Movements" is the term used by Gurd-jieffians for a group of sacred dances.
3. Hulme was a Gurdjieff student who wrote the novel *The Nun's Story* (1956); Neil Cassady was immortalized as Dean Moriarty in Kerouac's *On the Road*.
4. Basil Tilley was an influential leader of The Work.
5. O-Lan Shepard, née Johnson, Shepard's wife from November 1969 until their divorce in July 1984; sometimes called "Lo" or "Lonny."

The Shepard's first
visit from England in 1970
FAIRFAX Calif

That was an exciting family event
They arrived by train from New
York + we met them at the
station in San Francisco, Sam
was carrying their new son on his
back.

& our trip to which I drew an almost total blank. Pictures flashed across my head of my Dad, Wyoming, Fairfax, John, Scarlett, Kristy, Nana and I wound up saying something vague about time (in the abstract of course).[6] The air in the room was charged with that same mystery that was there before. Me and Lo went through the same nervous pre-meeting shakes—looking around for a place to have tea because we were too early. The funny feeling of being alone together without Jesse (at home with the Nanny).[7] Looking at every clock in every shop to make sure we're not late. Ordering a cup of tea, taking one sip, paying the bill & rushing to the meeting. Bang! There's Mr. Tilley with his face & his eyes & his moustache & we're back home safe. I forgot sometimes how far I drift from our purpose. Completely gone to another world. If only I could keep something from these experiences. I guess just to *be* there is enough of a task for right now. Mr. Tilley said that man always faces in two directions at once but we forget and pretend that we're one.

All our love to you all,
Sam

6. Kristy Johnson, O-Lan's younger sister. Nana was Johnny's dog.
7. Jesse Shepard, Sam and O-Lan's son, born in May 1970.

October 28, 1972—London

[HANDWRITTEN ON RMS QUEEN ELIZABETH 2 STATIONERY]

Dear John,

Just got back from Bray (7 A.M. to 7 P.M.)—your novel was waiting for me.[1] Another boost in the arm. I'm reluctant to tell you all the stuff that's happened and happening because it seems now you've probably already been through it. And yet it's impossible since every day brings a different experience & England must be another world from California. Although the ideas tie everything together like a bloodstream this particular morning will stick in me somewhere for a long time to come (I hope).[2] I want to share it but there's so much in it that I can only give you pieces or it would go on forever. First off, after a series of tense conflicts in us about whether to leave Jesse alone all day with someone we hardly know, it was "decided" that I should go out to Bray by myself this first time & Lo would stay home since she's feeling a bit sick. So off I go on "the Dual Carriageway" in search of the miraculous. The morning fog is lifting off the river banks and covering the highway. White swans with long necks pushing quietly through the water. The morning's brisk & cold. I'm purring along in my little Anglia van with the heater going full blast & following this guy's directions to Bray. I arrive at this place but figure it must be a mistake because it appears to be an abandoned chicken farm from the outside and there's not a car in sight. So I go back down the road, make a few U turns & try to re-trace the directions. I arrive back at the same "chicken farm" except this time all these cars start pulling in & I recognize a couple people from the group. I'm escorted in by this friend from our group & the whole thing becomes quite amazing. Hot cups of boiling black coffee with hot milk. Everyone's standing around a strangely shaped stove. People coming in from the cold. Patches of conversation. New faces but no Mr. Tilley. Three other teachers I'd never seen before but each one with some special twinkle in the eyes & litheness of body. A society of people striving toward the same aim. An easy silence falls on everyone for a while then like a bolt of lightning the action begins. Everyone knows exactly where

1. Unpublished novel; all of Johnny's letters to England have been lost.
2. According to Shepard, "the ideas" is a term for Gurdjieff's work.

to go and what to do. I follow Xavier (this friend) around all day helping him build cabinets. Managing to create double the work for him. Everything in me is in turmoil, irritated, exhausted, the whole bit. Lunch is food for the belly, head & whatever else you need. Words from a book I'd never heard of on silence. Back into the work with new inspiration soon to turn into more of the same swimming emotions and dreams. I came close to so many things but they seemed to slip away just as I almost grabbed them. The day is over in a flash. Night falls completely black. Everyone vanishes & I'm left there. Hanging around. Not wanting to leave yet having nothing more to do with what happened. Now I'm back & trying hard not to tell Lonny any of these strong impressions so as not to spoil it for her first time out there. One thing I'll never forget was the way I was shown how to use a saw. The most delicate strength I've ever seen in a man. Listening to the sound the saw made. I can remember watching my Dad saw wood with about a dozen curses for each stroke. Much the same way I've done it up 'til now. I'll never be able to saw wood the same again. (No double entendre intended).

Thanks for the long letter. I'll be reading it over again *before* the night's thru. Your letters are always well cherished by us [. . .]

December 15, 1972—London

[TYPED]

Dear John,

This morning our Christmas puppy arrived from Northern Wales in a box with straw. We've been telling Jesse about him coming for days. He's a baby black and white Border Collie. The kind that work sheep by hand signals and whistles. Very smart little dogs. His name's Banjo. We'll send you a picture of him and the Kid. It's like one of those Norman Rockwell paintings looking at them play in the back yard.

Last night we went to our last meeting with Mr. Tilley before the Christmas holidays. It was one of those times that'll last for a long while. First we had the meeting then we went to movements and later we came back to Mr. Tilley's for a Christmas drink. I gave him a big bottle of Cognac then we went downstairs to the room where we always have the meetings except, within the time we'd been to the movements it had been transformed into this black cave with orange Xmas trees decorating the walls. Lots of people crammed into a tiny space with cigarette smoke, drinks, nuts, crackers and cookies being passed around. Mr. and Mrs. Tilley moving through the maze acting as host and hostess in a powerful active-passive way. I felt very uncomfortable and crowded. Nowhere for a breath of fresh air. Then suddenly we were all swept upstairs to the living room. As each one of us entered the room Mr. Tilley told us individually whether to sit on the floor or sit in a chair. The living room was filled with us sitting in a half moon shape with Mr. and Mrs. Tilley sitting at the front of us. His home is hard to describe but you get the feeling of incredible warmth and paternal love. On the walls are tiny sparkling Christmas lights with dozens of Christmas cards from all over the world. A big white fireplace with potted plants around it. On the mantle is a gold fish with tiny red jewels, a ceramic donkey with a man seated on its back facing the tail end. Mr. Tilley began to read a Christmas story about a tiny brown mouse who lived in a mouse hole in the kitchen of somebody's house. The story was written from the mouse's point of view. How the smells drifted into his mouse hole at just the right angle to the way he was sitting. The sounds of the people living in the house. The cat. The

That summer Scarlet and
I were married. (1972-Sept 18)
At the Civic Center in
San Raphael CA.

Christmas tree in the corner with the golden angel on top. Three chocolate mice sitting in the branches. I won't tell you the plot in case you haven't heard it before. Then Mr. Tilley told about Mr. Gurdjieff and about what Christmas was like with him. He read from *Undiscovered Country* (I think) about Christmas with Gurdjieff.[1] I felt like a little kid through all this. At last I'd found a father. I felt protected and sheltered from the world outside, as though nothing in the world mattered but this experience, this huge family with Mr. Tilley at the head. And behind him, in the shadows I could almost feel Mr. Gurdjieff smiling on us from above. Then he stopped reading and smiled on us all. In a way I've never seen anyone smile. There was a kind of never-ending silent love that he sent out to all of us. It seemed to last forever. Then he said: "Well, my friends, have a happy Christmas." I clutched the paper wrapper from the Cyprus candy that he'd handed out to us and stuffed it into my pocket. I hope some day when I look at that wrapper with the exotic writings on it that it'll somehow remind me of being there with Mr. Tilley. Then we all filed out of the house, each one stopping in front of Mr. Tilley to wish him Merry Christmas. When we got out into the cold air and the pitch black night, O-Lan was crying. We drove back through the streets of a foreign city that seemed like it could be a civilization from another planet. Everything outside, the traffic, the shoppers, the buildings, the lights seemed like a tiny meaningless event that was doomed to repeating itself over and over. Now it almost seems miraculous that we find ourselves under this kind of an influence. There's no way of thanking you for putting us in touch with this man but somehow I feel we're all very lucky to be in the world together at the same time. Merry Christmas!!

Love to all the Darks from all the Sheps

1. *Undiscovered Country: In Search of Gurdjieff* (1967) by Kathryn Hulme.

meanwhile ... Sam and Jesse in
London England
around 1973

January 20, 1973—London

[TYPED]

Dear John,

Got your letter with the Godfather routine. The Dark against The Hippie Mafia. My heart started pounding as I read it, remembering similar situations where I've felt myself to be deeply wronged by somebody or other, having my violence take over, making threats, the challenge, the face off and then it's all over. Fantastic. Maybe necessary for the old blood once in a while. Sure wish I'd been there with my shades, and my black cowboy hat, just lurking in the shadows ready for action. Maybe even fiddling with a bike chain for extra effect. We could've done some nifty strong arm tactics like cruising their places of business very slowly in the white Chevy.[1] Parking right in front of their office and reading newspapers, every once in a while peeking out from behind, chewing gum slowly and then cruising off down the street. Real terror stuff. Yeah boy! Stink bombs through the window. The whole bit. Maybe even practiced some knife throwing on a nearby tree. Painting black swastikas on their car. We could've had some real fun.

Meanwhile, here in boring london we're freezing our ass off. Along with the central heating we got a paraffin heater, an electric heater and we're all wearing sweaters around the house. Last night, it snowed lightly. This morning it rained. Forecast for tomorrow: Light rain with heavy snow turning to fog with a slight slush and freezing frost with occasional bright patches. It's like that every day. It's only dog racing and consciousness (the promise of) that keeps me here. Sorry to hear yr having so much money problems. The idea of you having to hock yr pretty car really pisses me off somehow. It seems unfair. Money's not exactly raining on us either. I just sold a play to the BBC which should keep us going for a month or so.[2] How we're all gonna get together for the summer is still a mystery. Right now we really can't afford any marathon trips either. Lately we've been thinking of Spain as a possibility. Ireland seems a bit too damp. I'm really yearning for the sun about now. Things will probably change a dozen times before the summer arrives. We're all in good spirits though. Meetings with Mr. T.

1. Johnny's 1971 Chevy Nova.
2. The play was *Blue Bitch* (1973).

have started up again and it's like joining the human race again after being in zombie land for the past few weeks. the birthday party was something really extraordinary and seemed like the strongest dose of medicine I've had so far.[3] We arrived at Bray which is way out in the English countryside on a particularly cold and drizzly night. We're ushered into a room where we all have hot mulled wine to warm us up. After that, we go to a bazaar where all these people are dressed up like Arabs in robes, sandals, turbans etc. It's quite a shock. Like walking into the middle of an unexpected Off Off Broadway play. The people are gathered in different small groups involved in various activities like: weaving, book binding, printing, wood carving, pottery making, steel foundry, and each group is trying to sell their wares for the most they can get. At first it seems ridiculous, all these proper English people trying to act like soulful Asians, but then it turns into just good spirited fun almost in the memory of one who did all this for real in real life. Me and Lo buy a couple of interesting prints, one of a fisherman and the other of a Dervish prayer. Also a tea pot which was intended for coffee. Later we move into the dining hall and find our table which is designated by a color. The food is nothing special. Served on paper plates with wine and afterwards we get a small glass of Armagnac which burns like a fire. Then Mr. Tilley's voice comes over the speakers. There's so many people that the tables have to be arranged in a huge "L" shape with Mr. G.'s picture at the apex of the "L." Looking down the long table at the picture it seems to shimmer in the heat from all the candles. It's a picture I've never seen before. Gurdjieff sitting at a table with a tall fez hat staring at a bottle of wine. I think to myself it must be a café in Paris. Mr. Tilley announces that he just received a phone call from Madame de Hartmann saying that she was "concerned about us all" and that she had good wishes for us.[4] Later he announces that he's going to read some words from Mr. G. which will be followed by some of his music to close the evening. The words begin. They are from the last book which I've never seen. They concern the death of Orage and the phony attitudes which people wish on the living at the death of someone who they never even knew.[5] How in the old days people would gather together after the death of someone close to them and expound all the negative sides of the dead man's character. All the wasted events of his life. They would use the death to remind each of

3. Gurdjieff's birthday is January 13.
4. Shepard's note: teacher from Paris whose husband, Thomas de Hartmann, composed music for Gurdjieff.
5. A. R. Orage, a student and translator of Gurdjieff.

them of their own impending death and then drink and eat for a few days. There was much more to the words which I can't put together right now but they're recorded somewhere on my tape. Then the music began. It was like a tidal wave taking me over. My heart started beating like a chicken being led to the slaughter. I felt just like I used to when approaching a girl's door for a date in High School. There was nothing I could do but sit there and take it as it came. A flood of terror and ecstasy all at once. I didn't know whether to run or come inside myself. Then suddenly I heard some loud weeping and a girl burst out of the room slamming the door behind her. I looked up and the whole thing seemed to me like some bizarre magical sacrifice. The black table cloth, the people staring silently into themselves, the incredible music that brought some longtime sadness to me. Like everything we do in life is so pathetic and trivial in the face of this man who's handed us this gift like a big chunk of his own flesh. Then it was over. We drove back with something quite different than we brought with us.

Love from us all,
Sam

Dear John,

I'm getting really tired of writing these fuc
letters all the time. I want some real live flesh
blood stuff. You know, us in the white Chevy crui
around, looking like detectives and talkin philoso
Suddenly having a moment of thinking we're REALLY
IN THE FROZEN FOOD DEPARTMENT and then some creamy
floats by making sure not to look like she's on th
Ah yes, yer so right, food for fantasy. Let me ex
the depth of my dreaming lately. : We go through
the pros and cons of buying a house together and w
finally settle for this nifty little ranch somewhe
the outskirts of one of those suburbs. Not too fa
from all the newstands and supermarkets yet just f
enough so that we have a couple acres or so. We
divide the house up evenly between Darks and Sheps
sort of float back and forth but each of us has ou
own special room where we can get obsessive and is
if we have the inclination. Out in back through h
plate glass windows with the golden sunshine glari
in we get a view of a neat little corral. An Appa
mare with foal is peacefully nibbling on some fres
alfalfa and whisking away a blue bottle fly with h
tail. Off to the left is a long green paddock ful
about six varieties of purebred hounds with puppie
nipping at their heels. Scarlet and Lo and Kristy
fighting over a jigsaw puzzle on the huge kitchen
table. Jesse's trying to hold down a G chord on h
guitar. You're taking pictures of yourself as you
type and smoke a cigar. I'm waiting for you to st

January 25, 1974—London

[TYPED]

Dear John,

    I'm getting really tired of writing these fucking letters all the time. I want some real live flesh and blood stuff. You know, us in the white Chevy cruising around, looking like detectives and talkin philosophical. Suddenly having a moment of thinking we're REALLY HERE IN THE FROZEN FOOD DEPARTMENT and then some creamy chick floats by making sure not to look like she's on the make. Ah yes, yer so right, food for fantasy. Let me explain the depths of my dreaming lately: We go through all the pros and cons of buying a house together and we finally settle for this nifty little ranch somewhere on the out-skirts of one of those suburbs. Not too far from all the newsstands and super-markets yet just far enough so that we have a couple acres or so. We divide the house up evenly between Darks and Sheps and sort of float back and forth but each of us has our own special room where we can get obsessive and isolated if we have the inclination. Out in back through huge plate glass windows with the golden sunshine glaring in we get a view of a neat little cor-ral. An Appaloosa mare with foal is peacefully nibbling on some fresh alfalfa and whisking away a blue bottle fly with her tail. Off to the left is a long green paddock full of about six varieties of purebred hounds with puppies nipping at their heels. Scarlett and Lo and Kristy are fighting over a jigsaw puzzle on the huge kitchen table. Jesse's trying to hold down a G chord on his guitar. You're taking pictures of yourself as you type and smoke a cigar. I'm wait-ing for you to stop fucking around so we can go down to Lucky's in my new customized Hudson Hornet. Yessir, we're on our way boy!

S.S.

January 25, 1974—London

[TYPED]

Dear John,

    I'm getting really tired of writing these fucking letters all the time. I want some real live flesh and blood stuff. You know, us in the white Chevy cruising around, looking like detectives and talkin philosophical. Suddenly having a moment of thinking we're REALLY HERE IN THE FROZEN FOOD DEPARTMENT and then some creamy chick floats by making sure not to look like she's on the make. Ah yes, yer so right, food for fantasy. Let me explain the depths of my dreaming lately: We go through all the pros and cons of buying a house together and we finally settle for this nifty little ranch somewhere on the out-skirts of one of those suburbs. Not too far from all the newsstands and super-markets yet just far enough so that we have a couple acres or so. We divide the house up evenly between Darks and Sheps and sort of float back and forth but each of us has our own special room where we can get obsessive and isolated if we have the inclination. Out in back through huge plate glass windows with the golden sunshine glaring in we get a view of a neat little cor-ral. An Appaloosa mare with foal is peacefully nibbling on some fresh alfalfa and whisking away a blue bottle fly with her tail. Off to the left is a long green paddock full of about six varieties of purebred hounds with puppies nipping at their heels. Scarlett and Lo and Kristy are fighting over a jigsaw puzzle on the huge kitchen table. Jesse's trying to hold down a G chord on his guitar. You're taking pictures of yourself as you type and smoke a cigar. I'm wait-ing for you to stop fucking around so we can go down to Lucky's in my new customized Hudson Hornet. Yessir, we're on our way boy!

S.S.

The family on the side porch.
meanwhile a big pot of
somthen' was bubbling on the
kitchen stove and the whole
house smelled of dinner.

BeFORe PAINting

and in the midst of
repairing the roof and
windows. 1975.
Ranch house where
Johnny + Sam + Family
all lived. mill
Valley Calif.

In 1974, after three years in London, Sam, O-Lan, and Jesse returned to the United States, moving in with the Darks (Johnny, Scarlett, and Kristy) in Marin County, California. Later, as Sam predicted in his letter, the two families rented a horse ranch in Mill Valley, California (the Flying Y). After the lease was up, both families moved to a house on Evergreen Avenue in Mill Valley. Between 1974 and 1983, the two men exchanged few letters, though some of their conversations (especially in the early 1980s) were taped by Dark.

The Shepard/Dark house!

In November 1977 we moved off the RANCh and down the mountain to where SAM hAD bought a house on EVERGREEN Ave. in mill VAlley. CA.

33 EVERGREEN AVE

Sam — Nova Scotia   1973

Sam and I went out shooting' bottles
around the barn in the afternoon

" I'm finished with all
your silly foolishness"

John and Sam

<u>Mill Valley</u> CA.

1974

Sam
1975
Mell Valley
Calif

After touring with Bob Dylan's
Rolling Thunder Revue in the fall
of 1975 as screenwriter for the film
that became *Reynaldo and Clara* (1978)
and chronicling the experience in
Rolling Thunder Logbook (1977),
Shepard was approached by Terrence
Malick (director of the critically
acclaimed *Badlands* [1973]) to star
alongside Brooke Adams and Richard
Gere in Malick's next feature, *Days
of Heaven*. Often, Shepard would
send letters while on location;
where possible, the film has been
identified.

Sam

1976

Mill Valle
Calf

October 22, 1976—Alberta, Canada

[HANDWRITTEN]

Dear Scarlett,

Thanks for all the super-efforts with the eggs for Pinto & the foxtail in the toe etc.[1] I really do appreciate it a lot.

Today I was perusing *Newsweek* Magazine during part of my 'off hours' & came across a big review of Peter Brook's new theatre piece entitled *The Ik*.[2] It's based (ironically enough) on that charming book that Dan was raving about one day at the house.[3] You remember? The starving people in Africa & shoving each other into the fire so there'll be fewer to eat the food? Anyway, it's surprising how fast your opinions can change about something depending on the person involved. As soon as I saw Brook's name attached to the material I thought "maybe there's something to this after all." When Dan talked about it I was inwardly putting him down for some reason. It seems that Peter is opening this piece in N.Y. then touring with it to colleges across the country & finally winding up in Berkeley. We ought to try & get some tickets at the University when I get back & all go to see it. Might be an 'inneresting experience.'

Right now there's a thick blanket of snow covering everything outside. It snowed most of the day & is getting very cold up here. I just can't believe I'm still doing this thing. Evidently this is an unusually long time on location. The old hands working on the film say that the average schedule for a picture is 6 to 8 weeks—we're going into the 11th week now! Terry (the director) got sick from inhaling too much smoke from the fire sequences—so we've been delayed even more. I'm still hoping to get back by my birthday though.

The roughest part of this whole experience is having so much spare time. It's not like having unscheduled time when you're home because here you're

1. Shepard's note about Pinto: my whippet at the time.
2. Brook is the Tony Award–winning founder of the International Centre for Theater Research and the director of such films as *Lord of the Flies* (1963) and *Meetings with Remarkable Men* (1979), based on a work by Gurdjieff. Shepard met Brook in London.
3. The book is Colin Turnbull's *The Mountain People* (1972); Dan is, according to a note by Shepard, a friend of Dark's.

really in limbo. Sitting in a trailer on the high plains of Canada day after day starts to do things to you. I go through orgies of reading then writing then back to reading then I think "maybe I'll take a walk"—but you walk out and there's nothing there. Just plains as far as you can see & a few crazy humans huddled around a camera yelling things at each other. Anyway, give my love to one & all & tell everyone I miss them a lot.

Love,
Sam

The ShepARDs
1977
In front of Sam's old TRUCK

C 58 856

Scarlett and John
Calef 1979

On September 29, 1979, Scarlett
suffered an aneurysm deep in her
brain's basilar artery. Her slow
recovery is mentioned often in the
following letters and described in
the final section of Shepard's *Motel
Chronicles*. The next few letters
were sent to Shepard at the Holiday
Inn in San Marcos, Texas, while he
was filming *Raggedy Man* (directed by
Jack Fisk, written by Bill Wittliff,
and starring Sissy Spacek).

California   1979

                    Jesse and Sam in
                    the livingroom —

October 1980

[TYPED]

Dear Sam:

As you know O-Lan is busy getting her play together (although by her own admission she has never been this busy) so that she is gone early each morning, returns briefly after picking Jesse up from school and then vanishes out into the not-so-wild-Calif night not to be seen again until 8:15 the next morning as she stumbles and shambles out the door on another morning assault at Jesse's school.[1] I am cleaning Mon, Wed, and Fri for a few hours and spend the rest of the day with Scarlett. I could not have imagined that we could have grown closer than we were but this past month or so our relationship seems to radiate through our skin. She is feeling well and getting about alright and going to the house with me for meetings and lectures and sittings and I am attempting to go on every other Sunday, switching off afternoons and mornings with Nancy Silver.[2] That surprising "sweetness" (almost childlike) is still with Scarlett and she still sits entranced, sometimes for hours while Jesse spins her yarns from school or great football stories. Really, there is no one who does or could sit for such a long wide-eyed time listening with delight to a little kid. Of course in the evenings we are all together . . . the three of us and I take them to the Upstart Crow . . . we are a known trio like some odd gently floating chemical compound making our way in and out among the tables and the books. Sometimes I wear my combination false eyeglasses-nose and moustache. The other night we all went in with yo-yos. But I am, as I promised, looking after him, getting him to wash and making his dinner every night.

The dogs are fine. No worry there. And I'm keeping the patio moist.

Pentland is arriving this week and this weekend is a "work-weekend" which I'm attending.[3] Jesse and Scarlett will be with O-Lan at the theatre.

---

1. In 1981, with the Overtone Theatre, O-Lan constructed the play *Superstitions* by using elements of Shepard's work that he later published as *Motel Chronicles*. She went on to appear in such films as *Edward Scissorhands* (1990) and *Natural Born Killers* (1994).

2. Silver, a member of the Gurdjieff group in San Francisco, helped watch Scarlett.

3. Lord Pentland (born Henry John Sinclair) was a pupil of P. D. Ouspensky (Gurdjieff's first major interpreter) and Gurdjieff himself, as well as president of Gurdjieff Foundation from 1953 until his death in 1984. Pentland was an important figure to Shepard and Dark; Shepard attended Pentland's funeral.

Scarlett and her two daughters
in the kitchen   1979
Calif

My relationship to the ideas, my "work" has remained in the same vein, in that way which Krishnamurti speaks when he says "The understanding of oneself is not a result, a culmination; it is seeing oneself from moment to moment in the mirror of relationship."[4] Of course, I am finding this very difficult. It is possible to be interested in almost everything else. Outside the house I find I take this as natural and come to allow it, to sanction it until I no longer even care about the effort needed. But at the house this turning outward is much more noticeable and seems out of place. The "values" which St. Elmo stand for are different or seem to me to be different values from the values of the world, from my life.[5] Of course the dangers at The House are everywhere too. I came across a line in the Needleman book which describes it beautifully . . . "The overwhelming problem is one of attachment to the teaching itself; the 'love' of one's own religion, spiritual egoism—"[6] For me . . . it is all a question because it is an unknown, that is *I* am unknown from moment to moment to myself. Not that there is not "reaction," but that reaction can be experienced. Not that there is no discontent but that discontent can set one aflame. [. . .]

This is from Scarlett who is next to me in the bedroom. "Hello. More than hello."

Johnny Dark

4. The quotation is from *The First and Last Freedom* (1954).
5. St. Elmo was the name of the house (on St. Elmo Way in San Francisco) where the Gurdjieff Foundation of California was located.
6. Jacob Needleman's *Lost Christianity* (1980).

8 AM I'm sitting in your big leath
chair in your room downstair
listening to someone (Jesse
probably) clumping back a
forth over the Kitchen. I'm
escaping the morning diologe
which this morning centers
around whether Jesse can take
the bus back from school sin
O Lan's car is in the shop to
getting a new clutch. When i
sounded as though things wer
going to get noisey, I came dou
here. This is the first time
I've sat down here since y
left. It's very quiet and
comfortable but at the same
time inveigles me to separate
myself too much from the
rest of the house.
     There are three birds

October 30, 1980

[HANDWRITTEN]

Sam

8 AM I'm sitting in your big leather chair in your room downstairs listening to someone (Jesse probably) clumping back and forth over the kitchen. I'm escaping the morning dialogue which this morning centers around whether Jesse can take the bus back from school since O-Lan's car is in the shop today getting a new clutch. When it sounded as though things were going to get noisy, I came down here. This is the first time I've sat down here since you left. It's quiet and comfortable but at the same time inveigles me to separate myself too much from the rest of the house.

There are three birds outside the window pecking at themselves on a limb. I haven't seen Mr. Rat recently. The dogs are frolicking in the back.

Scarlett and I went to see *Resurrection* and without a doubt thought you were terrific; that you played it loose and natural and have a natural presence on the screen that's very attractive.[1] There's a slight tendency toward monotone at times—but nowhere near as much as you have in real life [. . .] I hope the film does well and that a lot of good stuff comes out of it for you after its release.

I'm spending quiet days with Scarlett, walking, talking, reading, going to the "house" etc. Even I can see how much she's improved, how well she gets around and yet her temperament remains very gentle and sweet [. . .]

Well—Happy Birthday to you [. . .]. I hope we can get together out there before long. Keep it together meanwhile.

John

---

1. *Resurrection* (1980), directed by Daniel
   Petrie and starring Ellen Burstyn and
   Shepard.

1980
Calef

Sam took us all for breakfast
to a resturant named Sam's.

November 1980

[TYPED]

It's an extraordinary New England wood fence crab apple golden leaf kind of day with the birds twittering and the sun beating down through a gentle meadow breeze. O-Lan left late tearing out of the house like Lucy in the *Peanuts* cartoon with scarves and hairpins and tiny bits of papers streaming behind her in the air to get Jesse to school and head for Santa Cruz where they're doing some more filming. She hopes to get back to S.F. in time for Movements and then go off to the theatre so I am to pick Jesse up at school and get his dinner and mail off her package to you and pick up a box of pet-meat in M.V. since we are out as of today.[1] I can see she has some feelings about asking me though she knows I will usually agree and I have eased her conscience somewhat by requesting the price of a movie in return. Aside from her conscience, I will do almost anything for the price of a movie and I enjoy going with Scarlett and Jesse. [. . .] Scarlett and Jess and me have a special "hiding" coat that we take along with us and in the scary parts we all get under the coat together and make "finger forts" until the scary parts are over. You will read more about this in Jesse's yet to be written "Memories of my Grandparents." I'll kid O-Lan about being put-upon sometimes but for the most part it gives me great satisfaction babysitting, getting good meals for Jesse and Scarlett, keeping the house clean, and all the laundry washed all of which seems a small lot in return for being the barely-working-non-paying failure of the family.

Last night we sat around the living room (O-Lan was out) listening for hours to some wonderful readings from Tom Sawyer and Huck Finn and a good deal of my associations about those books were dispelled as I began to acquire a tolerable sense of respect for Clemens, his style, his ear and his acute social-psychological observations surrounding a time (South pre-civil war) you don't generally hear much about. It was impossible to escape the recurring impression that the Sawyer-Finn books were without a doubt, in style and character the direct forebears of Kerouac and Cassidy as though this was the story of them as children growing up in the rural South over a hundred years ago. This morning I was up early, cleaned out the icebox, put

1. Mill Valley, California.

out the trash, washed all the towels, washed all Jesse's shirts and underpants (found finally under a poster in his closet) went out with Scarlett for coffee at the Upstart Crow, mailed O-Lan's package, stole a four volume set of *Peanuts* cartoons for us all to read this afternoon, went to another store and stole a two volume set of incredible Astronomy books (lots of pictures . . . one called Planets and Moons and the other The Galaxy and Quasars . . . and what staring at photos of the Milky Way does to your sense of scale and personal perspective cannot be adequately conveyed) picked up the dog meat at the M.V. market, came home and helped Scarlett down for a nap and here I am at 1:00 p.m. writing this and keeping one eye on the clock for when we have to pick Jesse up at school and other adventures.

Once again . . . you can put your mind to rest about everyone here. O-Lan, who misses you of course is obviously keeping herself furiously busy and is well. Jesse is definitely not at loose ends, looks very well, is healthy and appears very happy. He's doing well in school and afterward has his route and in the evening he is usually with us and we are fixing a big dinner well balanced but to everyone's taste or going to the movies or reading or listening to a story. Neither Scarlett nor Jesse are in any way neglected. I see to it they are frequently washed, bubbled and toweled and that their clothes are clean and that they get at least one good balanced hot meal during the day. I don't understand it but I am well equipped for the job and as I mentioned earlier it gives me satisfaction.

On the bed, Scarlett is completely encased in our afghan. She says she's hiding from a fly. She burnt her finger on a cigarette this morning and cried like a baby and I had to hold her and put cream on her finger until she felt better. She said she wasn't crying so much because it hurt (which it did a great deal) but because I wasn't in the room when she got burnt and she felt terrifyingly alone.

Lord Pentland, I think, has gone and I think I have pretty much brought you up to date on what's been going on at St. Elmo. This is the first time since I've been in the work I haven't been keeping notes and I don't think I will for a while. For one thing I don't have the same interest in it although an interest of another kind may well appear [. . .]

Well that's all for now. I will be speaking to you soon I expect.

Johnny

November 1980

[TYPED]

Dear Sam

  Scarlett's progress is such a relative thing. It's so easy to forget what she used to be like. I find myself surprisingly used to the way she is now and attuned to any slight progress in the way of walking or talking or her being able to do some small thing for herself for the first time . . . something which of course would have been an unthinkable issue when she was normal. Measured from the operation onward, she has made great progress. Compared to the way she used to be . . . She has a great long way to go. Being with her all the time day after day, I see that the psychological disabilities are not gone . . . those moments when she suddenly will begin to cry or suddenly become very afraid that someone will be coming for her to take her back to the hospital, or simply some terrible feeling of frightening helplessness at being alone

in the house even for a short while in the morning. I have had to take care of that one by leaving her in a restaurant while I go off and clean houses. It's so easy to forget on a day to day basis that this is someone who's had her head opened and her brain turned and jarred . . . not to mention the initial shock of a rupture inside the head spilling blood into the surrounding cushioning fluid. The physical difficulties are probably the first to go. As you know, the doctors speak little of the psyche. But still, there has been no anger, no irritation. The worst of that seems a year away, a year behind us.

Just now O-Lan is playing the piano and Jesse is sitting on the arm of Scarlett's chair with a postcard of Jesse James, telling her the detailed history of his murder and also, how to kill a buffalo. She's looking at him, nodding and smiling and he's talking on and on.

So, her healing process goes on. You can't stand in the way of that . . . plus she wants to get well, to be normal. It's still clear to me that a person in her situation needs as much love and affection and support and security and I can possibly give them. And it's made me see that it's something an awful lot of well people could use. People, animals, and plants thrive on it but it's so easy to slip into a kind of life of self-centered activity which we take to be natural and which makes such considerations impossible. In myself, I see a tremendous fear rise up in relation to extending myself to most other people and something closes against them for fear of being abused myself. I've been studying "listening" and I see ramifications of it there as well.

Shem

Fool for Love, 1982

s: This is the situation. There's three characters on stage. Picture this, okay? Two of the characters are in the present. One of the characters is in the past, like a memory. Okay?

J: A visual memory.

s: Yeah. He talks to one of these characters who's in the present as though it was a memory. That character hears his voice and relates to the memory but he talks to him directly. He talks to the other character only in the present and the other character doesn't know that the one in the past exists for the one he's talking to. See what I mean? And they're all present.

J: Now wait a minute. Okay, they're all present. Let me see if I got this. They're all present.

s: There's another character. An actor who—

J: I got that. I got that.

s: Okay.

J: And that actor talks to you as a memory.

s: Yeah.

J: And you talk to him as though he's in the past.

s: Right.

J: But—

s: He doesn't exist for you.

J: He doesn't talk to me at all.

s: He doesn't talk to you at all.

J: But the two characters talk.

s: Yeah. You ignore him.

J: So this character only exists for one other of the characters.

s: Right.

J: And obviously he's in that character's mind.

s: Right. It's like the old ghost thing like in *Our Town*.

J: Or *Topper*.

s: *Topper*. Yeah, right. But it's live. Live acting. [. . .] So that's the situation, right? Now . . . would you buy it if your character all of a sudden started talking to that one and came into the same relationship with that one—as this character? Or should he stay like that. You see what I mean?

J: Oh yeah.

S: What? He should stay like that?

J: Absolutely.

S: He shouldn't suddenly start talking to him? He should maintain that always.

J: From the audience point of view . . .

S: It would be clearer the other way?

J: Yeah.

S: You wouldn't buy it?

J: No. Not at all.

S: O.K. I just wanted to know.

California, September 1982

s: Well, are we going to get real creative?

J: You know it. Plus, you know what's the amazing thing is that . . . you know all those times we sat around and got stoned and thought up all those ideas—thousands of ideas we don't even remember? You remember?

s: Yeah.

J: "Boy, I got a great idea. What if we get a film or wrote a thing . . ." Well, all that stuff is not lost—it's all in those tapes. I mean, all one would have to do is listen to those tapes and you'd hear all those ideas again.

s: Yeah, but when you hear those ideas back, do you get as thrilled about them as you did when you had them? So what's the point?

J: No, but you could just hear the ideas. Like for instance, I had totally forgotten that we were . . . we thought it was a good idea to make a film of people just facing the camera—

s: Nicknames.

J: And talking about their nicknames. We thought that was the greatest idea of all time.

s: We did, didn't we? We must have been out of our minds. [. . .]

J: Oh, another thing, another conversation is you're talking about *Wild Child*—Truffaut's *Wild Child*.

s: I'm talking about that?

J: Yep, and you're saying that was great. "I saw that and Truffaut was in it." And I said what happens at the end? Does he—

s: Oh, I remember that conversation.

J: You said, "He gets him civilized. He tries to get him civilized." And then I said, "Wasn't there a whole part of you that was rooting for the wild side?"

s: The wild side? What was my reply?

J: You said, yeah. And then we started talking about—

s: Wild versus—

J: Yeah, those two things.

s: Restraint. That's a good subject. The unrestrained and the restrained—what's the opposite of restrained?

J: All of your plays have that in it. That's like one of the major characteristics.

s: That's one of my favorite themes.

J: Right. Now we didn't even mention that it was one of your favorite themes when we talked about it in *Wild Child,* but it was the same thing in a way.

s: That's one of my very favorite themes. The whole primitive thing versus the other thing.

J: I mean, every play that I've seen has that as the major—

s: Don't you find that interesting?

J: Yeah, I find that interesting but it doesn't interest me to that extent.

s: To that extent. [. . .]

J: That really interests you.

s: It's fascinating.

J: Holy mackerel.

s: I feel like that's my problem, that's my major problem. Reconciling—

J: Is that something that gets mentioned? I mean, is that obvious to every-body? People see the plays and then they write things.

s: Yeah, I guess it is.

J: It seems like it's so obvious that almost every article would start off talk-ing about it.

s: It's funny. It's funny how people miss the point.

Prospector Play, late 1982 or early 1983

s: Why don't we just start with the dialogue? I mean, we'll just agree they're in some place. Because if we get into describing where they are and all . . . that's boring.

J: Yeah, that is boring.

s: So we have two prospectors.

J: Then everything on the set has to totally pertain to prospectors. I mean people's ideas of what prospectors are.

s: Cliché prospector props.

J: Every cliché prospector thing you can think of. The burro, the pick, the hat, the sourdough bread.

s: Now wait a second. Wait. This is great. Cliché prospector props.

J: I already got it all down on this tape machine here out of the twentieth century.

s: Yeah but that's not writing. I like to write. A burro, a pick . . .

J: The guy's determined to write. Nothing will stop him.

s: A pick. What else?

J: You going to write all that . . . sourdough?

s: I'm writing a shorthand version, you know.

J: Sourdough bread.

s: Sourdough bread.

J: I don't know. A plaid shirt and suspenders. A Gabby Hayes hat.

s: Plaid shirt and suspenders. Okay.

J: The wardrobe to take care of.

s: Gabby Hayes hat. Gabby Hayes hat. Cavalry boots?

J: Right. Long red underwear.

s: Long red underwear. Underneath the plaid shirt?

J: Well, he's got the sleeves rolled up.

s: Oh, right, right. Long red underwear. A gold pan?

J: A gold pan, right.

s: Oh, sacks of gold?

J: No, we're not doing Rumpelstiltskin here. We're two prospectors.

s: Okay. You got a burro, you got a pick, you got a sourdough bread, you got the plaid shirt and suspenders, you got your Gabby Hayes hat, the cavalry boots, the long red underwear and the gold pan. Is that enough?

J: That's enough to give the general idea.

s: How about a cactus?

J: That's a good idea.

s: A saguaro cactus.

J: And a one-eyed dog.

s: A one-eyed dog? What type of dog?

J: A cur. A mangy cur.

s: A one-eyed mangy cur. What size?

J: Medium-size. Jesus, for a guy who wanted to get to the dialogue . . .

s: All right. Now what happens?

J: Okay. Now, they're standing around a table. They're both standing facing the audience.

s: Standing around the table.

J: One guy is unpacking cans from a knapsack.

s: Unpacking cans from a knapsack.

J: Now you start off the dialogue.

s: What's the other one doing?

J: He's just standing there looking at him, like they're having a conversation.

s: Just standing there.

J: The other guy is like this—he's, he's, you know, listening to him.

s: The other one is doing nothing.

J: It's very meaningful.

s: Nothing but listen.

J: Put "doing nothing meaningfully." The other one is "doing nothing meaningfully."

s: [*laughs and claps*] Do you want names for these guys?

J: They've got to have prospectors' names.

s: Prospector names. The one who's unpacking is who?

J: Well, let's see. What are prospectors' names?

s: How about Mobe—

J: Jeb?

s: Jeb unpacking. Now what does Jeb say?

J: You start. You do Jeb.

s: Okay. He's unpacking cans from a knapsack. That's what he's doing. Okay. He says . . . he's unpacking cans from the knapsack. He says . . . He could say so many things.

J: That's a great first line.

s: No, no, no, no, no. That's terrible.

J: Why, what was I going to say?

s: You were going to say that I could say anything or something like that.

J: There are so many things I could say.

s: No, no, no, no. Okay. I get to say Jeb's lines. And you can say whosever lines you want. Okay, here's what he says. He says, "I thought"—as he's unpacking, right?—"I put that damn thing in here last fall." That's what he says.

J: Okay. And now the other guy's name is what. What's the other guy's name?

s: Who you're going to be? How about Lenny?

J: Lenny?

s: Or Vinny.

J: Vinny. That's great. Jeb and Vinny. But they're both dressed as prospectors. There's no let-on, right? He's disguised as a prospector but his name is Vinny.

s: Not Winny. Vinny.

J: Vinny. That's what I said. Vinny.

s: His name is Camille. Jeb and Camille.

J: Read Jeb again. What does Jeb say?

s: All right. As he's unpacking the items from the bag—"I thought I put that damn thing in here last fall."

J: "What damn thing?"

s: Jeb says, "That thing." Now, what do you say?

J: All right . . . he looks at him. He stares at him for a while and then he says, "Oh, that thing."

s: "Oh, that thing"?

J: Yeah.

s: And then Jeb says, "Yeah."

J: Man, that's great. I love it!

s: Page two. Okay, now what?

J: The curtain closes.

s: You want the curtain closed?

J: Yeah.

s: Close the curtain? No. But a person dressed as a meat butcher comes on and closes the curtain.

J: A meat butcher?

s: Yeah, you know. All white. He just comes on pulling a blue curtain, and he just pulls it across the stage.

J: A meat butcher, great. And there's got to be a spotlight on him.

s: Dressed as a meat butcher.

J: A spotlight has to follow him. That's what makes it so exciting. Remember that feeling in the circus? Where the spotlight came on?

s: Hot white spot.

J: And he sings as he goes across.

s: Okay. What does he sing?

J: Ah, he sings . . . ?

s: Now wait a second. Pulling a blue . . . half curtain, right?

J: Half curtain. Right. Right. Singing a Polish folk song.

s: No. We gotta write a song. A meat butcher comes on in hot white spot pulling a half blue curtain across the stage, totally concealing the prospectors. Okay, he sings this song as he crosses.

J: I've got a great idea. We have to write the song?

s: Yeah. Yeah. We write everything.

J: God.

s: It can be a short song.

J: All right. What kind of song? Is it a melancholy song?

s: Whatever. How do you see it?

J: A guy dressed as a butcher. What would a butcher sing? A butcher would sing . . . That's why I saw him singing. I saw him as a foreign butcher.

s: Singing a German song. Or in Polish?

J: Yeah, yeah. In the language. [*Johnny sings in Polish.*]

s: That's ridiculous. That's absurd, Mr. Beckett. What does it mean? All of a sudden, he comes out singing a Polish song? What have you got in mind?

J: What the hell does the butcher mean?

s: I don't know. Do you want to cut the butcher out?

J: No. I think we should follow whatever image comes up.

s: Okay, okay. Sings the song as he crosses. Now what happens? He exits?

J: The curtain is closed.

S: The curtain is closed. He exits?

J: He exits with a white spot on him.

S: He exits . . . pulling blue curtain.

J: That's it. That's the name of it. *The Curtain*.

S: Wait a minute. It's *The Prospectors*.

J: Oh, yeah. That's right. *The Prospectors*.

S: It's the prospector play.

J: I've got to remember it's the Prospector Play.

S: Now what happens?

J: I know what!

S: What?

J: The curtain is closed, so what I see is . . . what year is it? It's obviously 18—what?

S: In the prospector deal?

J: Yeah.

S: It could be any time. Well, it'd have to be . . . 1849.

J: Okay. It's 1849, right? So an 1849 line of showgirls comes out.

S: Okay.

J: Because the curtain is closed now. As far as the audience is concerned, someone has closed the curtain on the play. But ya know what can happen in front of a curtain? Well, a guy could come out and tell jokes, or you could have the showgirls come out—from that period—and they do a period dance.

S: Yep. Or one of the prospectors could stick his arm out through the curtain with a puppet on it. And a spotlight comes up on the puppet. And the puppet starts talking.

J: Boy, is that absurd. Okay. The curtain is closed. A puppet comes out.

S: A puppet appears.

J: A puppet appears. Let's just follow that however it comes out. Just follow it out.

S: A hand puppet appears between the curtain. In spot. Okay, what kind of puppet? I mean like a snake or . . . what is it? A dinosaur?

J: I don't know what the fuck it is. The puppet is a . . .

S: A chicken.

J: A chicken? A chicken comes out between the curtain. All right. A talking chicken comes out. A guy in a chicken suit comes out. A guy in a chicken suit comes out and does a little dance. You know they actually had that in a Gene Wilder movie. Somebody wrote that into the script. They were hired by a bank.[1]

s: Oh well, let's not do that then. A hand puppet appears between the curtain in a spot. What kind of puppet? I know . . . let's go back to that chorus line. If the hand puppet doesn't work out, let's go to the chorus line.

J: All right.

s: A chorus line of 1840s showgirls.

J: Come out and do a—what do you call those—a dancehall act. You know, wearing tights. Garters.

s: Do a dancehall act. Now, what's the dancehall act?

J: You know, it's like those girls come out and—

s: Oh. You know what you could do? You could do that, and then you could have one of those old melodrama plays happening in front. And the two prospectors are playing the parts.

J: Yeah. Yeah. So what happens after the dancers exit?

s: The dancers leave and the two prospectors come out in front and they're doing this old melodrama thing.

J: Like what? That would be great.

s: You know, those old westerns. Stick 'em up.

J: Just with each other? Okay, okay. Here's an example. At a certain point, you see the two prospectors come out and they go . . . okay, they go . . . God, this is bizarre. Sheew.

s: This is the kind of activity I've been involved in for eighteen years.

1. The film was *Stir Crazy* (1980, directed by Sidney Poitier and costarring Richard Pryor).

On St. Patrick's Day 1983, Shepard
left his home in California to move in
with the actress Jessica Lange, his
costar in Graeme Clifford's *Frances*.
The couple stayed in Minnesota before
settling in Santa Fe, New Mexico.

Spring 1983

[HANDWRITTEN]

Last Night of the Play[1]
Sun night

Sitting in J. Lion's office writing this to you as May and Eddie thrash out their "relationship" (little knowing that "in time" it's been already thrashed out, done and settled and that they're living happily ever after in Minn.)[2]

— (so stop all yr screaming May)

In the audience we have on this final night—Scarlett, Jesse, Fredricka, Beresford, Bill Jordan and his wife, Amy, Val and Kathy's boyfriend (what's his name?) I'm going by Tosca's to speak to Jenette afterward—everyone is supposedly going over there (woops—here comes Linda with a joint) to celebrate closing night.

I spent the morning at St. Elmo and the afternoon in bed (I'm still sick) listening to our "lost" tape about the Squeamish Indians and Rights for the Bashful (and a long rave about the psychological significance of "sidekicks" (Tinkerbell and Peter Pan—Pinocchio and Jiminy Cricket.)

Wherever you may go, always remember that you are in some way representing the Garcia Vega club and all that we stand for.[3]

Johnny Dark

I just went out front. The actors are going flat out. This is it! Kind of attitude and the audience is loving it. They're digging the lines.
* This is Letter #1 in The Johnny Dark Sam Shepard Complete Collected Letters Pub. by Doubleday

---

1. San Francisco's Magic Theatre's production of *Fool for Love* with Ed Harris as Eddie and Kathy Baker as May.
2. John Lion was the founder and, for many years, artistic director of the Magic Theatre.
3. Sam and Johnny's cigar club, the Garcia y Vega club, was founded when they told Jesse that a leftover cigar band from that brand was the token of a special organization.

Spring 1983

[HANDWRITTEN]

"What a man knows well. That is his preparation."
—GURDJIEFF

Dear Sam

That I might drink, and leave the world unseen,
And with thee fade away into the forest dim
—KEATS[1]

This made me think of you and the way you were feeling around the time you split.

It's 7:30 morning on a Wednesday. Nana just pushed her way into my room. Scarlett is sleeping next to me. I'm at death's door. This is what I've done to myself. First, as you recall, I took all that speed lowering all of the body's resistances. Then I immediately contracted some kind of viral chest infection. With my lungs & chest in this condition I proceeded to begin scraping the caked dirt from the garage floor causing the fine dust to flow into my system and by 8:00 last night I had a full scale Asthma attack under-way with me lying on my bed gasping. This morning finds me dividing up my will between 10 minute coughing spasms.

Scarlett is fine. I spend almost all my time with her, even take her to some of the cleaning jobs with me. I love being with her. I don't have to feel crazy with her. It's like we're two halfs of one person. We have long conversations over coffee. She's got three desires in the whole world—me, coffee, and a pack of herbal cigarettes. Everything strikes her funny. [. . .]

By the time you read this I expect you'll be in N.M. Hard to believe that me and Jess will be seeing you there. Will I be breathing again by that time or will I have to show up on a respirator? The other day me and Jess were talking about

1. The lines by Keats are from "Ode to a Night-ingale"; the Gurdjieff quotation used as an epigraph is included in P. D. Ouspensky's *In Search of the Miraculous: Fragments of an Unknown Teaching* (1949).

what outlandish outfits we could wear for the flight out . . . patches, bow ties, canes, that sort of thing.

As you see I have sent you a tape I thought you'd like to have. It's one of our classic conversations which will bring a smile to yr eye. Listen to it with earphones for best results. I hesitate to send it to you because you are such an impatient bastard. You're always too "busy" for such things. Well then let Jessica listen to it and you can wait for such a time when you've somewhat immobilized your body through drink or disease—but don't try playing it in yr truck and then tell me you can't understand the fucking thing [. . .]

I was thinking the other day—will we ever ride again on the Harleys, stoned out of our minds, discussing the human condition at 80 MPH?? Yes—I'm sure we will—and *more*. There are *even* better days ahead I'm sure of it. New things in store, not just for us separately but together as well. Stealing bathrobes at Macy's. The Samurai and the Flycatcher etc. is just the beginning, son. America—open yr thighs! I'm real glad you and Jessica found each other at last. You couldn't have sat at the dining room table flipping horse magazines forever. I think it's great. Romance wins out! What could be more fulfilling? That's what *Singing in the Rain* is all about and all those kind of films—remember when she wrote to you after you thought it was over and we walked to breakfast and you were so happy instead of yr usual grumpy self—"my girl wrote to me—listen to the birds singing" and you were smelling blossoms on the trees and looking into rain puddles and we leaned against the car back home and you said "I wish I could enjoy being alive like this every day" and then I started singing

"The way you wear your hat.
The way you sip your tea"[2]

and for a moment, I thought, or felt that you understood something about Crosby, Astaire, and Jolson.—But alas—the next day you were putting snake oil on yr cinch and saying "I'm going to set in the yard a spell."

Wednesday Night: Back in bed coughing. Too sick to work. In the afternoon prowled through the Goodwills. Need a costume to fly to N.M. in (Remember our White Suit idea years ago?) Why am I always so broke? Because I am a fuckup. If I had any money, would I be any less a fuckup? Of course not. Still—it's nice to be able to buy what you

2. From the song "They Can't Take That Away from Me," by George and Ira Gershwin (1937).

want. I've been trying not to steal. I suppose I could get more cleaning jobs. Perhaps I'll put another ad in the paper.

Today Scarlett and I were talking about the women at St. Elmo. She said, "The trouble with them is that they all think they're the toffee on the toffee apple." Scarlett is my one constant motivation for trying to grow up. But I'm generally such a dismal failure. (For example, I drank half a bottle of cough syrup in the aisles of Thrifty today for want of a joint or your company). Now—time to turn down the light. Hope you are o.k. I'm sure that you must be. Funny how one runs down at the end of the day. One's thoughts and feelings . . . [. . .]

I realized for the first time this morning how possible it will be to get accustomed to all of this. After the initial shock of your leaving I can feel the new life flowing in a little at a time, feel the way life begins to adjust itself. I didn't see that when Scarlett got sick but I see it a little now. [. . .]

Thurs: O-Lan called tonight from LA. Events are changing so rapidly that no doubt you will have spoken to her and much will have happened by the time you read this. My sympathies go to whomever I'm speaking to at the time so that I am with you when I speak to you and with her when I speak to her. She is doing alright and says she suffers at least once heavily a day. She says Jesse is quiet and seems mainly concerned about comforting her. We all probably have him still as a little child but when I talked to him on the phone tonight—I was talking to a sensitive and intelligent teen-ager. I'm trying to find a relationship with O-Lan and have to start at the beginning. She has always been for me a satellite for someone else, first Scarlett and then you. I don't think we have ever related to each other as people in our own rights or given each other our due and now I feel the need to discover that from the beginning as I'm having to discover with Jesse on an almost daily basis. I told her I had spoken to you and that you might call her. I told her that although I was not commensurate with her loss, I felt the empty place your leaving had made, the loss of your influence upon me and all the ways I had come to depend on you, as no doubt it has been for you to some extent as well.—It's strange, because at the same time it makes life more vivid, that emptiness seems to punctuate the moments, revealing them and myself in the midst of them. No one knows what will happen. It's a kind of frightening and yet exciting realization which often jolts the present into focus. I walked to the corner this afternoon and remembered how often I had seen you walking toward the house from the corner slowly and sadly over the past year, always turning something dark over in your mind and never seeming at home or content, either dreaming or on your way to another place, another chore—and I thought, he must be happy now, at least for the time being, it must be a welcome respite from those slow sad morning walks. [. . .]

There's something that feels awkward talking to you on the phone and hearing you talk about your new place. I guess it comes from the strangeness of so suddenly not knowing anything in your life yet when you speak to me, everything in my life, the people, house etc. is all familiar to you. And at the same time you can see its an inevitable "stage" that can't be avoided.

I felt like such an asshole after I talked to you and Jessica, regardless of how I may have sounded.

Sam: You sounded like an asshole.

Johnny: Thanks.

But regardless of that—*inside* I felt like an asshole. I knew myself to be an asshole and it pricked my vanity. I didn't like it. I couldn't even see any value in it at the time. Don't forget, just because I'm so fucking cool most of the time, what a Schmuck I am. And try to be forgiving. You don't think Mozart wouldn't have been a Schmuck to live with? O.K. The fucking guy is great with the music but he's such a pantywaist and he always goes into a snit when he doesn't get his way.

I just ran across these amazing sentences *again* of Gurdjieff's which in the light of all that's recently happened, has acquired new meaning—new dimension.

"Only he will deserve the name of man and can count upon anything prepared for him Above, who has already acquired corresponding data for being able to preserve intact both the wolf and the sheep confided to his care."

Yrs—JD

March 1983

[TYPED]

Dear Sam

Had breakfast with Dennis.[1] It was raining. [. . .] Kristy was down the other night. She told me, "I feel sorry for Lonny but I say more power to him for doing what he wants."

I've been off drugs and booze since I almost killed myself on speed two weeks ago. But my gratitude for being alive can't last for ever.

O-Lan went off for a fiddle lesson this morning and won't be back till 5:00 so I'm here with Scarlett and Jesse all day. Jesse still has a cold and is taking a nap now. Here I am while you're running around North America with an abandoned wife, another woman who keeps laughing out of context, a sick kid, a deaf dog and a leaky roof, not to mention a room full of stuffed animals and a basement full of windup toys . . . and no fucking grass any-where in sight.

O-Lan was telling us this morning, not without some sense of humor, about the whole Patti Smith episode, how it started, how it ended and what it was like.[2] I asked her where she was with *this* whole scene and she said it changed daily for her, that she was concerned for you because you sounded like you didn't know what you were doing and any information she got from you she had to pull out of you because you were only saying yep and nope and that maybe for the time being she'd just let you tell her whatever you had a mind to tell her and let it go at that. Also that she didn't think you were away because of her or because of Jessica but on the other hand maybe it would turn out it really was because of Jessica and we'd all just have to wait and see I asked how long you were gone with Patti (thinking it was a month at the most) and she said six months, but that she had written you off after two weeks. So I asked how you got back and she said, you called one day and said you were through with Patti and that if she didn't move back in

1. Dennis Ludlow, friend of Johnny and Sam's, played Martin in the Magic Theatre's premiere of *Fool for Love*.

2. In 1971, Shepard separated from O-Lan for a few months to move in with the artist and singer Patti Smith at the Chelsea Hotel.

with you, you would do something drastic like go to South America. (Not the most drastic thing I ever heard) So she said, o.k. she'd move back in with you. So I said, "Well, I guess you hadn't written him off after all" and she said no, she guessed she hadn't. [. . .]

j.d.

March 25, 1983

[HANDWRITTEN]

Sam

The only good that may come out of this is that I'll finally have someone to write to and send tapes and photos to once again (since Sharon) and have someone to visit once in a while.[1] Well I'll send you tapes and photos soon but for now a brief note.

I've more or less covered what I wanted to tell you on the phone the other day which is that Jesse is absolutely fine (in fact at this moment he's sitting on my bed with me looking through volume 10 of the family album and karate-kicking my feet.) He's in good spirits—he seems to understand and of course is used to your being away in any case. So it will be a good thing and good timing if it works out that we all are able to get together at the end of May.

O-Lan is o.k. going about her business as usual. You've probably talked to her more than I have and of course she doesn't know the whole story (past or present) so it's still not the shock it could be or will be.

Scarlett is the same—of course she's been following this thing all along and even though she's concerned about her daughter, she has great feelings for you too and will no doubt break down in tears when she sees you.

Ace is howling in the front, Banjo is rooting in the back, Nana is shedding in the house and the last of the canaries is dead. (Remember that mad morning when you left—"Where's my fucking bag?" racing around the house. And then right after you left I went home and the women marched in singing in French and I thought—"holy shit—he left me here in the middle of all this" and I started looking to see if there was a matinee I could go to. I went to Market St. and watched something like "The Mummy Eats Your Brains Alive" or something all afternoon before I could face going home. 12 fags tried to cop my joint and I was drunk on cans of Tequila Sunrise. What a day!!)

1. Dark's note: Sharon Doubiago, poet/author and girlfriend of mine.

I'm just going off doing my cleaning (I can come to N.M. and clean yr place if you want) and going to movies. Not stealing too much. Made it with Dan's sister when she was in town but she went back to Vermont. She's very nice, very pretty except she's about 6'9" or some absurd height [. . .]

So . . . Everything here is OK under control. Don't worry about that. Everyone's thinking you'll either come back or you'll never come back. It probably won't be as big a shock to them when the time comes as you think.

Remember—whatever you need and what ever you want me to do at this end—I'll take care of. Between the both of us we can take care of *everybody*. You and me, we're family—like brothers—so there's never any problem. Jack and Neal.[2] Keep me posted on yr whereabouts in N.M. and if you don't want to call—put it in a letter. So far, I think it's all working out

Johnny

2. Jack Kerouac and Neal Cassady.

March 29, 1983—Wrenshall, MN

[HANDWRITTEN]

John,

Just got yr 2 letters yesterday & have read them thru several times. I'll try to describe something of my situation here, although the sweep of events over the past couple weeks is so awesome and jam-packed that I get that sense of total failure in the ability to describe it with language—(One of the main reasons I'm such a lousy storyteller.)

I'm sitting right now in Jessie's remote cabin hideaway in the deep forests of Northern Minnesota surrounded by snow.[1] Everything's white & silent as far as the eye can see & the ear can hear. It's like sitting in the middle of a Christmas postcard & it's almost the end of March. Very cold outside but warm as toast in here with the wood fires burning. We've been absolutely alone up here for about 3 days until yesterday when we picked up her baby & two nephews from her parents' house. That's when I got your letters which arrived at her Dad's place—He's this gruff old country guy with a black plow horse out back & broken down tractors all sitting around the yard buried in snow. He comes up from his downstairs room saying: (in a loud voice)—"Is Sam here! I got a couple a' letters for him here." And he goes into the kitchen & starts thumbing through all this fan mail for Jessica until he arrives at these 2 envelopes which I recognize as your handwriting. Everything strikes me on the raw nerves these days—even the recognition of your handwriting—to see that I recognize this whole person thru the way he writes letters on paper suddenly seems like a miracle to me.

So anyway, we return to the cabin with 3 kids now all jammed into the cab of the truck (ages: 2, 4, & 6) & I'm four wheeling the truck thru mud, slush & snow down this back-country road surrounded by White Birch, Pine & Spruce trees & we arrive at the cabin with this gaggle of kids—which is very different than being alone with the one you love. First thing that happens is the little boy, Mattie, falls head first down a steep flight of stairs & cracks his head so bad there's a welt down his forehead the size of a large Night Crawler. So he's crying like crazy & calling for "Mommy" & we're applying icepacks to his head & wrapping him in blankets & telling him he'll be all

---

1. "Jessie" is Jessica Lange.

3

Cheaps 5 & dime Woolworth
stores & faces - especially
old faces with high cheek
bones, deep set blue eyes
all descended directly
from Swedes & Finns &
Norwegians. It's really
the far north of Americ
& as different from say
Texas as Africa is fro
England. I can't descri
the feeling I had walkin
side by side with her
down those streets, knowin
this was her home town &
she was a child in this
place & she was describin
buildings she remembere
& places she grew up in,
here I was with her &
we were really together
after all those agonizing
months of being seperated

Inside, my world keeps
shifting always. I miss

right & he's screaming for his Mom the whole time. The nearest doctor is 30 miles away & I'm worried the kid might have a concussion so we keep waking him up every 15 minutes to make sure he's not dead. It turns out he's fine & the swelling went down & things settled down for the nite.

Yesterday, me & Jessie drove into Duluth which is a town right out of Kerouac.[2] You wouldn't believe this town. Right on the shores of Lake Superior with brick industrial buildings. Ice & snow on the sidewalks. Cheap 5 & dime Woolworth stores & faces—especially old faces with high cheek bones, deep set ice blue eyes—all descended directly from Swedes & Finns & Norwegians. It's really the far north of America & as different from say Texas as Africa is from England. I can't describe the feeling I had walking side by side with her down those streets knowing this was her hometown & she was a child in this place & she was describing buildings she remembered & places she grew up in & here I was *with* her & we were really together after all those agonizing months of being separated.

Inside, my world keeps shifting always. I miss the family & Jesse & O-Lan & all of you—sometimes with a terrible sadness that seizes me completely. The thing that hurts me the most is knowing I abandoned everyone. That I ran off & left everyone high and dry. Even though I know that everyone is self-sufficient more or less & resilient & able to continue no matter what—I still get swamped with this feeling of betrayal.[3] Especially for O-Lan. I keep remembering your telling me once that Scarlett had told someone that the reason they were feeling guilty is because they *were* guilty. That seems true to me. Even so, I know I can't turn back now. There's still a "rightness" to this new direction that I can't deny. I love this woman in a way I can't describe & a feeling of belonging to each other that reaches across all the pain. It's as though we've answered something in each other that was almost forgotten. I look back on that whole ten years in California & I see myself hunting desperately for something I wasn't finding. I know the Work point of view is the only true one. That life is inside. That nothing outside can ever finally answer our yearning. I know that's true but, in some way, finding Jessie has reached something inside me. A part of me feels brand new—reawakened. I know even this will change. There'll be moments of deep regret maybe. But life is a gamble. I felt the weight of that the first time I left home for good. I walked out of that house into the unknown & it scared the shit out of me but the adventure of hitting life straight on was

2. Shepard's note: where Bob Dylan was born.
3. Shepard's note: being the betrayer.

69

a thrill I'll never forget. I feel that now—along with the fear. But I see the fear stems from being alone in the world & it has a new meaning for me now. You can be alone in the midst of people or you can be alone & join with the other one's aloneness. There can be a real meeting between two people at the point where they always felt marooned. Right at the edge. And that's how it is with me & her.

4/2/83 (Pueblo, Colorado)

It's late at nite here—& another motel. The girls are asleep. We've been driving 3 days from Minnesota—across Iowa, Nebraska & now Colorado—thank God for the West! I never really realized the sharp distinction between the Mid-West (where I was born) & the West (where I was raised). The Mid-West is like death—real death—it's on its way out—everything is being abandoned—at least in the rural areas. It's freezing cold (minus zero degrees are common throughout the winter). The cities all have the feeling of communist countries. People are super depressed & very poor. All the small farms are being auctioned off. Every cafe you stop in there's notices up for farm auctions. It looks like it's going to become one huge tract of government-owned agri-business & all the people will have vanished for the Sun Belt. It's definitely the end of an era. A perfect time for the chronicler & documentarian. It's all going to be gone very fast and no one will remember what happened except through photos & tales passed down. One thing that struck me—I stepped out of the truck to put some gas in the tank—somewhere outside Omaha, Nebraska—& this bitter cold ferocious wind hit me. I mean this wind was like ice & blowing with a vengeance. Just a few yards away from the gas station was the Platte River—now I've done a lot of reading on the history of the Plains & the Platte was one of those momentous rivers where a lot of Indian wars were fought with the Cavalry. You read about that stuff but you don't realize the weather conditions they were conducting these battles under. Those Indians had to have been as tough as leather to live out in that cold—not to mention the white settlers. And now, the descendents of those very people are finally giving up the ghost—not because of the weather so much as the economics. It's an amazing sweep of changes. Who knows what's up ahead for this country.

I talked with Mathew tonite since we're only about 4 hours north of Santa Fe & he's arranged us hotel reservations & is working on getting us a place to rent.[4] He switched right into high businessman gear & talking with him is like talking to a travel agent or something. He's great though & working his ass off to find us a place without letting anyone know "who" it's for. We've only run into the "star" bullshit once—in Denver—but it was a real drag with all the waitresses and customers coming over to get her autograph. I hope it's not going to be a big deal that way in Santa Fe but who knows. We arrive tomorrow at Mathew's and he's going to fill us in on the possible houses we can rent. As soon as I know where we'll be I'll let you know so you & Jesse can make plans to come down. I'm really looking forward to seeing you both. We'll have a great time down there re-instating the "Garcia y Vega" Club. I gotta get some sleep now. More later.

4/6/83 (Tesuque, New Mex.)

Here we are ensconced in a fancy condominium hotel on the outskirts of Santa Fe. We've nailed down a real nice place to rent in town for 2 months while we look for something to buy. It's snowing here too cold but very beautiful. Will Spring never come???

Last nite we got a baby sitter & went out for dinner & a movie—*Max Dugan Returns*—very corny Neil Simon melodrama but Marsha Mason and Jason Robards were great.

Had a great talk with Jesse last nite on the phone. I'm glad he's calling me. He sounds real excited about the trip down here. I suppose the most practical thing is to put you & Dennis up out at Mathew's place (he volunteered) & keep Jesse with me in town. The place we've rented is real small, otherwise you all could camp in there. I can pick you all up at the airport in Albuquerque. Just let me know the time of arrival & flight #.

I'm now strongly considering *not* going to New York but don't let on to Dennis or anyone in the cast until I've made a real decision. The main problem is finding someone to take care of the production for me.[5]

I think I should wrap this letter up now before it gets out of hand. I'll keep in touch & send me more letters when you get a chance. My love to the whole bunch.

Your pal,
Sam

4. Mathew, according to a note by Shepard, was John's cousin.
5. *Fool for Love* opened in New York at the Circle Repertory Theatre on May 26, 1983.

Dear Sam

Got your letter — description
of being in Minn. in the cabin,
the woods, the cold brick towns
of the midwest. I could really feel
the icy wastes of depression shuttering
through the town. You should think
seriously about becoming a writer.

We watched the academy awards
last night over at Vals — me,
jesse and Scarlett. Me and jess
were setting together and got
real excited when Jessica won
(I can still hear L.P. "Oh theres
Sam who won the prize)

With jesse it was like
someone in his family had won
the oscar. He really let up.

Me and jesse are setting in
the bakery on a bleak Tues
morning 7:25 AM He's doing his
homework. I'm taking him to school.

Two parts in yr. letter that
I remember from reading last
night — the part about the

April 12, 1983

[HANDWRITTEN]

Dear Sam,

Got your letter—description of being in Minn. in the cabin, the woods, the cold brick towns of the Midwest. I could really feel the icy wastes of depression shattering through the town. You should think seriously about becoming a writer.

We watched the awards last night over at Val's—me, Jesse and Scarlett. Me and Jess were sitting together and got real excited when Jessica won.[1] (I can still hear L.P. "Oh there's Sam who won the prize)

With Jesse it was like someone in his family had won the oscar. He really lit up.

Me and Jesse are sitting in the bakery on a bleak Tues morning 7:25 AM. He's doing his homework. I'm taking him to school.

Two parts in yr. letter that I remember from reading last night—the part about feelings of abandonment which I can understand and yet what seems to balance the truth of that is your feeling for Jessica, which as we both know was always extraordinary. I was always excited by the specialness of it and felt way back in the beginning that you had come across something that was missing in your life and I found myself encouraging you to it in spite of the obvious disastrous side.

I'm rushing this letter a little because school time is approaching and we have to go back and get the car. I'll continue later this afternoon. This will give you time to have a cigarette, cough, blow yr. nose and throw the napkin in my plate.

—At the Post Office

about to go to work. Dropped Jesse off. He said "Isn't it great Jessica won the award." I asked him if he was pissed at you. He said—"no, not at all but O-Lan sure is." [. . .]

Won't be long we'll be seeing you. [. . .] These are racy weeks for me. Cleaning & taking care of Scarlett etc. by day—the house by night and away every weekend. Last week Catalina then this week

1. Academy Award for Best Supporting Actress for her role in *Tootsie.*

I'm going back to L.A. to see Ces, then the week after that to New Mexico.[2] My cleaning people are starting to think I'm peculiar.

— well we're looking forward to seeing you & to the whole visit thing and to seeing Jessica and talking and getting loaded etc. We miss you but I feel *great* that you got all this going for you.

Johnathan Darkness

---

2. Ces was a girlfriend of Johnny's.

JESSICA   SAM

Champagne and beer were served.
Johnny played piano. 1983
                        N.M.

April 18, 1983

[HANDWRITTEN]

Sam

I'm embarking toward something that resembles health (tomorrow) in the hopes that I shall be able to walk erect by the time I see you, and breathe without the artificial lung. [. . .]

When I arrived home yr fat typewritten letter was here and a very fine stoned letter it is too, my boy. The further adventures of Huck Finn as written to his friend Tom, in which Huck goes to the American Southwest and begins to get along with himself.

Actually a very heartening letter because your feelings for Jessica and her feelings for you and the ways in which yr. life is being affected, are all quite touching and, to me, who's watched you grow from a miserable asshole into a renowned asshole, it's extremely heartwarming and actually fills me with gladness to hear that your love for each other is such a force against the awful kind of desperateness you were used to living with. I'm really happy for you, and I can say that fully because I am happy with my own self and fulfilled in the ordinary sense and so am not in this case envious of your situation but feel instead that in fact we may be *sharing* another one of those parallels we've been sharing for the past few years.

I haven't talked to *anyone* who understands your scene. Certainly not O-Lan or Kristy or Sandy or Doug etc.[1] I think Dennis does and I think Scarlett does. But in Scarlett's case, even though she understands, her emotions are divided.

I spoke to O-Lan when I called long distance last night. I asked her how everything was with her. She says "O.K." and won't say much more than that or if she does, she says, "What's there to say? It's all very obvious!" And then she said she wanted to have a meeting with me. About what?—Just a general meeting, she said, about *everything*. (If there's one thing that really makes me nervous it's a general meeting about everything with O-Lan.)

1. Sandy Rogers was the older of Shepard's two sisters. She wrote and performed the songs in Robert Altman's film version of *Fool for Love* (1985).

There's a lot to say and less now as my mind has gone to the Bahamas or someplace. Of course we'll speak soon about flights and times during the week. This is just to help stuff your New Mexican mailbox.

Aside from at least one good stoned session at some time in which I think we need to welcome Jessica personally to the glorious intelligence of the Garcia Vega club—it's all wide open and I'm cool, you understand.

Be speaking to you soon. (Don't forget to make the arrangements for the hot baths, peanut butter, and cigars [. . .] I think you know what I'm saying)—Now, I have to pause till my voice comes back to me because my heart is in the coffin there with Caesar.

J.D

1983   Calif

But even as the new play was
opening, Sam had plunged into
the writing of a film script with
German director Wim Wenders, due
to be shot in Texas that Spring

April 29, 1983

[HANDWRITTEN]

Johnny Buhunkiss,

Been having these incredible shifts of energy lately—possibly due to the old altitude—where I'll feel dog tired & then suddenly be up & jumping around like a jackrabbit. This is my jackrabbit phase right now—so I'll write until it begins to drag again.

Wim is here & we've been meeting every morning at his hotel & rewriting.[1] We've cut considerable pages out of the script now & got it down to regulation Hollywood size. We've also been discussing the possible cast a lot & the ideal one we've come up with turns out to be almost identical to *One from the Heart*: Harry Dean Stanton, Fred Forrest, Nastassja Kinski & Tuesday Weld—so far. Of course none of them have been nailed down yet. Wim is still very grim & reserved—also slightly odd I find. He gets easily distracted in the midst of work by the most ridiculous things—like suddenly getting very interested in where the wiring to a certain light in his motel room is leading. He'll get up in the midst of a conversation we're having on the script & just follow the wire across the room until he finds the socket it's plugged into. Then he'll stand there & sort of make these little noises of acknowledgement & return to the table. Weird. I still like him a lot though & he's great to work with, although I'm now getting real bored with re-hashing the script & just want to see it get into production.

Me & Jessie & the baby have entered some kind of new phase where it feels like a little family now.[2] It took Shura a while to really accept me, since I kept coming between her & her mother a lot but now she really has opened up & wants me to read her stories all the time & ride on my shoulders & get tickled & all that other stuff little kids like. Jessica just continues to amaze me. It's as though she's never really been loved or cared for before. She just keeps opening up to me in a way that causes the same response in me. We're closer now than we've ever been & much of the posing to each other that went on during our hot & intermittent affair has dropped away.

1. Wim Wenders, in town to work with Shepard on the script for *Paris, Texas*.
2. The baby was Shura, Jessica's daughter with the dancer Mikhail Baryshnikov.

I came up with a small revelation the other nite—(possibly on grass so there no danger of it being permanent.): *Guilt* is the opposite of *Acceptance*. It was very stark & clear—these 2 states in radical contrast. Of course there's absolutely no control over which one presents itself at any given time—but the idea suddenly came as a surprise & a help. Going further with it I saw that Guilt is always wrapped up with the past & Acceptance can only be arrived at in the present. Guilt is a habit. It's so strong & so intertwined with events from deep in the past when the emotions were raw that I've never really questioned its validity or usefulness. I've only just felt it. It's probably the single most powerful negative influence in my life & it's ruled me in one way or another for years—going back to my early childhood. To be free from Guilt would be to enter a whole new world of possibilities.—I've re-read Pentland's words from that meeting 3 or 4 times now & the part where he speaks about freeing the energies that are locked up in us through an action of unity must apply to these strange territories of guilt & tension that plague me all the time. Guilt obviously produces tension. A lot of tension. The energy is locked off. There's no flow or interaction between the parts—so everything gets messed up. Now I started to make attempts to look directly at this state when I discovered myself experiencing it. And what I saw was that I was totally unwilling to let go of the tension. It was such a strong sensation of clinging to this tension—almost out of a sense of self-protection—as though I'd lose myself if I dared to relax. That was "very inneresting," as they say in the old Wednesday circle but also I began to get a feeling for the really practical side of taking a look at my state instead of trying to figure it out or avoid it or change it.

In any case I have a renewed interest in the Ideas & I've written Pentland a letter about contacting the group down here. I can also see the truth of this point he made in that meeting of becoming superstitious about being on the good side of the Big Powers—which I think was in response to your question that night.

Right now I feel very much between 2 worlds. Both are interesting to me for a change. Both present a challenge & I have no real preference for either one. I just find myself fluctuating between them & sometimes I actually feel myself in both at the same time—which is very unusual to me. Probably all this has to do with the recent shock of events.

I sometimes miss our rampant conversations on every subject under the sun but I find some satisfaction in knowing neither one of us has kicked the bucket & we'll be meeting up in L.A. or Texas soon.

Say hi to Jesse & the family for me.

Your partner,
Sam

September 3, 1983

[TYPED]

Dear Sam

We have this puppy now all about the house, as if we haven't got enough stuffed animals in the bedroom. Very cute.

I took yr letter to the Crow to read.[1] I sat by a window. The place was empty and I had coffee and orange juice. The description of cutting yr finger.[2] It's amazing to have read that because I had just been sitting around most of the afternoon reading *Dracula*. Stoker was Irish. He wrote it at the end of the nineteenth century and he's got things like phonograph recordings and typewriters in the novel, which were absolutely new inventions then (You never think of *Dracula* and *Typewriter* as appearing in the same novel) I could just picture you getting cut because from having stayed with you out there it seems I saw you going up behind Jessica like that a hundred times.

Of course I was real curious about how it would go at the station with you and O-Lan. I could not imagine, when I first heard her plan, why she would subject Jesse to that. I thought she should have kept the image of his Mom and Dad intact a little longer. That was my reaction. But who knows what effects things produce. Things just happen, and so arbitrarily it seems most of the time. I mean, we're "compelled" to act one way or another just like we seem compelled to "react." I don't see how you killed six hours walking around waiting for the train. That's like walking around from midnight until the sun comes up. You must have *bought* something you're not telling me about. [. . .]

I just went into the living room to give Scarlett a kiss but she wouldn't let me kiss her because she said she didn't trust me because I've been reading "that book" (*Dracula*). So of course I had to start biting her on the neck.

About not staying at your place. It's not a problem because I talked to Mathew and we can stay at his place. I understand Jessica's feelings about it. And as far as Scarlett's reaction, after she read the letter, she said she really understood how Jessica felt and that as far as I was concerned she was willing to stay home while I went if

1. The letter has been lost.
2. Shepard writes about the event in "More Urgent Emergencies" in *Cruising Paradise*.

she would be in the way. I assured her that that wasn't necessary. It's *amazing*. When she says stuff like that there's not a trace of self pity or sarcasm in her manner or voice. She actually *means* it. I said to her, "It's o.k.? You don't mind?" and she said, "The only thing I mind is if it makes you unhappy." (Who am I living with?)

On the way back from the Crow, driving home I started daydreaming about the fact that I actually got a postcard from Jack Kerouac and that somewhere Kerouac was alive and writing a message to me (whoever he thought I was) What ever made him come up with the phrase ". . . all yr Connecticut Maytimes"?[3] And I thought, "the man's a poet." That's what I think about your writing most of the time. I think of you more as a poet who writes plays and prose pieces, than as a playwright.

You're right . . . we're going to have a hell of a time at this thing. (Remind me to get film for my camera.) Hope you can still pick us up at Lamy. And what are my chances of getting a car to drive. According to Mathew we're going to be stranded out there unless I can "make arrangements." I told him it would take care of itself and I'm sure if you guys don't have anything available to drive, it will still work itself out alright.

I hope we get a shot at a famous Uncle Henry meal while we're all together.

Thanks for the long letter (remember those long ones in England?) I've been watching your career with interest, public and private.

"The highway is for gambling,"[4] *is a*
great way of ending a letter. I got to hand
it to you for using it and to Dylan
for writing it. It reminds me of Kerouac's
". . . love is a duel."

j.d.

---

3. While Johnny was working as a dog-catcher in Milford, Connecticut, he wrote to Kerouac in Florida about what *On the Road* meant to him, and received a postcard in reply. The entire message reads:

"Thanks a lot, John. Regards to all your Connecticut Maytimes."

4. The actual line from Dylan's "It's All Over Now, Baby Blue" is "The highway is for gamblers."

SAM   JESSE

New Mexico
1983

October 10, 1983—Waterloo, Iowa[1]

[HANDWRITTEN]

Dear John,

Here I am back in the mouth of the mad movie machine. The externals are identical every time & I never seem to get used to them. Always some inner complaint about the insanity of it all. "Is it really necessary to make this much fuss & waste just to make a movie that's only going to disappear in time anyhow?" Anyway, I'm going thru the usual little period of adjustment which always resolves itself in me taking to my trailer & holing up like a woodchuck, dreading the sound of the A.D.'s walkie-talkie. Still, it ain't a bad way to make a lot of $ in a relatively short time.

I started this letter to you 5 days ago & I'm just now getting back to it. We're shooting nites now & it's rainy, windy & cold & I'm sitting in my trailer again. Just had a chicken dinner from the catering truck. We're getting set to shoot a tornado sequence where a truck overturns & one of the kids gets buried under a pile of corn.

I'm kind of worried about Jesse. I've had two letters from him that sound very sad & alone. Is he really all right? He never seems to tell me how he's feeling on the phone. Just talks about bikes & cars & stuff. It kills me when I put myself in his place for even a second. I just hope he can get out here with you for Thanksgiving. I miss him a lot.

Just found your letter about Sharon and Oregon trip today by accident. It fell out of a big envelope that had other mail in it. Don't know how it got misplaced like that. I'm sure happy for you that you & her have healed up & you're back on good terms. I know how much you suffered during that bad time when she got looney on you. I just can't believe the power of the female animal. I go through such inner dramas over Jessica—the whole spectrum of emotions from teen-age jealousies right up to the most tender love I've ever known. I just can't believe she gets to me like that. Lately I've come across something interesting & I think, in a strange way, it comes from your influence. I've found that it's possible to see (more or less), what's taking place inside me as far as negative emotions go—or the temptation to indulge in negative emotion by mulling over certain thoughts—*but* rather than

1. Shepard notes that he was in Iowa to shoot *Country* with Jessica Lange.

everything was oriented around that home ba
Now, it turns out, I'm with a woman who lik
to travel & move around. I still feel this who
resistance to that kind of life — almost like
became convinced that that was behind m
"I did that in the sixties". I don't really
the same restlessness as I did then, but st
it strikes me that I'm closed off in the who
area of adventure. I always thought I w
pretty adventurous but Jessica comes up
stuff, while we're driving along in the car, &
"Why don't we take the Orient Express ne,
summer & go to the Himalayas?" She
actually said that. I was stunned. "You
mean the Himalayas where Mt. Everes
is?" — Yes. That's what she means. Then
she starts plotting out the whole trip. We
take a boat to London then on to Paris —
I feel this tension come up in my stomach
where did this come from? What's wrong with
little travel? It might be nice to get out & se
the world a little with your favorite girl.
lot of this attitude must come from all the
years of being "in the Work" where the "hous
became the key fixture & the weekly schedu
was totally mapped out around the activit
there. Now, without that structure, everyt
feels open-ended. I'm not making any
judgements about either one — it's just ree
different knowing it actually is possible
pick up & go on a trip to the Himalaya

just sit in that state, seeing & not expressing—to move in another direction through humor. It's very difficult but possible & what's amazing to me is how other people respond to it. Like Jessie & Shura. This borders, I guess, on the temptation to *change* something but if the non-expression of negativity includes the possibility of behaving the opposite of the way you feel, it must still be possible to see the whole ballgame—inside & out.

I still haven't grown entirely accustomed to this new outer life. I feel more willing now to live with the idea of moving around a lot. Before, it was so set that home on 33 Evergreen was the main base—always a place to return to & re-group, get back into the work at St. Elmo, the family, the ranch—everything was oriented around that home base. Now, it turns out, I'm with a woman who likes to travel & move around. I still feel this whole resistance to that kind of life—almost like I became convinced that that was behind me—"I did that in the sixties." I don't really feel the same restlessness as I did then but slowly it strikes me that I'm closed off in the whole area of adventure. I always thought I was pretty adventurous but Jessica comes up with stuff, while we're driving along in the car, like "Why don't we take the Orient Express next summer & go to the Himalayas?" She actually said that. I was stunned. "You mean the Himalayas where Mt. Everest is?"—Yes. That's what she means. Then she starts plotting out the whole trip. We'll take a boat to London then one to Paris—etc. I feel this tension come up in my stomach. Where did this come from? What's wrong with a little travel? It might be nice to get out & see the world a little with your favorite girl. A lot of this attitude must come from all those years of being "in the Work" where the "house" became the key fixture & the weekly schedule was totally mapped out around the activities there. Now, without that structure, everything feels open-ended. I'm not making any judgments about either one—it's just very different knowing it actually is possible to pick up & go on a trip to the Himalayas—not that I'd ever want to.

Sat. morning—after 6 hours sleep—shooting all nite in wet suits to keep the synthetic rain out.—It's very beautiful here. Full Fall with the trees all golden & yellow. A real Mid-Western little town—Kids on bikes riding through the fallen leaves. I haven't been anywhere near the East for years & there's all this nostalgia from those days on the farm in Pennsylvania & my journeys up to New England when I first tasted the liberation of having a Rockefeller or Guggenheim grant & taking off in my little Volkswagen for places unknown. I was awful lonely then but still enjoyed the romance of the road.

Now it's early morning (1:A.M.) of the 25th of October—isn't this about the same time of month Scarlett first went into the hospital?[2] It seems awfully familiar to me. Shura's got a bad cold—all congested & miserable so she's sleeping with Jessie & I'm in another bedroom upstairs. [. . .]

Well, a lot of shit has hit the fan since I started this letter 10 days ago. The cinematographer has been fired, the director's quit & I've quit until they get a replacement.[3] They've threatened to sue me if I don't go back to work but threats always make me more stubborn. It's a strange situation to be in because Jessica has a big stake in this film & she wants to get it done come hell or high water. At this point I just want to go back home & ride my horses & shoot my new shotgun & maybe build a fire in the fireplace. I really can't stand this movie crap anymore—it gets harder & harder to do it. I don't really know what's going to happen now. The producers are frantically looking for a new director & trying to keep the film rolling so they don't lose money. I suppose this move on my part is going to brand me as "difficult" & "temperamental" in Tinsel Town. I really don't give a shit anymore. Jessie & me are closer than ever but life in the movies is just not my game so I guess I'll just have to accept this fact that I'm hooked up with a movie star & allow her to play that out & maybe just ride along beside her on the sidelines somehow.

In any event, Thanksgiving is still a ways off & any number of possibilities could develop but I still want us all to get together around that time—wherever it might be. I'll keep you posted for sure.

I've been doing some trap shooting with my 12 gauge on Sundays. Have you ever done it? It's great. There's this old Trap Shoot Club out here in the country where all the old boys show up & you stand 3 at a time—about twenty yards from a cement bunker & yell "Pull!" Then this clay disc goes flying out over a field in an unpredictable direction & you try to nail it before it hits the ground. You're scored from 0 to 25 for hits & you change positions about 6 times. It's your kind of activity—Zen & the Art of Aiming. You don't have to run or jump. Maybe we could do some of it together sometime. I'm getting Jesse a beautiful 20 gauge Remington.

2. Shepard's note: after her brain aneurysm.
3. The director was Bill Wittliff, who also wrote the screenplay. He was later the producer and screenwriter of *Lonesome* *Dove* and *Legends of the Fall*. Richard Pearce was eventually brought on to direct *Country*.

Have thoroughly gone nuts on shotguns lately. Bought every book I could find. Studying the old models & hunting through gun shops for them. I'm going to build a collection. It's the same kind of obsessive behavior as always—but I love it. I have yet to try shooting skeet but I'm going to try that too.—That's a whole bunch of clay pigeons projected out in various patterns—like the way birds fly. This Remington 870 that I've got is a pump action 12 gauge—holds 5 shells & will accept up to a 3" magnum so it kicks like a mule into your shoulder. It's the exact same gun the police use for riot control & the mercenaries use in Africa. A real mean mother. The pump action is so fast they say it can beat an auto load 12 gauge. It's a beauty too, with hand tooled walnut stock. I enjoy just looking at it across the room.

Well, I guess I've run off at the mouth enough here. I'll wrap it up for now. I'll be in touch soon about what develops here. Let's definitely get together for Thanksgiving though. More later.

"The brother you never had"
Sam

(This is also borrowed from Dylan—his song "Lenny Bruce is Dead"—
full line reads: "Lenny Bruce was bad
He was the brother you never had")

October 31, 1983

(Wait till you read these unbelievable Kerouac Bio. Excerpts I sent you)

Dear Sam

It's 7 AM and I'm sitting in the Bakery in Mill Valley stoned. Isn't that great! Here I am 42 years old sitting in a small Northern Calif town 7:00 on a rainy October morning and not just any morning but *Halloween*—and I'm completely ripped. So I was pouring my coffee and one of the "regulars" who I've never talked to is standing there and we say "Good Morning" and she goes on to make (our first) conversation. (She doesn't know she's talking to Zorro this morning.) She says, "Are you always up this early or did you forget to set your clock back?"

"No" I say "I always get up this early—no matter what, I always get up this early. No matter what time it is I get to bed I get up this early. I don't know why. I just pop up. I always wanted to be the kind of guy who slept till noon. I always wanted to wake up in the afternoon covered in newspapers sleeping in my clothes."

She says "why did you want to do that? You'd miss half the day."

"I don't know. There's just something so reckless about it."

Those were also the first words I've spoken today. [Just thought of a great exercise. For a week keep a record of your *first words* of the day.]

I wish you had been here last night. I walked into O-Lan's room (yr old room, like I used to do) and went into a whole bit about Noah and his ark and about how Noah walks out (this is a play) from your closet with a basket of animal callers, whistles and noisemakers—different callers for every animal in the world. Fish callers, butterfly callers. And I did Noah blowing all these callers and then freaking out when he sees what shows up. Then I went into a Noah monologue of Noah saying how he was 600 years old and how much the area has changed and how run down things had become. The Garden of Eden was all Blacks and gay bars were springing up along the Red Sea.

O-Lan was beside herself laughing. Then I read the whole Noah myth from the Bible for her as a dramatic radio show with musical background.

It's amazing how many nights we did that. It was strange doing that in yr old room for somebody else. With all respect to O-Lan it was a lonely substitute. There was no *Sam backflow*. It was like talking to another generation. [. . .]

Johnny

In November 1983, Johnny and his
then girlfriend, the poet Sharon
Doubiago, traveled to Iowa in a
van to visit Shepard on the set of
Country. (Johnny's extramarital
relationships were always undertaken
with Scarlett's knowledge.)

On the Set of Country—Iowa, 1983

s: This is totally her scene. This is like the way she always lived on the road when she was doing movies by herself. So I'm coming into it just completely like a visitor. This rented house has been totally renovated. Housekeeper, German one.

J: How do you find out how to be in this situation?

s: It's really hard. Sometimes I can accept it. I mean, this is just a temporary situation and then we go back to our home—wherever it is. And then other times I'm totally outraged. Totally pissed off it's a women's environment. It's totally run by women here. Gertrude's in the kitchen and Jessica's with the baby. We've had some unbelievable kind of—

J: Confrontations?

s: Yeah, I mean I get so enraged sometimes that I'll just go off and get a motel room. Then I come back. Then it would smooth out. "It's okay. I can handle it." [. . .]

J: Most occupations don't flow into one's life to that extent. Except a doctor. Say you ran off with a woman doctor. And the first thing that would happen. No, I mean . . . what occupations—where would that come up? That would come up. I'm sure a lot of women have experienced that. Something like "He was always at the hospital." [. . .] I feel that all the time. Especially with the thing . . . the women. Well, like after you left, there was one less man—

s: A lot of women.

J: There was a lot of women.

s: I've been coming to this real interesting thing that's still kind of in the background. If I can't handle this environment, you know—I mean, I love this woman, I really *love* her, and yet I might not be able to handle this situation she lives in. Well, okay, what have we got? I split? I just go? And then what do I do? I live *alone*? So, what do I do? You know this whole thing of what would it be like to just . . . and really just be alone? What would that be like?

J: That's incredible. That's the extreme situation.

s: That's where you'd really be up against something. If you're totally alone. I can't even handle the idea.

J: An incredible thought. You see these people. They go to New York, they get a room. It's like—you've seen these scenes a million times. I've come. This is the hotel. This is your room. And I'm visiting you. "How is it going, Sam?" I associate that with old age, though.

s: Old age and senility and turning in on yourself. Cutting everything off. It wouldn't be like living alone like a monk.

J: I would think that love would survive all that.

s: Yeah, it does, because that's what brings me back around. I'm kidding myself if I think I can live without her. This person. As outrageous as any of the conditions or situations get.

J: There's always the possibility that'll drop away—those prejudices will drop away.

s: Or something else will shift. It's like you're thrown together. I mean, we've been living together for six months. That's not very long.

J: It's been very intense though. [. . .]

s: Maybe you've done one gesture that you feel like you have to honor. I've done this one thing—I've walked out of the room.

J: Oh, I see.

s: I can't just drop that. Now I've got to go out the door. Now I've got to get in the truck.

J: And you don't want to do it.

s: It's kind of like "I'll show her who's boss." "I'll show her a thing or two."

J: I know that really well.

s: And you're out sitting in some fucking hamburger stand going through this thing—"I'm never coming back. I'm gonna get a motel." Then what do you do? "Maybe I'll go to California." Then what will you do, schmuck? "I'll go to live with Sandy." Oh, I see, and then you're going to go back to the house? "Uh, maybe." Pretty soon it all peters out.

J: So how do you resolve it?

s: Oh, God.

J: Is it embarrassing? [*Sam laughs.*] What's so fucking funny about that?

s: I'm totally embarrassed.

J: You are?

s: You come back and say, "I'm sorry. I'm totally embarrassed by my actions. I just want to sleep with you, okay? I want to hold you and fuck you and I'm sure sorry. It won't ever happen again."

J: But it's more than that.

s: Oh, yeah.

J: You just want to be with the person. You just want to be with the person.

s: But the sexual thing—you're just powerless in the face of that.

J: I know.

s: I mean I'm totally powerless. [. . .] When I first got with Jessica, I thought, "Well, this is great. I'm going to settle down, get in a home situation, have kids. Make a family and all that stuff." I had this whole idea. Then I realized, "I'm with a totally different woman. She wants kids, and she wants a certain kind of feeling like that, but she doesn't want to stay in one place too long." Six months in Santa Fe was enough. She wanted to go somewhere else. She said, "We can go to Europe next year. I'll get pregnant and we'll go to Europe and then we'll come back and have a kid and spend some time there and we'll go somewhere else." That's kind of like the way she wants to live. [. . .] What do you think of this theory of men turning forty and on past? Do you think it has anything to do with the age we are?

J: You mean midlife crisis?

s: Whatever they call it. It's not coincidental that this is all happening—

J: There's a definite thing that happens. You know how they say adolescence, everybody has the same kind of . . . "It's a difficult period, you know, adolescence." So it's a real thing, and it's generally thought of as being difficult. It's like a passage.

s: You feel like time passes.

J: There must be other kind of passages, like the one at forty.

s: I bet it is. I mean, you definitely feel that there's two sides—there's a youth and then a different kind of age.

November 28, 1983 November—late—snowing in Iowa—1983

[HANDWRITTEN]

Dear John,

I'm up late, very stoned. Everyone's asleep but me & I was down in the kitchen & started wondering if you ever made it back to Mill Valley alive. You must have. Looked like you were having a mixed bag of emotions when you left. It was great to see you but I know now that, aside from these infrequent encounters where there's always women to contend with in the situation—it would be great to every once in a while, meet up with just the two of us—on the road somewhere—no women—no kids—maybe a dog—but basically just you & me. That was when we had the most fun I think. (And what's the point of getting together if we don't have a little fun?) We always talked about that & never really did it. We ought to actually plan something, sometime for about a week maybe—where we just went down the road together & got stoned all the time & did dumb things like write notes in notebooks & take pictures & have revelations. Why not? I think maybe there's some fear about that—like I know it would be hard to leave Jessica and tell her I'm going to just get loaded for a while & wander around aimlessly—just like it would be hard for you to leave Scarlett. But if we know up front that we're coming back then what's the big deal?

I know I've got two sides in me that are very irreconcilable. One's totally undisciplined & just wants to wander into some adventure—even just the sense of adventure—that feeling of "life is a real adventure"—and the other side has this image of an orderly, disciplined life. This is like the stuff you were telling me when you were here—'life on the road' versus 'life at home.' Maybe they have to be lived parallel to each other & at the same time now that they're part of a whole. I don't know.

I've been thinking a lot about the Work lately. It goes in cycles. I'll go weeks without a single thought of work. Living totally automatically, swamped in dreams, delusions, in the grips of all kinds of emotions—then some little thought will come in about sensation or an idea from the books— like energy and I'll try something like sitting or working with the 3 foot atmosphere exercise. And that will go on for a while & slowly dwindle into oblivion until something starts up again. I really appreciate the ream of notes from the meetings. A lot of it was duplicates from what you'd sent me before but I re-read everything & found new stuff—or stuff I'd overlooked. Pentland's whole emphasis on search for truth seemed to be the cutting edge. Suddenly I saw on paper that he was asking for something in all that. It was as though he were proposing that the real search for the heart of the matter was being lost or overlooked in preference to a narrow view of work as a series of private investigations & then a 'show & tell' kind of session once a week at the meetings. He seemed to turn the whole sense of what a 'meeting' is in a new direction. But, I suppose, he always did that & I was unaware of the direction. I feel this real need at times for a discipline in my life. But a lot of it has to do with a kind of superstitious fear (like Pent. says in the notes) of not being on the side of the Big Powers. It really is a question to me now of what *work* actually is. What's really behind it? Did I ever work purely for the sake of self-observation? Did I ever carry it to the point where I saw what I need to see? A voluntary work is what he calls it. I never really felt it was voluntary—like "I'm going to *volunteer* for the Army—I'm not going to wait to be drafted, I'm actually going to volunteer!" I never felt that—except rarely—at work weeks. It was always this sense of obligation.

Anyway—enough raving. I've got to hit the sack.

More—later,
Sam

December 10, 1983

[HANDWRITTEN]

Johnny,

What a saga this life is! The ups & downs are staggering. Yesterday I got engaged for the 1st time in my life. I suddenly had this overwhelming desire to conform to all the social formalities of being "in love" in the old style. I wanted to give her a ring & ask her in the corniest way possible, if she'd be my wife & have my kids and live with me forever. I bought this great antique Sapphire ring set in gold. I stuffed it in my pocket & got all excited about asking her. I waited for her to come into the motel where we watch the dailies every afternoon & when I saw her coming I swept her outside into the cold wind & snow & popped the question. We jumped up & down together like little kids, giggling in the snow.

I've been thinking about your situation with Sharon for the past few days & even though you've probably arrived at what seems like "the end"—I wouldn't be so sure. Just looking back over my whole adventure with Jessica before we finally got together—I came to that same decision more than once—& it turned out wrong. I know you feel it's different with her because of her strange attachment to that guy but, even so, there may be a whole new area of feeling that will come up in her now. That's the thing that gets me is—no matter what you "decide" there's always the feelings that move in their own crazy ways without regard for any decision. Anyway, I'll bet dollars to donuts you haven't seen the last of her.

I've got about 4 more days here in the land of the lost. Then I'm on the road again. It's been unbelievably cold here lately—sub-zero temperatures every day. Wind howling. Snow blowing in your face until you feel like your ears & nose are going to fall right off. I'll be real glad to get out of it although much of the time here with Jessie has been great.

Here's some possibilities for us getting together over the next month or so:

If you can't meet me on the road to L.A.—we could get together in L.A. for a couple days. I might swing up through San Francisco on the way out to Boston. We could meet up there & you could even travel with me for a couple days—heading East & then fly back to S.F. I guess it all depends on when you can get free. Anyway, I'll call you in L.A.

Your partner,
Sam

Sam and Johnny

March 23, 1985

[TYPED]

Dear Sam

Phone calls suck and I can't seem to write a decent letter anymore. Maybe postcards are the way to go.

Scarlett is sitting at the other end of the table wrapping birthday presents for Kristy's twins to take to them tomorrow in Santa Rosa. She's going to stay up there for the weekend. Well since she's going to be up there, I didn't sign up for St. Elmo and Mary and I are going to get a place for the weekend, drink champagne, watch erotic movies, fuck, eat and talk about the work I guess since it looks like she's "in the work."[1] In any case she's been meeting with Needleman every week in S.F. and is about to enter one of his Sunday night reading groups. She seems very interested and can't be pried away from Fragments and is suddenly seeing herself and the world anew in a way that's both very unsettling and exciting for her. She comes to all this with about 200% more preparation than I did at 28, that's clear.

I've been riding the Harley all winter cause we haven't had much rain. This year "The terrible trio" as Jesse calls it (Me Jesse and Scarlett) have spent a lot of time together and I'm really thankful for it because it's always very light and filled with laughs and good feelings. A lot of watching video movies and going out for ice cream and walks . . . that sort of thing.

I signed a contract with the dog trainer for the new Golden which is due to be born this month. The contract has all these stipulations about the dog must be trained and taken to shows and bred and the splitting of stud fees. We have a name for him too. Scarlett thought of it. Teddy. Teddy, Tuppence, Honey, Ace and Banjo all lived together in a little house. In fact Tuppence is laying at my feet next to her catnip mouse. The dogs are in the back and Jesse is up at the ranch waiting for a horse to be born and O-Lan is in S.F. at auditions of her new play and Scarlett is taking a nap.

I'm a little nervous because I'm one of the three people who walks out and gets to speak about tonight's Theme question which is all about Impressions of myself as I am.

---

1. Mary was a girlfriend of Johnny's.

There's a young work at a place in S.F. on Balboa St. that I've been included in and I read *All and Everything* there last Friday night (part of the Arch Absurd chapter).[2] That's where this Theme meeting is. About 30 people. It's Phil Wood and Bill Jordan and a few others from G group and now Mr. Dark. And then there's this thing in Sacramento with Needleman's group which is quite an experience. He hasn't been back since the first time we drove up there so I've made the trip twice alone. (Well, actually the first time I went up with Mary and stuck her in a classy Motel during the meeting.) It's a lot of work and not what I thought it would be (I didn't figure on all the unflattering impressions of my self not knowing what the fuck I was doing) and of course for an hour I'm there trying to respond to people's questions and impressions. The second time I drove up with Scarlett and we were late so I pulled into the first Motel I came to and it turned out to be a super X rated motel with red wallpaper and the entire ceiling covered with mirrors and colored lights and porno movies on the T.V. (That's where I left Scarlett and Honey during the meeting.) We drove home the next morning. Needleman loved that story. However . . . all this has been very helpful for me, for the way I'm understanding the Ideas and am able to approach them in myself and I can see the relationship between these new activities and the crafts and group meeting.

Glad you got *Idiots in Paris*.[3] I read that aloud to Scarlett in our bedroom and she cried at the end. I got a strong feeling of "being efforts" when I read it a few years ago. I'd like to read it again. I should read all the books again.

So I guess you could say there's a strong Work atmosphere going on around this time in my life including my relationship with Mary now.

You probably feel funny when I say I miss being stoned with you, like we can't have a good time without being stoned . . . which isn't true of course but certainly has elements of truth in it. We've certainly never been as aligned for such a length of time, without disappearing into our own private obsessions when we weren't stoned. I think about that great trail ride a few years back. So, some day we'll have to do that again . . . when the time and place is just right.

2. *All and Everything* comprises "ten books in three series" by Gurdjieff; the parts of the trilogy were published in 1950, 1963, and 1974.

3. *Idiots in Paris: Diaries of J. G. Bennett and Elizabeth Bennett* (1949), published in 1980, describes, among other things, the last three months of Gurdjieff's life.

Sam
&
Johnny
and a lot of talking.
1984 N·M

I've been keeping busy along with The Work with the housecleaning jobs (I got about 5 houses) and with various photo and typing projects I've got underway. (I'm doing Scarlett's biography with her grandmother, from tapes I've made of her telling me the stories.)

I know what a pain in the ass it is to sit down and write, so don't worry about that. I got the envelope with the Nova Scotia stuff in it and gave it to O-Lan. By the way . . . did you ever come across my precious Ivory Chinese statue in those boxes. If so, I'd dearly like to get a hold of it. But maybe it was scooped up back there in Nova Scotia?!

It was good seeing you at dinner when you were here. Needleman said the same thing. Hope to see you soon.

John

March 30, 1985—Santa Fe

[HANDWRITTEN]

John,

Thanks for your letter & notes. Just finished reading the whole batch. Some very inneresting stuff in there. Must be quite a new dimension to be found in that situation of being the "leader."

It's very quiet here right now. Shura & Jessie are taking naps. The birds are chirping & a light snow is falling past the windows. I've been reading avidly lately—about six books at once, as usual, so it takes forever to finish one. Finally finished *Idiots in Paris* though—very simple & touching, particularly the ending stuff. What ideas we've all fabricated in our minds about who Gurdjieff was—those of us who never knew him! I got a whole new & different sense of him from that book. Also reading a great piece by Tolstoy called *Confession*—all about his tremendous moral & spiritual turmoil at the age of about 51. Talk about middle-aged crisis—this guy really put himself through the mill. Then, again, re-reading the 3rd series & going through all the notes from Pentland's talks that I have.[1]

I'm struggling along with my play, which is very difficult to write because, finally, I'm beginning to see the absolute hopelessness of all forms of negativity—but *hopefully*, this will be some kind of final definitive piece on my age-old themes of father & son, sister, brother, mother, family, etc.[2] Who knows? If nothing else, I feel as though, after twenty one years of writing I'm finally able to get down to the real essence of what's behind it. So many masks. Also doing some painting & re-kindled that old interest which has now manifested as yet another obsession for Western Art from the late 1800's to the turn of the century. Luckily, now—and I don't know whether this has to do with age or not, but these whirlwinds of obsession are much more short-lived, even though they have all the same characteristic intensity & blind lust behind them.

Me, Jessie & Shura have come into some brand new territory of togetherness now. There's a real sense of family & belonging to each other. It's a whole different

1. The third series of *All and Everything*.
2. The play became *A Lie of the Mind.*

ball park raising a little girl but it's quite incredible to see how it demands a different side of me & how positively she responds to it when I allow it in myself.

I'll write more later. We're getting set for dinner now. I miss all of you very much. Maybe one day I'll get over the sense of tragedy about my departure from you all & we can be together without the past hanging so heavy on my head.

Your old friend,
Sam

May 15, 1985

[HANDWRITTEN]

Sam

[. . .] I miss the long discussions we used to have.

This is a hard time for me. They come and go. I've come face to face with some of the things I can't bear about myself. These are the things that seem so insignificant to others and that's why it's probably so hard to talk about. I guess it's not the trait—it's the shock of the way it's experienced internally. In particular—my incredible lack of patience which seems to take all sorts of forms—jumping from one thing to another, never finishing anything for the most part or finishing it not exactly right, the continual sense of hurry in everything I do, the striving for results, the way it appears as short tempered-ness, irritability and other negative forms which I usually justify—etc. etc.

I can't tell you how much I don't want to be this person. But there it is. There's no escape from it. [. . .]

Last night I was up at Mary's place in the mountains. We watched *Body Heat* and fucked and afterward she went out into the woods over to this other cabin that her kitchen was in and came back with Baked Potato & cream & sausage and we lay in bed and tried to figure the movie out. She had missed her group meeting and I think eventually this "work" will not be for her.

Scarlett's been sick for a week but is better this morning. I think we'll be able to go to the same work week which is great. I'm going to spend most of the day with her. [. . .]

Me & Jess usually hang out after school. I look at him and realize he'll be grown—off on his own somewhere. I'm really grateful for the years with him—these years & those great Flying Y years when he was 6 and Nova Scotia etc.

I've been reading a lot of Henry David Thoreau—he's a great nature romantic. It's amazing how similar he seems to Kerouac. The romanticism and how life is only real if you write it in your journal. We both know a little of that feeling. Life is only real . . . etc. [. . .]

John

October 1985

[TYPED]

Sam

You must feel like one of those born-again people what with a new play underway and a new film coming out and a baby on the way.[1] How are you feeling? Is it all turning out or going in the direction you had hoped?

I'm enclosing some things I've been working on since I finished transcribing our talks, which is the letters . . . not just ours but I started with ours and going over them made me feel very nostalgic. It brought back so many feelings from those times. Looking back like that, you see so many things. I was struck reading again your letters from England the tone of excitement and the quality of "play" you had and wonderment about yourself (in relation to The Work) and I found myself hoping that's all still alive. You'll probably see much more about your own stuff. Also I'm enclosing some stuff from the last book I read which I thought you'd like. [. . .]

On the home front things have not changed too much and everyone is well. The days are beautiful October Mill Valley leaf covered clear cloudless days. It's nice having Dennis living nearby . . . I think I mentioned he has a place over on Sycamore St. and a lot of time I walk over there with Honey or with Scarlett. Walking through these streets I feel like Archie (or Jughead). Jesse and I hang out a lot after school, do things with the dogs or cruise into town for an ice cream . . . still sit around with Jesse and Scarlett at night sometime reading aloud etc. Of course it's changed in that Jesse isn't 5 anymore which is hard to get used to but there's a lot that's remained the same.

We never really got together since our long stoned horsey ride in NM what with one thing and another coming up. So I guess we still have those times ahead of us. I think of you often and hope you're doing o.k. Tell Jessie hello from me. I saw her last film with Eddie and enjoyed it.[2]

yr buddie
johnny dark

1. The film was *Crimes of the Heart* (1986; directed by Bruce Beresford and costarring Jessica Lange); the baby was Hannah Jane Shepard, born January 13, 1986.
2. The film was *Sweet Dreams* (1985; directed by Karel Reisz and costarring Ed Harris).

October 29, 1985—N.Y.C.

Dear John,

Glad to get all yr latest letters. It's very strange—the effects of time on everything. It's hard to see where I stand in time. How "old" I really am.

I think about you too, a lot. How come, out of all the people I've come across in this life that you & me somehow hit it off as partners in that odd way we had where we both understand a certain ridiculousness about things. It was great fun. I don't think I've ever had so much pure fun before with anyone of the same sex. Of course fun with women is different because you get to actually climb inside each other's bodies & that's fun of a different order. But there were times when the two of us just roamed for that wild adventure of the imagination—the "real" imagination—that I don't think can be duplicated.

I've always set myself up as a great enemy of sentimentality. But now, I see, that time brings a certain yearning toward past experience. That's the thing my old man got lost in. That & the bottle.

I think about Jesse a lot. How strange this whole thing must be for him. And yet, part of him must have already accepted it by now. I worry about what kind of mark it's going to leave on his life as a man.

I'm back here in N.Y. struggling with another play. Trying to make sense of it—and worse, trying to make sense of being a playwright. I still feel so goddamn awkward with it all. Like an imposter. The emphasis of my life changes from day to day. Some days I think, all the meaning I need is to be with Jessica & Shura & the new baby & some life in the country—far away. Then I come back to some attempt to accept the whole 9 yards. It's difficult. Even success is difficult. It seems so weird that I should find my life, as it is, so difficult to accept it in its totality. Why am I always partial & denying some aspect of it in favor of something else?

The work involvement here has been a big help. I've actually discovered something about my own personal needs & true questions. What I've found is that my curiosity about "the Work" is really in relationship to questions that were already in me about life & the work is the only avenue of true response to that part of myself that needs to know. It's no longer a quest for some secret that the others have the answer to. I suppose the death of Lord Pentland has brought that home in some way.[1]

I need to get some sleep now as I've got to get up early & take Shura to school—then off to rehearsals.

I'll write more later when I get a chance. Hope things are leveling out for you. Say hi to Scarlett & Jesse & everyone.

All my best,
Sam

1. Pentland died February 14, 1984.

December 21, 1986—N.Y.C.

[HANDWRITTEN]

Here I am in N.Y. again. In a dressing room out in Queens working on a Woody Allen film.[1] Life is strange & totally unpredictable.

Today's supposed to be my last day then I drive from here to Minnesota for Xmas. Another world—minus zero degrees with a thick blanket of snow—like a Xmas card. It's the place me & Jessie first ran away to & spent weeks holed up in her cabin building fires & realizing our lives had been suddenly and irrevocably changed. We were together at last. Five years has passed since that morning we had breakfast at Sam's Pancake House in San Rafael, then returned to Mill Valley & I packed & got in my truck & drove down the highway. Amazing. I find myself reminiscing much more now than I used to. Must have to do with time.

I've been taking long walks alone at night on the streets of the city. I really love it this time of year. The air is cold & crisp & all the Xmas lights are out. During the day the shopping madness is frightening but at night its oddly peaceful. Jessie's in Minneapolis with the girls, I can't wait to see them. We've been apart almost 2 weeks now. My life is so different without her. When I'm alone I feel lost & stupid & totally useless. I don't know what to do without her. She's my whole world. I never thought I'd be this way with anyone.

I guess Jesse told you about the situation with this filming & the train trip may be falling through. I'll know more about the state of things after Xmas. It would've been a great trip but actually it turns out to be much easier on me not to go back & forth so much.

I'll be in touch with you after Xmas. Hope everything is well with all of you.

My love to Jesse, Scarlett & O-Lan,
Sam

1. Woody Allen's *Winter Project* (ultimately titled *September*); Shepard replaced Christopher Walken, only to have his own part reshot with Sam Waterston.

June 1987—Virginia

[HANDWRITTEN]

Dear John,

Thanks for the letter. Yes—another tadpole has sprouted—Samuel Walker
is his name & a fine lad he is.[1] Here's a picture of the whole crew. Hannah
Jane is going to be an Olympic shot-putter by the look of it.

Things are really jumping around here now. Lots of shitty diapers &
sleepless nites but a rollicking good time nonetheless. Every once in a while
Jessie & I just stare at each other with kids in our arms & break out laughing.
Hard to believe a scant 5 years ago we were chasing each other from hotel to
motel.

I hope one of these days we can meet up like you said you wanted to
in Calif.—some anonymous place with no associations & just have a good
old get-together with no big moral dilemma hanging over our heads—like
"should we get stoned or shouldn't we"—just have some fun & talk a lot.

Seems to me our friendship was always something that was strictly between the two of us anyway. We should have a lot of stuff to talk about now. I
don't even mind if you bring a camera & tape-recorder & all the pot that'll fit
in your truck. That's all a part of it anyway.

I've been reading King Lear again & working on my screenplay, which
is set to start shooting in Oct. with Charles Durning, Jack Warden, Tess
Harper, Patricia Arquette & Jessica.[2] Should be a good line-up.

Hope all is well with you out there. Say hi to Scarlett, Jesse & O-Lan.

Yr Pal,
Sam

---

1. Samuel Walker Shepard was born
   June 14, 1987.
2. The screenplay was for *Far North*
   (1988), which he also directed.

June 1, 1988—Virginia

[HANDWRITTEN]

Dear John,

Great to hear from you. I was beginning to wonder if you'd finally given up on our long alliance.

Sounds like all your pursuits are as strange & idiosyncratic as mine. Mostly now our lives are consumed by raising three little kids. It's a 24 hour task with hardly any let-up. It runs the full gamut of emotions & the rewards & failure are absolutely immediate. Our little girl Hannah Jane loves singing—she loves to be sung to & told stories to. She's at that age (2) where every story or song takes on mythic proportions. I've dug up a lot of my old Cowboy songs which she can't get enough of—especially lines like "The Fiery & the Snuffy are rarin' to go"[1]—I take her out on one of my old Quarter Horses & we ride around the farm—she likes splashing through the creek on horseback. By the way—isn't it great that Jesse's working with horses up in Santa Rosa & making money on his own! I'm really proud of him.

Our little son, Walker, is just turning a year old & has just learned to walk (hence the name). He's cut a bunch of teeth that go six ways to Sunday in his mouth.

Shura is a tall, elegant 7 year old now—playing violin & going to school.

Summer is now upon us. Very hot—in the hundreds. We've been planting lots of gardens. Vegetables & roses. In fact the activity is non-stop.

I'm trying to write another screenplay which I'd like to shoot maybe in the winter.[2] It's a period Western in black & white—something I've always wanted to do. This production company is very happy with my last film so they say they'll put up the bread for another one. I can't believe I can actually make films now.—If you get a chance to see Wim's new film *Wings of Desire*, try to see it. It's incredible. All about Angels. The best thing he's ever done & shot in beautiful black & white.

I don't know what to say except occasionally I do miss those amazing days where we'd get stoned & just wander

1. From the nineteenth-century cowboy song "I Ride an Old Paint."
2. According to Shepard, the screenplay was for *Silent Tongue* (1993), the second film he directed. It starred Richard Harris, River Phoenix, and Alan Bates.

around through shopping markets or ride bikes or just stare at life & go on mental journeys. There was something so great about that time but I guess it's gone. Hard to believe things just pass like that but I guess you just go on to the next saga of one's life.

Hope all is well with you & Scarlett. Say hi to Jesse & O-Lan.

Your friend,
Sam

November 3, 1988

[HANDWRITTEN]

Sam

    Although late—I wanted you to know I was thinking of you on your birthday. This is a birthday card. Happy Birthday Old Man.

    It is doubtful that I'll be in a position to meet you in New Mexico this winter owing to the time away from home it will take to drive and the money—which I'm saving to take Scarlett and Magic to Hawaii.[1] So more time will pass.

    From time to time I meet people in "The Work" in the street and it amazes me how far into the past all that has receded. I guess it has taken another form altogether.

    I send you the last episode in the section entitled "women" (which actually begins with my Mother.) Well—everything changes but this is what's happening now. Try writing Cowboymouth today and see what comes out [Great idea: Hemingway is forced to re-write *For Whom the Bell Tolls* 30 years later.] Everyone's *New* work is the re-writing of their old work. The ultimate on "calling yr shot."

    Be of good health and cheer. Scarlett & I send Birthday

Love
John

1. Magic was Johnny's girlfriend for
   a few years in the late 1980s.

October 3, 1989—Virginia

[HANDWRITTEN]

Dear John,

Funny—I was thinking of you too, right about the time *your* letter arrived. Must be the weather. Those crisp Fall days when we'd be aimlessly stoned, wandering the streets of Mill Valley & goofing on anything that happened to jump into our heads. Those were some high times! I was thinking, last time I was up there, that we'd just somehow miraculously fall back into that way of being with each other but I guess everything changes. Still it was good to see you & Scarlett, although there's a sadness in it that I can't seem to get over. How we all just become separate from each other, after all that time of being so close.

I'm having one hell of a time with my writing lately. Can't seem to finish anything. I've got four incomplete plays on my desk & seven stories—but nothing is finished.

The kids are all in amazing form. The girls both going to school & Walker T-Bone discovering he's a boy—crashing around making airplane sounds & diving into the furniture.

We've had 32 inches of rain this year so horse activities have been cut back to a minimum. Trying to get some Foxhunters started for the winter season.

I have to return to L.A. on the 14th thru the 16th of this month for a re-shoot of *Defenseless*.[1] I'll be staying at the Four Seasons Hotel on Doheny—if you want to give me a call down there. I really don't want to leave the farm now that Fall has arrived but I guess I have to go. It would be great to see you if you happen to find yourself in L.A. around then.

Love to Scarlett & keep writing those juicy autobiographical memoirs—they're great!

Your pal,
Sam

1. *Defenseless* (1991) was directed by Martin Campbell and starred Barbara Hershey, Mary Beth Hurt, and Shepard.

October 11, 1989

[HANDWRITTEN]

Dear Sam

Got your letter—nice letter and yes I puzzle over the same fate that befell us, first being in one life and then suddenly in another, hardly ever seeing each other, speaking or writing. I think we achieved a kind of openness of communication [. . .] by the proximity of us living in the same house, passing from room to room etc. [. . .] we generally pursued our own varied interests which have always been dissimilar from each other.

I too—always hoped, (after you left) that each time we met (here, Santa Fe, Virginia) we'd fall back into those great states—ie: that incredible horse ride we took—stoned—on the desert in N.M. or—stoned—sitting in the bedroom in Santa Fe contemplating shooting up the new wall with shotgun or—stoned—at the gun show and later in the upstairs room of the house in Iowa that time I came with Sharon.

So at first of course I kept pushing for us to get loaded and (therefore crazy) when I first came to Santa Fe—which must have been unsettling for Jessica and maybe the reason she didn't want me to visit.

But for the most part I never could understand why we couldn't manage to be free somewhere for a day or days at a time as on that proposed trip we were one time going to make camping out, riding the highways [. . .] instead . . . we always met "by the way," always with other people. Even last train visit to Virginia, we were never once alone away from Jesse or people in the editing room. Or here . . . aside from ½hr meeting in Denny's, never just you and me walking the beaches or hiking or riding or swimming all day alone because it needed to get worked in with Jesse and Sandy and other obligations.

And now, due to one thing and another I can't smoke anymore and don't drink yet I refuse to believe we can't somehow hit those states between us on the natch and I still feel that one day we will be able to meet in some "neutral" place and just amble around digging things and each other the way we used to do because my feelings for you, my admiration love remains intact in spite of limitations of time and situation so regardless of "how long" I'll never let us lose touch.

Me and Scarlett are taking a trip at the end of November. From here up to Reno—through Donner pass, down other side of Sierra thru Owens Valley to Big Pine, visit friends there then on to Shoshone in Death Valley arriving Thanksgiving. Two days there and then down to Palm Springs to meet up with my girlfriend Magic who'll be there having just come off a week's hike in the desert. Then over to (don't know how to spell it but it's pronounced 'Oh-Hi') where Krishnamurti foundation & library is (that's where he died) and then home. Having both Goldens with us the whole way.

So in honor of the trip I just bought a beautiful little 38 police special Smith & Wesson. Very small & light. Undercover like the kind the cops wear tied to their ankles or down the back of their pants.

I may have mentioned am reading for first time *Moby Dick* and don't laugh if you haven't actually read it through word for word but I think still it's the greatest thing I've ever read. One of those pieces you can't imagine a human writing.

I wanted to tell you about my trip to Arizona to see that first love of mine—of which I told you a bit over the phone last time. But it'll keep.

Meanwhile I am writing away at the never to end Bio.

"An old jazz piece was on the player. Marion and I started dancing. I laid her back on the white marble table, where the vet used to kill the dogs, and pulled her pants down. She held on to the sides of the table while I ate her but I was drunk and impatient to climb on top of her. It was a short fuck. We could hear Jerry's Harley coming down the dirt road just as we finished and we pulled ourselves together before he walked in—"

That's part of that same introduction-to-letters-from-women section I sent you last time (except in some cases there are no letters)

Hope yr stay in L.A. is good and you get back to the family O.K. Understand you took the train. *And* you have a birthday coming up. Me too before long. Another year and I hit 50. "Interesting" (as we used to say in the work).

With affection,
John Dark
President of the Lisa Vale Fan Club[1]
Secretary of the Garcia Vega Club

1. Lisa Vale was a successful fashion model in the early 1980s, appearing often on the cover of *Cosmopolitan*. Shepard and Dark wrote her a joke fan letter as the "Lisa Vale Fan Club."

October 29, 1989—Virginia

[HANDWRITTEN]

Dear John,

Glad to hear you all survived the rumbling earth.[1] That must've been spooky for a while. I tried to call you at the house for 2 days but the phone lines were down I guess & couldn't get through. Jesse's description of it was pretty vivid with his truck shaking like silly putty & all the horses galloping around.

Due to your on-going influence I've been reading *Moby Dick*—another classic I avoided for no good reason. It's an amazing piece of work. How does a man sit down & decide to even attempt something like that? He must've been on speed.

Life here is in the 'kids-go-to-school' mode. Both Hannah & Shura have to be trucked back & forth twice a day, so there's lots of driving. The weather's beautiful now—Fall here is my favorite time of year. Went foxhunting yesterday on one of my retired polo ponies.

Don't get paranoid about the letter writing. I just sometimes can't get motivated but I enjoy the exchange.

Give my love to Scarlett.

All the best,
Sam

1. The Loma Prieta earthquake (6.9 on the Richter scale) struck the San Francisco area on October 17, 1989, killing sixty-three and interrupting the World Series.

Sam and John

Nova Scotia
1973

September 4, 1990—Virginia

[HANDWRITTEN]

Dear John,

Funny I should get your letter on the very same day I'm cleaning out one of my many neglected filing cabinets—full of old letters, manuscripts, notes—piles of papers & I came across your huge book of notes you sent me of our endless dialogues—other letters from you, dating clear back to England & a great black & white photo of the two of us destroying the front porch in Nova Scotia—me leaping off the steps with a hammer & you in the background with bushy black hair like the early Bob Dylan—we look like we're in High School or something & I thought what a great friendship it was! Truly great. I miss the very same things—just riding around in the white Chevy talking about any old thing that floated into our demented imaginations & then, momentarily, actually becoming characters & acting them out as we wandered through grocery stores or the streets of San Francisco or San Rafael on a brisk stoned afternoon. Somehow, it always reminded me of drunken Irish characters from Flann O'Brien—stumbling from bar to bar, spouting poetry, singing ballads & making up outrageous stories—always in trouble with women & ultimately pathetically alone. I hope some way we can again strike up our own private dialogues—hysterically funny to us only—maybe as *very* old men on a bus stop or a park bench in some place like Lincoln, Nebraska where we're equally lost.

I, too, have been going through the same heart-wrenching stuff you describe—(maybe not the same but with the same results) & each time I come out the other end of it I think—aah, at last it's over—I can get on with my life again but it keeps coming back. I'm convinced now it has nothing to do with women although I make myself believe I wouldn't feel this way if it wasn't for "her."

Writing is such a pain in the ass. I'd like to just talk & maybe walk—that's about it. I'm exhausted from it all. Hope we can find a way to meet up & have a good time one of these days. It would be great to see you. Love to Scarlett & my ex-wife if you see her. And tell my son to call me—I've left messages all over hell for him. I remember the last words my Dad ever wrote me in a letter—"See you in my dreams."[1] How 'bout that.

Your on-going amigo,
Sam

1. Shepard used this phrase as the title of a chapter in *Cruising Paradise* loosely based on his father's death.

Calif
198.

Bill   Johnny   Sam

Then Bill Hart (left) arrived from
New York for a visit and stayed
most of the summer like a mole
in Sams basement den, drinking
beer and reading every night till
dawn.

May 27, 1991—Virginia

[HANDWRITTEN ON TOTIER CREEK FARM STATIONERY]

Dear John,

Thanks for your sudden flood of letters. Always good to hear from you & your latest state-of-mind. I've been all over the shop lately—running back & forth to N.Y. with the new play.[1] Very strange shifts where I'll be mowing hay on a tractor in the middle of 60 acres of open field with crows circling over head & rabbits jumping out in front of me then suddenly cut to West 46th St. in Manhattan—picking my way through a million alien beings & spending 12 hours a day inside a theatre with a bunch of actors. It's been very thrilling though to get back into theatre after a 6 year hiatus. I forgot how much simple fun it is to work with a play—lights, costumes, props—all the down home hand-madeness of it, as opposed to movies where it's all about the camera. Bill Hart directed this one.[2] You remember Billy—standing by the refrigerator in Mill Valley—staring into it & finding nothing to eat. That photo of the three of us straddling bikes like giant retarded children out by the marsh.

It would be great if we could get together this summer. I agree. Right now I have no idea where events will take me. I need to find an acting job soon as I'm in deep shit again with money. Can't seem to earn enough of it these days. Looks like I'm going to direct another one of my screenplays this Fall.[3] Amazing luck considering I got fried by the critics on my first one.[4] If that becomes real I'll be on location, possibly in New Mexico or Texas. Maybe we could meet up then if this summer doesn't work out.

Right now I'm working on yet another play, re-typing the one I just did & doing general farm labor.[5] I love sitting on a tractor & plowing or bush-hogging. It's one of the great pleasures in this life. Never monotonous. I have 14 head of feeder steers to sell this summer plus 7 head of horses. This farm

---

1. *States of Shock* premiered at the American Place Theatre in New York on April 30, 1991.
2. Bill Hart, a director and literary manager at the Public Theater, also directed Shepard's *Tooth of Crime (Second Dance)*.
3. Shepard's note: *Silent Tongue*.
4. Shepard's note: *Far North*.
5. The new play was *Simpatico* (1994).

I'm going to get to direct another one of my ___ this fall. Amazing luck considering I go ___ say the critics on my first one. If that be ___ real I'll be on location, possibly in N ___ Mexico or Texas. Maybe we could meet u ___ if this summer doesn't work out.

Right now I'm working on yet an ___ play, re-typing the one I just did ___ general farm labor. I love sitting on ___ tractor & plowing or bush-hogging. ___ of the great pleasures in this life. Not ___ monotonous. I have 14 head of feeder ___ to sell this summer plus 7 head of hor ___ This farm is beyond my wildest dreams. ___ Kids are all developing into very head- ___ individuals — "spoiled rotten" would be ___ way my Dad would put it. They do ha ___ strong sense of themselves though & none ___ carry that horrible fear of retribution ___ with them — which is fine by me. They ___ swimming & would spend the whole da ___ pool if we let them. The stifling summer ___ hit us. Those Southern nights where everythin ___ with humidity & you seek out a rocking ___ the back porch with a fan overhead, sip ___ & listen to the frogs wail away. Something ___ Tennessee Williams. Me & Jessie are in lov ___ again & everything is hunkey-dorey. Give ___ hug for me & a peck on her furrowed brow ___

Love to you bu ___

is beyond my wildest dreams. The kids are all developing into very head-strong individuals—"spoiled rotten" would be the way my Dad would put it. They do have a strong sense of themselves though & none of them carry that horrible fear of retribution around with them—which is fine by me. They all love swimming & would spend the whole day in the pool if we let them. The stifling summer heat has hit us. Those Southern nights where everything drips with humidity & you seek out a rocking chair on the back porch with a fan overhead, sip iced-tea & listen to the frogs wail away. Something like Tennessee Williams. Me & Jessie are in love once again & everything is hunky-dorey. Give Scarlett a hug for me & a peck on her furrowed brow.

Love to you both,
Sam

Sam

1992   N.M.

January 9, 1992—Virginia

Dear John,

Here's some xeroxed letters from Kerouac to Ferlinghetti which you may already have. They were sent to me by the people who are making that documentary I took part in & read some of the selections you sent me. Also, some info on the Chinese poet Li Po who pops up in that wino poem you got from City Lights.

I mentioned your name to the film makers when I was there in N.Y. & told them you did the photos for *Motel Chronicles*—they would like to know if you have any "road pictures" to use in their film (see bottom of letter enclosed). If you do—contact them at the address & phone on letter.

Enjoyed your latest piece of writing. Wonderful to see you've discovered the use of *paragraphs*! And your spelling is almost impeccable! I'm proud of you, son. Not to mention you've developed a real knack for a turn of phrase.—I remember an interview I saw a film of once of Charlie Parker & they asked him what he thought set him apart from all other tenor sax men. His reply was stunningly simple—"The octave, man. Just the octave."

Warm Regards,
Yr. pal
Sam

where SAM WAS directing
A FILM he HAD WRITTEN..

1992

March 17, 1993—Virginia

[HANDWRITTEN ON TOTIER CREEK FARM STATIONERY]

John—

It was 10 years ago to the day (St. Paddy's) that we met in that Pancake House in San Rafael & I was completely strung out about whether to go or stay & you suggested I might as well go & I drove back to Mill Valley & packed, threw my guitar in the trunk, you took a last picture, I plugged in Hank Williams & headed south on Hwy. 5 for L.A. & an unknown future. It seems like an eternity ago. Since then my father has died, Pentland died, Jessica's father died, Joe had a stroke & can't speak, two of my kids were born & the world has turned upside down.[1] Who knows what lies ahead. I'm glad though that there's an on-going dialogue & friendship between us, as broken & intermittent as it might be, still there's a sense of some kind of continuity— maybe the only real impression I have of continuous time.

We had a monster blizzard here ("the Storm of the Century" they're calling it). More than a foot of snow in mid-March. No power for 2 days which was kind of fun. Heating the house with wood fires, cooking in the fireplace, hauling water up to the house & livestock from the spring—Just like the old days. The best part was no *T.V.*! Right now it's raining & turning the snow into brown sludge that runs in long muddy streams downhill toward the swollen creek. If we get any more water here we're going to have to build an ark. The wild birds are searching frantically for food so we've been feeding them off the back porch. All kinds—Cardinals, Jays, Sparrows, Red Wing Blackbirds, Robins, Crows, Black Capped Chickadees, Bluebirds, Purple Martins—it's like a sanctuary. It's Spring Break for the kids—no school—so they're running like maniacs through the house—chasing each other with wooden spoons—making pretend potato soup & living in fantasy land. I've been reading them the whole C. S. Lewis collection of the "Narnia Chronicles" which starts off with *The Lion, The Witch & the Wardrobe*. They're the perfect age right now for this stuff.

1. Joseph Chaikin, founder of The Open Theater, collaborated, as cowriter, with Shepard on *Tongues* (1978), *Savage/Love* (1981), *The War in Heaven* (1985), and *When the World Was Green* (1996).

Well—I'm off to Scottsville to collect the mail & buy some milk. Talk to you soon. "May the road rise before you & the wind stay always at your back."

Happy St. Patrick's Day
Love to Scarlett—
Sam

P.S.:—Good Reading Tip: *The Texas Rangers* by Walter Prescott Webb.

Johnny AND Sam

Noodle, Texas
MARCH-1994

Le Parker
MERIDIEN
NEW YORK

rm # 4109
(nose bleed section)

2/15

John —

Got your letter. Just returned from V
by train — back to work in the Big Apple. I'm
on the 41st floor of this mid-town Exective
type hotel that's so high up you can bar
see the street. Good view of Central Pk.
though, every morning. I'm enjoying N
like I never thought possible & realized
the nite while walking along Columb
that I lived the entire decade of the six
+ part of the 70's in a state of chronic
paranoia — i.e. — it was impossible to
enjoy anything back then. I've been
checking out all the restaurants in tou
going to plays, movies, museums — li
a regular tourist. I love walking the
streets — just the absolute non-stop
diversity of humanity. Incredible.

Glad you like Pete's book — I thou
you might connect with it. I'm now on
RING LARDNER, who I'm su
you've read but I neve
had before & I'm complete
stunned by this guy. Just finished a

February 15, 1994—N.Y.

[HANDWRITTEN ON LE PARKER MERIDIEN—NEW YORK STATIONERY]

rm. # 4109
(nose bleed section)
John—

Got your letter. Just returned from Virginia by train—back to work in the Big Apple. I'm on the 41st floor of this mid-town Executive type hotel that's so high up you can barely see the street. Good view of Central Park though, every morning. I'm enjoying N.Y. like I never thought possible & realized the other nite while walking along Columbus that I lived the entire decade of the sixties & part of the 70's in a state of chronic paranoia—i.e.—it was impossible to enjoy anything back then. I've been checking out all the restaurants in town, going to plays, movies, museums—like a regular tourist. I love walking the streets—just the absolute non-stop diversity of humanity. Incredible!

Glad you like Pete's book—I thought you might connect with it.[1] I'm now onto RING LARDNER who I'm sure you've read but I never had before & I'm completely stunned by this guy. Just finished a short story he wrote where he speaks from the P.O.V. of a 14 year old girl. Great stuff. Another reporter type–newspaper guy from Michigan who wrote a Sports column. It's fascinating to find how different writers pick a "voice" to speak in & Lardner had a great ear for that old twenties Mid-Western vernacular that I remember my Grandpa & Uncles used all the time. Stuff like: "Whitey, your nose looks like a rosebud tonight. You must have been drinkin' some of your au de cologne."

Gotta be at work at 7:A.M. so must sign off for now. Thanks for the pix. Talk to you later.

Your old Pard.
Sam

---

1. Shepard's note: Pete Hamill's
   A Drinking Life.

April 12, 1994

s: Ah God, I don't know. Today I was ready to fold up shop.

J: Why? What happened today? [. . .] Why were you ready to pack it up?

s: Oh, I don't know—I had one of those falling-outs with the old lady again just as she was going off to Chicago of all things.[1]

J: Oh, shit. That's the worst time. That's what makes it so shitty, because the person's not there and you have to wait . . .

s: You'd think after eleven years things would level out.

J: Why don't they level out?

s: I don't know.

J: It must be the same reasons over and over again.

s: Yeah, you know, there's this weird thing, some sense of like holding a grudge that comes up every once in a while.

J: When *you* have it?

s: Both of us. I don't know what it's about. It's weird. Very weird. We get along great for a while and then this other thing raises its ugly head.

J: You mean something from the past?

s: No, just these feelings, as though there's some grudge or something. But I don't know what the grudge is about.

J: Maybe it's not a grudge. Maybe it's . . .

s: It's the feeling of a grudge.

J: When you say grudge, that means against the other person.

s: Yeah. [. . .]

J: The last time I remember that happened, you were getting ready to pack it in and go to Texas—"Well, I guess I'll just go and move to Texas."

s: Woe is me.

J: Remember that? I said, "What? You're moving to Texas?" "Yeah, that's it. I've had it. I have totally had it. I'm moving to Texas." I said, "Oh, Jesus. Well, keep in touch." And then the next thing I heard, you guys were going away on a vacation somewhere. And then there was the time you drove back to Santa Fe nonstop. You had a fight, and you

1. Lange was going there to shoot *Losing Isaiah* (1995; directed by Stephen Gyllenhaal).

drove all the way to Santa Fe before you cooled off. And then you got there and just as you pulled into Santa Fe, it wore off and you ran to the phone—"Hello sweetheart. I'm sorry. And not only am I sorry but I'm in Santa Fe for Christ's sake. I got to drive all the way the fuck back now."

September 22, 1994—Virginia

[HANDWRITTEN]

John, ole pardner—

Good to hear from you once again. There's that old sting of nostalgia whenever I get one of your letters about our days back in the 70's, bopping around Marin County like a couple of misplaced beatniks. Sounds like things are changing rapidly out there for you—I've almost given up on the notion of "settling down" & "having roots" & all that stuff that emotionally I love to cling to. My whole life has been composed of nothing but transition sometimes to the point of feeling I was born in the back seat of a car. I have this terrible dread of packing a suitcase & yet at the same time, a great excitement about what might lie up ahead. I've always done my best work (i.e. writing) when I'm in the middle of some turbulent change. Being constantly uprooted always brings up the old basic questions about identity & reasons for being etc. Right now I'm home in Virginia on a drizzly day but come next week I'll be up in New York starting rehearsals on my new play, then off to Santa Fe to do a film then up to Minnesota for Xmas then back to Virginia.[1] It's endless.

Still working on my book of stories & piano.[2] I love piano & sometimes sit there slamming away at it for 3 hours at a stretch. Don't know if I'm improving but it's a great feeling just to play & let your fingers do the talking.

My youngest son, Walker, has become a chess genius at age 7. He beats me every time now (which isn't saying a whole lot about his talent) but he seems to have an amazing ability for seeing the abstract patterns of moves & all their consequences.

All the kids are back into the school routine & our lives are pretty much circumscribed by it. I don't mind it though; getting up at 6:00, fixing their lunches, feeding them breakfast, driving them to school. It's a good way to start the day off.

I hope you & Scarlett find a nice little nest somewhere & keep in touch.

Buena Suerte,
Sam

1. The play, *Simpatico*, was produced by the New York Shakespeare Festival in November.
2. The stories were collected in *Cruising Paradise* (1996).

May 13, 1995—Virginia

[HANDWRITTEN]

Dear John

Thanks for the letter. [. . .] Just got back from taking Walker to his Sat. soccer game. He's become quite an athlete super fast & coordinated—runs circles around all the kids on the field & scores these amazing goals like you see the European pros do on T.V.

I took the whole family to the Kentucky Derby & we had a great time. All the girls in their straw Derby hats & finery, Walker in a suit & tie. Got Eddie Arcaro's autograph for Walker (I guess I told you.)

Funny you mention Zen again. I've been re-reading *Beginner's Mind* by Suzuki—one of the most no-nonsense books I've ever come across on actual practice without the frills of philosophy.[1] I flipped to the front of the book & there was this inscription: "For Sam, April '75, Johnny Dark"—exactly 20 years ago. Good God, twenty years!, I thought. Back when we were running around San Rafael with replica model pistols, playing cops & robbers, stoned & stealing bathrobes. It's all too amazing.

Me & Jessica have decided to get married this Summer, up in Minnesota. If this becomes reality, I was wondering if you'd consider being best man. Kind of an odd request of a former father-in-law but I guess we've all done weirder things in this life.

Meanwhile, we're gearing up for the big move & so far, things seem to be going smoothly.[2] I'll be sending you the book toward the end of the month since I want to hold onto it as long as possible, just in case I strike lightning in a bottle before the official due date: (June 1st).

Hope everything is well with you & yours. Hi to Scarlett.

Yr. Old Friend,
Sam

1. Shunryu Suzuki's *Zen Mind, Beginner's Mind* (1970).
2. Shepard, Lange, and the children relocated from Virginia to Stillwater, Minnesota, not far from River Falls, Wisconsin.

September 1995

Still recording my book and at the same time, beginning "Part Two" to it, which is an idea I've had about the reworking of letters. So far I have twenty 90 minute tapes recorded.

I'm at a part in the recording where we're writing letters furiously back and forth to each other (in the early years of you and Jessica, when Mathew was looking for a house for you in Santa Fe and then later, when Sharon and I arrived in Iowa, your night out with Harry Dean and later on a veranda in L.A.)

Tremendous sense of time passing, as always. Lots of stuff about polo and musings about The Work and stories about meeting Pentland in New York and your letter about going to his funeral. [. . .]

Not everyone enjoys going back over the past and recording the present (which is really the past) but I sure get a kick out of it. I remember as a teenager sitting at my bedroom desk writing letters with carbon paper and filing the letters away in a special metal file my mother bought me for that purpose.

You're not the only one who doesn't write back. Out of about five or six people I write to on and off, only one (this guy in Idaho who's a college English teacher) writes back. I guess people go through a stage where they write letters and then one day it's over.

I'm still in school. In fact it's 6 a.m. on a warm Thursday morning and I have to be at school down in Marin at 9:00 for a couple of massages in the clinic. It takes me about an hour to drive down.

Scarlett and I got invited to a "Gurdjieff dinner" up here in Sebastapol a few weeks ago. Apparently there's a "Work" up here complete with house and movements room, farm, crafts etc. We didn't know anyone there except the people who invited us. They invited everyone to do movements before dinner. (I was the only one who declined.) I went straight and it was kind of boring. The thing about being stoned I guess is that I have a great time on my own thinking everything is so interesting. I wish I could find that same level of interest on the natch but when I'm straight I'm a lot more closed.

Jesse was here for a day. He stored his truck tool box with us before going off to Texas. We took a walk and talked about Bunny.[1] He thought that maybe he should break up with her (again) and said that she had told him she thought they should break up because she couldn't take his going off all the time. He was surprised to find that her saying that was a big relief to him. I advised him to do nothing and we talked about "many I's."

Scarlett is well and sends her love.

I was re-reading yr. new book the other day and enjoyed it even more, Good stuff. I like dipping into it now and again. [. . .]

J.Dark

1. Jesse's girlfriend.

Dear John—

I'm writing you this on the back of yr own letter as I got a sudden spark
that I should write & have no paper but this. I'm sitting in a tiny coffee shop
in River Falls Wisconsin having a Cafe Latte & a sandwich, after spending a
couple hours chain sawing firewood up on the new land I bought near here.
This is a town of 10,000 souls—college town & summer home of the Kansas
City Chiefs football team. Nice, quiet little burg with wide Western streets.
Me & Jessica are going thru an incredible common realization that we both
come from almost identical transient backgrounds, children of alcoholic
fathers & that neither one of us know where we want to live & call "home."
This morning I took her out for coffee & she said she was suddenly profoundly depressed about returning to the land of her childhood & that everything she'd imagined about being here in Minnesota was a total fantasy &
the actual reality of "being" here was something she couldn't foresee. I think
your advice to Jesse about "do nothing" is exactly right. I told Jessica we
should at least stick it out thru the winter before we picked up sticks again. I
mean seeing as how we've both invested close to 2 million in land & houses.
(What was that notion of *'many I's'*?) Anyhow I never would've guessed that
she'd be the first one to get sick of this place. I was just beginning to get into
it. In any case so long as we stick together I told her we can't stray far from
what's right. Where we ought to be is together & so far, that's holding. The
beat goes on.

Your Perpetual Buddy,
Sam

January 24, 1996

[HANDWRITTEN]

Sam

    I thought of yr old man, of course and of you and you and me at the height of our conviviality & late night sessions. Here's John Holmes writing in his previously unpublished journals abt his pal Kerouac (plus a few pages from Holmes' early essay about K.) I always get a fire in the belly when I read this stuff and wish there were some crazy friends around. Apparently they too used to plan to "meet up somewhere" for sessions of drink, smoke and mad dialogue.

    By the way, Scarlett—(a big fan of yours) sends her love.

John

Handwriting becoming even more senile. (Spelling *couldn't* get worse.)

John, mi amigo,

If I don't write now I never will
so — here goes. Thanks for your
latest 'news' letter. Always interest
your keen observations of stuff
around you.

Recently got back from the
most amazing trip with family
to deepest Mexico. (Tolum in the
Yucatan). Haven't been down there
since 1965! You know how I love to
fly — well, for about a week befor
this trip we scheduled, I was
teetering back & forth between
going / not going — incredible
inner turmoil about it — you
know, the kind of conflict where
life itself seems to be hanging
in the balance & all along you
absolutely know that something
along the way is going to tip the
balance & bingo — you'll end up
35,000 miles above the earth,
flying to the tropics or sitting
alone at home, hovering over
coffee, wishing you'd gone. Long
story short — I went &, of cours

March 1, 1996—River Falls, Wisconsin

[HANDWRITTEN]

John, mi amigo,

If I don't write now, I never will, so—here goes. Thanks for your latest 'news' letter. Always interesting, your keen observations of stuff around you.

Recently got back from the most amazing trip with family to deepest Mexico (Tulum in the Yucatan). Haven't been down there since 1965! You know how I love to fly[1]—well, for about a week before this trip we scheduled, I was teetering back & forth between going/not going—incredible inner turmoil about it—you know—the kind of conflict where life itself seems to be hanging in the balance & all along you absolutely *know* that something along the way is going to tip the balance & bingo—you'll end up 35,000 miles above the earth, flying to the tropics *or* sitting alone at home, hovering over coffee, wishing you'd gone. Long story short—I went &, of course the moment we landed in Mexico—sun, Spanish, palm trees, blue Caribbean—I couldn't believe I might have missed this out of some old, idiotic mind-habit about not flying. We stayed on this remote beach, pure white, saw maybe 6 people all day—mostly Mexican soldiers jogging down the shore. Swam every day— no T.V., no phone & random generator-driven electricity. Studied Spanish, played chess with Walker (who beat me 6 out of 7 times & always asked me if I was really trying, which I really was). Anyhow, it was about the best trip I've ever had & it was over all too soon.

On the return flight I'm feeling pretty full of myself now—if not courageous at least more macho. 'I can do this. You just get on, strap yourself in & go!' I'm getting a little help from Jessica in the form of small pinkish pills called "Zanex" or something—takes the edge off the anxiety. So—we take off from Cancun for a 3½ hour routine flight back to Minneapolis. Everything's sailing along nicely until somewhere over St. Louis, Missouri, the man in the chair directly behind us *dies!*[2] His wife is calling for help, so I stagger to my feet in a semi-drug stupor & go back to where they are. There he is—deader

---

1. Shepard details his distaste for flying in *Cruising Paradise*'s "Falling Without End."

2. According to Shepard, this incident forms the background to "Land of the Living" in *Day Out of Days* (2010).

than Road Kill—mouth agape, some kind of black intestinal bile spewed out across his chest and arms. She's in a white state-of-shock, pleading with me to help get him out into the aisle so she can administer mouth-to-mouth & palpitate his heart. So I stumble in there and grab the corpse behind his knee, throw one of his dead arms over my shoulder & haul him out to the aisle. Luckily, (though the man is quite dead) there's 2 doctors on board who set to work on him right away, trying to pump air & life back into him—but to no avail. The stewardess announces that we're now going to make an emergency landing in St. Louis—so we begin to descend. They pull this guy off the plane & proceed to hook him up to electro-shock equipment & zap him half a dozen times but he's not coming back to the land of the living. We leave the poor wife in St. Louis, alone with her dead husband, in a strange city, & proceed back home to Minneapolis. Everything about this trip was remarkable.

Now, we're back. It was -5 degrees this morning. Images of Mexico still haunt us all. The kids' sunburns are peeling & I'm out breaking ice in my cattle tanks. They say *spring* is on the way!

More later—
Buena Suerte!—
my good friend
Sam

July 25, 1996

[TYPED]

Sam

Book received, and a neat little thing it is too, with devastating picture on the back.[1] Amazing how much more "authentic" it reads than it does in manuscript form. It is finally distanced from the author in some wonderfully official hard cover way. Scarlett and I thank you.

Odd dinner coming up this Sunday in Marin at Eugene's house for an old friend from Conn. named Marion. In the early 60's Marion had affairs with Eugene, me and Dan over the space of a few years and Eugene is bringing us all together, now with our wives (but Marion without husband) 35 years later for a meal. Dan will be arriving from work at his S.F. gallery, natty in his tie and jacket, white beard and portly girth. Eugene will most probably be in T shirt and stoned out of his mind and I'll be coming from the spa in Calistoga in an image as yet undecided. I first fucked Marion on the "treatment table" of the dog pound in Milford Conn. late one night at the edge of the city dump. Other than that, I don't remember what she looked like except that she was close to six feet.

George called me from New York and wants to come out to Calif. for a few days so he can have me record all the stories that he's been storing in his brain about this one particular character we all used to live with in '59 on 116th st and Riverside and with whom, in fact, he's once again living down on the lower east side.[2] If he comes, the book will grow larger I'm afraid.[3] When I die, see that it gets to an editor. There's a good fellow.

I send you copies of some old photos I thought you might enjoy having. I've probably sent you some of these over the years—I can't remember. Maybe there are some you haven't seen.

Napped half the day;
No one punished me!
warmest affections

John

1. *Cruising Paradise*
2. Dark's note: George Ganzle, a friend of the poet Eugene Lesser's and mine from New York.
3. The book is Johnny's long work of vignettes and observations, published in part as *People I May Know* (2006).

Summer 1996

[TYPED]

Sam

And here I am between books again. I know very few people who read at all—almost none of the thirty or so women I work with read books. An occasional magazine and the newspaper is all. Scarlett reads anything that comes her way and when nothing is coming her way she reads science fiction. Jesse reads pretty much what you read (once he finds out what you're reading) and Dennis reads nothing but Gurdjieff books. I massaged a guy from Canada the other day who said he was a writer and we spent the hour talking about 19th Cent. English authors. The guy was a bit of a literary snob and hadn't much muscle tone. [. . .]

Why is it so difficult to read the writing of someone you know well? Do you find that to be the case? Others don't seem to have that problem but I do and I notice how hard it is for people who know me to want to read what I've written. And yet letters are acceptable. I find I have that trouble with your writing although once I actually begin reading, the resistance disappears. [. . .]

Here are all of my Lord Pentland tapes and a Lord Pentland photo among others which I thought you'd like to see although I may have already sent you some or all of them before over the years. Enclosed also—photo of me with some of the spa staff. Sexual encounters with two—blonde in black dress standing right behind me who nearly drove me mad (I wrote a little chapter about her for the book. She still has a kind of 'hold' on me and is a terrible tease but if you magnify her you'll see how great she looks) and Japanese girl at my right elbow was after hours thursday night bath partner. I'm making sketchy spa notes for later chapters should I live that long. People are still intolerant of my recording. And I can tell you, after a lifetime of it, I'm being very careful about not allowing myself to get swept away again by a pretty face, because I remember the pain. And I remember what Krishnamurti said—something to the effect that the mind is always pursuing pleasure, consciously or unconsciously and that our life is made up of desire into action and the sustaining of pleasure by thinking about the activity that's given pleasure. Well, I know first hand the kind of suffering that that pursuit can bring about, although in the beginning it seems impossible it could come to that. [. . .]

You know, we're still driving the old white Nova ('71) (immortalized in the first line of *Rolling Thunder Logbook*). I found a guy up in Geyserville who restores cars and I've made a deal with him to restore the Nova to it's almost original condition (plus power steering.) Paint job, seat covers, new dash etc. etc. Jesse (being very 26 and having grown up partly in that car) said . . . "Not power steering. Then it won't be cool anymore. And you'll lose the 'feel' of the road if you have power steering."

I said, "I've been feeling the fucking road with that car since 1971. It's time for a change."

I hope we can sit down to that brandy/joint etc. one day. Meanwhile—I hope all is well.

with affection
John

1/13/97

Dear John —

Can't hardly believe it but finally in
Ireland. Jessica's doing 'Streetcar Na
sire' in London, so I've brought the k
e for a week in the emerald Isle. We
nt walking around the streets near Trin
lege of the River Liffey. Everything s
teped in history & literature you can't
th your breath. Dublin seems to be th
osite of London — very alive & pulsing —
ch more youthful. Absolutely devasta
sies on every corner! I've rented a car
e going to make a little tour over to G
into Connemara then down through the
Limerick & Kilkenny & back to Dublin

Needless to say, I wish you & Jes
ng for the trip but — who knows — me
ll make it before we're both 80 ?? I'll
e the Blarney Stone a peck for you &
n some fine token back. Reading my c
Irish short stories along the way. By the w
ranks for sending me that John Cheev
y fine. I read every inch of it. Looking
hooking up with you & #1 son in Fe
ue to tip a jar of guinnes together.

Fond Rega
Yr Old Pa

January 13, 1997

Dear John—

Can't hardly believe it but finally made it to Ireland. Jessica's doing *Streetcar Named Desire* in London, so I've brought the kids over here for a week in the emerald Isle. We all went walking around the streets near Trinity college & the River Liffey. Everything so steeped in history & literature you can't hardly catch your breath. Dublin seems to be the opposite of London—very alive & pulsing—also much more youthful. Absolutely devastating lassies on every corner! I've rented a car & we're going to make a little tour over to Galway, up into Connemara then down through the Burren, into Limerick & Kilkenny & back to Dublin.

Needless to say, I wish you & Jesse were along for the trip but—who knows—we might still make it before we're both 80?? I'll try to give the Blarney stone a peck for you & bring you some fine token back. Reading my collection of Irish short stories along the way. By the way—thanks for sending me that John Cheever story. Very fine. I read every inch of it. Looking forward to hooking up with you & #1 son in Feb. We'll have to tip a jar of Guinness together.

Fond Regards,
Yr Old Pal
Sam

June 18, 1997

[HANDWRITTEN ON A POSTCARD FROM THE OLD LIBRARY, TRINITY
COLLEGE, DUBLIN, SHOWING THE BOOK OF KELLS]

John—

Suddenly I'm reading Chekhov—all his short stories—(13 volumes).
Can't believe I overlooked this guy for so long. He's like the Mozart of fiction
writers. One little gem after another. I keep harking back to our great time in
Healdsburg this Spring. How perfect it seemed to be. I'm still sober but, of
course, the edge of amazed enthusiasm has worn off. I suppose inspiration is
always destined to tail off & then you get to start all over. Some aspect of the
Laws which I still don't comprendo. Life is good here. Fishing, golf, good
weather.

Say howdy to Scarlett—Yr Pal—
Sam

Trinity College Library Dublin   6/8/97

John—
Suddenly I'm reading Chekhov—
all his short stories—(13 volumes). Can't believe
I overlooked this guy for so long. He's like
the Mozart of fiction writers. One little
gem after another. I keep harking back
to our great time in Healdsburg this Spring.
How perfect it seemed to be. I'm still sober
but, of course, the edge of amazed enthusiasm
has worn off. I suppose inspiration is
always destined to tail off & then you get
to start all over. Some aspect of the Laws
which I still don't comprendo. Life is
good here. Fishing, golf, good weather.
Say howdy to Scarlett— Yr Pal—SAM.

Book of Kells (c 800 AD)
fol 30v (enlarged detail)
© The Board of Trinity College, Dublin

August 20, 1997

[TYPED]

Dear Sam

I think I've come to the same point with letter writing as you and will probably make this one my last. Good talking to you again. Wonderful story about yr old man and you watching the ewe giving birth to twins on the grass. Could have been a piece of a Frank O'Connor story. And oh, by the way, thanks for the tip about the stories—I went right down to the library and got a collection of Chekhov's short stories and the collected short stories of O'Connor. Read Chekhov's "Anna on His Neck" (something like that) and O'Connor's "Don Juan's Temptation," I think it was called—which strongly reminded me of you.[1]

I also appreciated yr story about thinking about being present and then having to go back to see if you turned the water off at the trough.

There's only two places for us to be. We're either in "thought" or we're present. Most people live their whole lives in thought. But presence is unmistakable—like this moment now that you're reading this line—in which you're aware of the print on this page. It's like being a blind man who can suddenly see everything in front of him.

But yr story was wonderful—I could see the truck going slowly down the driveway and then stop and then return to the trough. That sense of being out of touch is one you've mentioned many times before. [. . .]

Mathew's daughter Sarah was here the other night. We took her out to dinner. She stayed until eleven and we all had a nice chat. I hadn't seen her since she was 13 and here she is 26. And yes—Kristy is 36 because O-Lan is 46 and I'm 56 and Scarlett just turned 64. In fact, O-Lan is coming by on Friday for a visit. She's coming to see Scarlett, actually. We don't have much of a relationship, as you'll recall. And Kristy no one ever sees. She's like one of those kids who somehow got into the wrong family and gets away as soon as she's able.

No—I'm not what you'd call a family man. I was only ever interested in finding the one woman and by God I found her.

---

1. The title of Chekhov's story is "Anna on the Neck" (1895).

Everything is well here. Trying to eat right and stay fit and healthy for my own sake and the rigors of the job. Scarlett is well and I'm writing every day—though it's a different kind of writing than you do I suspect; more documentary. I believe I sent you something not too long ago.

Maybe, as I say, if the lad ever gets married, we'll see each other again.

as ever—
John

1997

Sam and
Scarlett

All in all it was a wonderful
visit which brought us all closer

October 6, 1997—Minnesota

Dear John—

So glad you haven't decided to make good on your threat to stop writing letters. I would have missed them, even though that might be hard for you to imagine since I rarely write back. Got your last one about quitting your position at the Spa.[1] Somehow it didn't really surprise me. I'm always amazed by your resilience & ability to take things as they come. Maybe it's a gift of some kind or maybe you've earned it—it doesn't matter.

Just got back from a big cattle drive in Oklahoma with some friends of mine. Huge, open country—horseback for 3 days straight—big campfires under the stars & cooking with dutch ovens, cowboy style. This may be the very last decade of anything even resembling that old-style wide open range life. I'm not really nostalgic about it but it sure is great to get a real taste of it now & then. [. . .]

I have *no* job. I haven't worked for a year & there is *nothing* on the horizon. I call my agent. She says there's nothing out there. Things are dead in Tinsel Town. What am I going to do? Then it occurs to me. I've been running this "acting" scam for twenty two years, never even imagining that one day the well would run dry. Now it's come. I start going through things in my head—"liquidate my assets—sell the horses—sell the truck"—all this shit. Then I start getting a little perspective—'of course this was bound to happen—things go in cycles—you've had your day in the sun & now the rug's going to get pulled out.' Amazing! What was I thinking? So here I am feeling now slightly liberated & I don't know why. I have absolutely no idea what's up ahead & it's o.k. Something will happen. [. . .] I'm completely in the grips of forces I can't control.

This has been a sensational month of glorious fall weather. Fishing with Walker out on the river. Fiery golden trees, glistening water & fish as long as your arm. It's all a blessing & somehow I'm beginning to get a glimmer of how transient it all is & the real meaning of being here in the moment by

---

1. The letter has been lost.

moment. I think of you & Scarlett & Jesse & tiny Healdsburg from time to time & feel all our lives just pushing on. It gives me a time of sadness but now the miracle of it all seems to outweigh that & I'm real glad our friendship seems to sustain through time & all the ups & downs of 'ordinary life.'

Buena suerte, mi amigo—
Your friend,
Sam

November 7, 1997—Minnesota

[HANDWRITTEN]

John,

Thanks for the birthday letter & pix. Great one of you walking, head down, toward camera, hands in pockets, white hair gleaming in Calif. sun. What is this man pondering about so deeply? Look up man! Look up!

Yes, another birthday! I took the whole family out to a neat little restaurant in a small town nearby. The walls of the place are lined with glass cases containing a huge collection of salt & pepper shakers. Every time the train passes or the door opens & shuts, all the salt & pepper shakers rattle & tremble in unison. It was a great meal, surrounded by the ones I love & I kept having little glimmers of the truth (that's all I hope for now) of how incredibly selfish I've lived my whole life—everything geared toward what I might gain out of it—even in my relationships with family & those I think I'm closest to. The insanity of it boggles the mind &, of course, there's always this censorship going on; always this internal self-criticism—"You shouldn't be like that. You should be more generous—open-hearted—" etc. It's sickening & yet this amazing truth of 'seeing' comes on now with a force far greater than I ever felt it during those periods when I thought I was 'In The Work.' It must have to do with time. Maybe so much time has to pass before the real nitty gritty starts to leak in through all the dreaming & self-deception. So— aging isn't so bad if this accumulation of a force toward seeing myself actually grows along with the degeneration of the physical body. Who knows what dream we're caught up in now!

I've finished my play on my birthday—auspicious.[1] Took me almost exactly one year to complete. I can remember when I used to write a play a week. (Of course, they were shorter back then.) Also, working on more stories. I love the form & see many new possibilities in it. Came across a Mid-Western writer by the name of William H. Gass who wrote a collection called *In the Heart of the Heart of the Country*—very strange almost hypnotic style that every once in a while explodes into some vivid image of experience. You might like him or hate him—depending on

1. *Eyes for Consuela* (1999), which was based on the story "The Blue Bouquet" by Octavio Paz.

your mood. Reading the Pentland book every day—always something vital to glean from it. Always returning to the same question of attention.

Life compels me now. I must eat! I must have coffee! I must smoke & become engaged in the activities of the day. I must be pulled inexorably out of myself in order to be reminded again & again of the need to come back. I never saw that before. The two-headed monster. When they used to talk about 2 directions I had no idea what they were saying. Double arrows & all that Ouspensky stuff. And now I'm really spinning out—the ego-mind gobbling up every scrap of a real idea, a real experience & turning it to shit. It's wonderful, isn't it? (Jimmy Stewart—*It's a Wonderful Life*).

Regards to you & yours.
Your aging friend,
Sam

November 23, 1997

[HANDWRITTEN]

John—

Found this among the cracks in the library downstairs, trying to cull out some old books.[1] Thought you might like it. Could possibly be a rare collector's item! Worth millions—you may have it already.

Winter here now—snow & ice but actually amazing to be in these radical changes of seasons—(being a child of the desert country). Things like sledding, ice skating, skiing & ice fishing—never heard of before. It's like being transported to some exotic land where they eat seals & dance under the Northern Lights.

Working on stories now. I'm almost possessed by it. Reading voraciously—mostly contemporary stuff—occasionally come across a rare jewel (which I pore over & over, trying to decipher the formula. Of course there is no formula for great writing—it's a question of being & that can't be bottled or pinned down—Thank God!

Here's hoping you & Scarlett have a great Thanksgiving.

Warmest—
Sam

---

1. The book was *Old Angel Midnight* by
   Jack Kerouac. Shepard had a copy of the
   pirated printing of parts 1–49 published
   by Booklegger (Albion, UK) in 1973.

November 1997—Thanksgiving

[TYPED]

Dear Sam

We finished reading the play.[1] I thought it was a beautiful little number, clean, well written and funny—that old familiar tone of yours, the ever present "old man" off to the side and the trademark two sides of yourself talking to each other, the one laconic, crisp, Raymond Carver or Peter Handke–like in its no-nonsense brevity and the other slightly comic/hysterical man-caught-in-a-dilemma he cannot understand (which in fact I read aloud to Scarlett as Jimmy Stewart.) And then always that slightly abstract-mythic quality that gives the piece a tone which makes one feel after finishing it that you've just read a description of a dream.

But I was also struck afterward and remembered again how close to the vest you play it, on a personal level, and that in all the conversations we've had, with the exception of one conversation—stoned in the basement of your house in Iowa about storming out of the house in the midst of an argument, you've never talked much about your relationship with Jessica, although here in the play is somewhat of a main theme about a man and his woman in Minn. their difficulties, his emotional attachment to her, their separation and his apparent return as the play ends. And I realized that of course, this has always been one of the obvious differences between us, this tendency where I usually tend to say too much and you tend to say too little (a quality which, because it was so different from myself, I've always greatly admired, taking into account of course that we probably don't do anything "on purpose")—except at that amazing juncture—now a long time ago—where we'd get stoned together and find a kind of balance of openness in communication between our two extremes.

If the casting goes well it should be a wonderful piece to watch; its sparse, clean, funny and thought provoking and I wish I was sitting with you on opening night in the last row when the lights go down. Thanks for sending it.

And of course many thanks for the Kerouac book. No, I don't have it though I've heard about it for a long time. Great going to the post office to pick up an unknown package and find that along with your winter-in-Minn

1. *Eyes for Consuela*

Dear Sam

We finished reading the play. I thought it was a beautifu.
little number, clean, well written and funny - that old famil:
tone of yours, the ever present "old man" off to the side and
trademark two sides of yourself talking to each other, the one
laconic, crisp, Ramon Carver or Peter Hanke-like in it's no-
nonsense brevity and the other slightly comic/hysterical man-
caught-in-a-dilemma he cannot understand (which in fact I read
aloud to Scarlett as Jimmy Stewart.) And then always that
slightly abstract-mythic quality that gives the piece a tone
which makes one feel after finishing it that you've just read
description of a dream.

But I was also stuck afterward and remembered again how c:
to the vest you play it, on a personal level, and that in all
the conversations we've had, with the exception of one
conversation - stoned in the bedroom of your house in Iowa abo
storming out of the house in the midst of an argument, you've
never talked much about your relationship with Jessica, althou
here in the play is somewhat of a main theme about a man and I
woman in Minn. their difficulties, his emotional attachment to
her, their separation and his apparent return as the play ends
And I realized that of course, this has always been one of the
obvious differences between us, this tendency where I usually
tend to say too much and you tend to say too little (a quality
which, because it was so different from myself, I've always
greatly admired, taking into account of course that we probabl
don't do anything "on purpose") - except at that amazing
juncture - now a long time ago - where we'd get stoned togethe
and find a kind of balance of openness in communication betwee
our two extremes.

If the casting goes well it should be a a wonderful piece
watch; its sparse, clean, funny and thought provoking and I wi
I was sitting with you on opening night in the last row when t
lights go down. Thanks for sending it.

And of course many thanks for the Kerouac book. No, I don'
have it though I've heard about it for a long time. Great goir
to the post office to pick up unknown package and find that al
with your winter-in-Minn letter. Reminded me of the time I can
home from the dog pound in Conn. and found a post card from
Kerouac..."Regards to all yr Conn. Maytimes." Nice inscriptior
you put in there. I recall we made a rule up long ago that we
always had to put an inscription in any book we were going to
give each other. (One of our better ideas.)

Raining like a sonofabitch this morning. Scarlett in the
other room throwing a towel for Webster and laughing. We just
back from the coffee shop (8a.m.) where I was reading Proust
aloud to her. She went up to get a coffee refill and came back
(in typical Scarlett fashion) all excited saying, "I just an a
adventure with a man with a hideous ring." And then later wher
finished reading another amazing Proustian sentence where the
author is looking at the envelope of a love letter he's sent t
some young girl:
       "I had difficulty in recognizing the futile, straggli

letter. Reminded me of the time I came home from the dog pound in Conn. and found a post card from Kerouac . . . "Regards to all yr Conn. Maytimes." Nice inscription you put in there. I recall we made a rule up long ago that we always had to put an inscription in any book we were going to give each other. (One of our better ideas.)

Raining like a sonofabitch this morning. Scarlett in the other room throwing a towel for Webster and laughing. We just got back from the coffee shop (8 a.m.) where I was reading Proust aloud to her. She went up to get a coffee refill and came back (in typical Scarlett fashion) all excited saying, "I just had an adventure with a man with a hideous ring." And then later when I finished reading another amazing Proustian sentence where the author is looking at the envelope of a love letter he's sent to some young girl:

"I had difficulty in recognizing the futile, staggering lines of my own handwriting beneath the circles stamped on it at the post-office, the inscriptions added in pencil by a postman, signs of effectual realization, seals of the external world, violet bands symbolical of life itself, which for the first time came to espouse, to maintain, to raise, to rejoice my dream."[2]

Scarlett looked over at me and said, "Wow, it just goes to show you what lives in the souls of moustached men."

Enclosed is a passage I just read from my Ali biography about him cheating on his wife and how it got back to his wife in print just before the Frazier fight. I see we're all in the same boat and women just don't get it—except I must say, Scarlett who was just explaining to me how men are so different sexually from women and I said, "In what way" and she said, "Well men will fuck at the drop of a hat but women have to be wooed." [. . .]

Happy holidays to y'all
warmest regards and many thanks,
Johnny D.

2. From Marcel Proust's
   Swann's Way (1913).

John Boy — I love this
photo - it exudes 'completeness'
I think - male - female
to the core. I'm on my way
to N.Y.C. to start the play.
Gray, drizzly, snowy
highway - just stopped
for catfish & coffee. The
mind keeps racing. I'm
seeing now, more than ever
this seduction of day-
dreaming which I've

always indulged
in. It's where
all the writing
comes from. What
would it be to be
a conscious day-
dreamer?
On the Road
SAM

TO: JOHN DARK
637A Healdsburg Ave.
HEALDSBURG
CA., 95448

(forgot to send this to you —
Thanks for the thing on McSorley's
great little essay!

January 19, 1998

[HANDWRITTEN ON POSTCARD LABELED "A MEXICAN ARTIST RECORDS
HIS FIRST IMPRESSIONS OF SAN FRANCISCO"]

John Boy—

I love this photo—it exudes 'coupleness' I think—male-female to the core.
I'm on my way to N.Y.C. to start the play.[1] Gray, drizzly, snowy highway—
just stopped for catfish & coffee. The mind keeps racing. I'm seeing now,
more than ever, this seduction of day-dreaming which I've always indulged
in. It's where all the writing comes from. What would it be to be a conscious
day-dreamer?

On the Road
Sam

(forgot to send this to you—Thanks for the thing on McSorley's great little
essay!)

1. *Eyes for Consuela* opened
   on February 10, 1998, at the
   Manhattan Theatre Club.

January 30, 1998

[TYPED]

Sam

That stuff we were talking about on the phone to do with seeing the incredible drama of yr life as it takes place all the time, I realized afterward is of course what we'd been talking about all along and what in fact "The Hero Is In His Kitchen"[1] is all about—the fact that your dreams are always coming true at the moment except nobody realizes it because they're not present, they're in "thought." Yeah, I think you can move out of thought so that for the most part, you're walking around just looking out through your eyes. What we used to call self remembering was just more thinking about "I am here" followed by thinking about "How am I going to describe this at the group meeting?" So much seems to have fallen away. My whole obsession with women and impulse to try and "get them," the impulse to want to get stoned, to run away from the ordinary suffering, my fear of other people and the submersion in the continual "thoughts" day after day.

How that has happened I don't know but I think it's connected with stumbling across for the first time about five years ago, the fact that thought is the enemy when I started studying Krishnamurti which seemed to really open up during the time I was having those anxiety attacks and I started living again from my feelings instead of from my head, which I feel I'd been conditioned to do through The Work for all those years. Everywhere I looked I could see that my thoughts were at the root of my problem. I'd meet a girl, for example, and instead of just looking at her and listening to her, I'd be thinking about how to fuck her. Or I'd meet some guy and instead of just listening to him and watching him while he spoke I'd be thinking about who he is, how much does he know, can he kick my ass etc. I was always thinking about that stuff. And it seems that over the last five years through dealing with that realization, this whole new orientation to thought has changed and along with that, everything else changed. And now this latest thing of there not being any escape from discomfort

1. A dialogue in *Cruising Paradise*; the two characters, Clayton and John, are approximations of Shepard and Dark.

(suffering, loneliness, boredom etc.) means that . . . there's no escape. That's it. You stop moving and just "have" your stuff and that too seems to bring about tremendous changes.

Is this sounding like a lot of philosophical bullshit on paper? You know what it's like trying to put words to all this shit. The point is I don't think you necessarily have to "struggle" with these things the rest of your life which means always being in conflict. This stuff does drop away so that the whole subject of struggle becomes irrelevant.

Well it's good to know I have at least one friend even if he's all the fuck the way out in Minn. Stay healthy.

John

SAMUEL BECKETT, LONDON, 1965
PHOTOGRAPH BY DMITRI KASTERINE

Dear John,
 Feeling somewhat as
stunned & perplexed as
this photo of Mr. B. but as
the great man said: "I can't
go on. I'll go on. Something
is taking its course."
 Having finished work
on the play I return to
find myself immediately
falling into same old
habits of thought & behavior.
Now & then a glimpse of
what "seeing" might be.
Maybe it's an art form!
 Your Amigo,
 Sam

© DMITRI KASTERINE
© FOTOFOLIO, BOX 661 CANAL STA., NY, NY
F386   ISBN 1-88127-

To: JOHN DARK
637A Healdsburg Ave
HEALDSBURG
CALIF., 95448

ST PAUL MN 551
FEB 1998

HUMPHREY B

February 14, 1998

[HANDWRITTEN ON A POSTCARD DEPICTING SAMUEL BECKETT]

Dear John,

Feeling somewhat as stunned & perplexed as this photo of Mr. B. but as the great man said: "I can't go on. I'll go on. Something is taking its course."[1]

Having finished work on the play I return to find myself immediately falling into same old habits of thought & behavior. Now & then a glimpse of what "seeing" might be. Maybe it's an art form!

Your Amigo,
Sam

1. Beckett's novel *The Unnamable* (1953) ends with the line "You must go on, I can't go on, I'll go on." "Something is taking its course" comes from Beckett's play *Endgame* (1957).

March 2, 1998

[HANDWRITTEN ON SAM SHEPARD STATIONERY]

Dear John,

First of all, thanks for the great bundle of various esoteric & otherwise material. I am reading some of it avidly; some I've set aside until later. I just realized why it's become so difficult for me to write letters—it's a mental thing—the thought comes in that it's going to be a very long & arduous task, setting down all these details, some of them not very interesting &, in the long run, who cares? Very negative kind of block. I don't know why. I will try to go at this piece by piece & hope I don't end up boring both of us in the process.

Last time I talked to you on the phone in B.C., Canada, explaining my need to get back here on account of Jessica's mom.[1] So I take off driving back on the very same route that me and Jessie had driven coming out, except now I'm alone & thinking how odd to be re-tracing the same trip in reverse but without my partner (we had a great trip coming out). I'm making good headway; bright skies, the road is dry & wide open, all kinds of the usual revolving day dreams, amazing country—going through the Bitterroot Mountains of Idaho—down into broad, endless expanses of Montana with the Big Horns jutting up in the distance—grand American landscape! I spend a night in Coeur d'Alene, Idaho by a lake; next night Billings, take off on day 3 of the trip, heading hopefully for Rapid City South Dakota when I run straight into the most awesome blizzard I've ever encountered—wind blowing the snow at 50 m.p.h. across the highway, visibility zero so I'm forced to stop in Sheridan, Wyoming, having made a pathetic 105 miles for the day. I check with the truck stops & weather advisory & they all say this is a monster storm blanketing the Black Hills with over 48" of snow & the drifts are getting up to 16 feet high in spots. I'm stuck. So, I spend the night in Sheridan, great old cowboy town with one of the truly great bars I remember fondly from my long-ago boozing days, called the 'Mint Bar.' Funny thing is I'm not even tempted to go in. I don't know why. The thought of entering a bar full of drunken strangers just suddenly

1. Shepard was in British Columbia shooting *Snow Falling on Cedars* (1999; directed by Scott Hicks and starring Ethan Hawke).

seemed like the worst idea in the world. I have lunch at a little dive called the 'Palace Cafe'—bacon, lettuce, tomato sandwich—very fat waitress but pretty in her face—mounted heads of dead animals on the wall—buffalo, antelope, deer—the usual Western motif. I check into a Best Western with a room that has a view of the alley & a bright blue garage. I haul all my books into room & throw them on the bed: Chekhov stories (4 volumes), John Cheever & a whole mess of Spanish language learning books—which I've really come to enjoy. (I'm getting to the point where I start translating my own thoughts into Spanish—kind of double-clutched associating. It's fun.) I call Jessica & tell her the news that I'm stranded in Wyoming & I can hear the disappointment in her voice—(of course she's back home dealing with the kids & the horrible hospital vigil with her mother). Then she says she's sorry she caused me to start off back home when she knew I wanted to go down & visit you & Jesse & Scarlett in Calif. Of course, it's not her fault but there you have it—a blizzard has erupted directly in my path. I turn on the weather station—one of those cute weather reporter girls in a red suit, strutting back & forth in front of a huge map of the U.S. with swirling satellite pictures of clouds, snow, rain; flicking her fingers & sweeping her skinny arms up the length of the Mississippi where a gigantic serpentine green tongue of stormy weather licks up into the plains & explodes into white dust, marking the exact spot where I sit on my motel bed surrounded with books & papers. I mean it is a wall of snow covering both Dakotas & half of Wyoming. The weather girl says something pert like: "If you're planning any travel tonight on I-90 East, better take your survival kit because it may be days before they find you." Then she moves nimbly on to the West Coast (where I'm supposed to be!) to tell me that the weather has turned absolutely gorgeous in California!

Next day, hell or high-water, I head east again. It's not looking good. Wind still blowing like a banshee—snow coming sideways & the road has an eerie glassy look to it. I persist for some reason & start daydreaming about the Charles Grodin Talk Show, I guess it must have been one of the last things I saw on T.V. or something. I don't even like the Charles Grodin Talk Show, in fact I really dislike it. Suddenly the car is completely out of control. The whole rear end is sliding sideways on a sheet of ice & I'm heading into the center-divider ditch, which luckily is very wide but very deep with snow. I manage to pop it into 4 wheel drive & haul myself back up onto the highway then crawl another 5 miles or so wondering how it could be that a man's whole life could be snuffed out in the midst of an idiot day-dream about the

Charles Grodin Show. Up ahead, through the driving snow, I see a patrol car with all its blinkers on, parked sideway in the highway. I pull up next to it & a cop, dressed in an icy parka, icicles dripping from his nose tells me there's two semi-truck & trailer rigs jackknifed up ahead. He says there's no way through to Rapid—have to spend the night in Gillette. So here I am again—another one horse Wyoming town for the night.

(I have reached that inevitable point where I'm flat bored & need to wrap this up.) Long story short—it took me a full 6 days to traverse the distance from B.C. to Minneapolis & there were times when I thought I may never get off the motel circuit, but here I am, back again home.

I will make another stab at a coherent sustained correspondence but for now, I've had it. [. . .]

Your Partner on the Open Road,
Sam

June 21, 1998—Minnesota

[HANDWRITTEN]

John—

It's Father's Day morning & officially the first day of Summer on the calendar. Glorious morning with the sun breaking across the river & all the robins chirping their heads off. Walker's asleep upstairs & all the girls have gone off to the cabin up north so I'm sitting here having coffee in this semi-contemplative bliss right now.

Got your letter about your bout with anxiety & odd how I relate to that state. I feel like it's always around, lurking, even when the outside circumstances seem to be peachy-keen. Maybe it's some deep-seeded childhood phantom that we'll never get shed of. In some ways I think it was probably this very state of anxiety & fear that brought me initially to ideas in the Work & Zen & my interest in writing & art. So it's a double-edged sword maybe. Some mornings I can't believe how strong it is; like something's terribly *wrong* that I can't put my finger on & yet there's nothing terrible at all. It takes me half a day to recover from it & usually that "recovery" is through getting totally identified with some function or set "interest" like the cattle or horses or writing & slowly the anxiety fades into the background. I was raised on a steady diet of fear & guilt. That's plain to me now but no easier to swallow. I'm convinced there's no intellectual way out. The great appeal of the "ideas" is this possibility that right now, in this instant, I can come in touch with a presence that transcends & at the same time includes all this confusion about myself; that makes me whole instantaneously.

It was great to see you again, even for a short spell. I'm grateful for our strange long-term connection. I had the feeling something was unsettled about you but didn't know what. Scarlett looked great & I met up with Jesse next morning who was into his feed-store drill but seemed happy with himself. I love that small town atmosphere up there although it borders somehow on being counterfeit. I guess that's the best we can do in modern day America—pretend that life is as simple as it was in the fifties. Maybe it is.

Walker's stirring upstairs & we've got a day of fishing planned—out on the river in the boat. He's eleven now & lives completely in his body. If it isn't physical, he has no interest.

Hope to hear from you soon.

Love to Scarlett.

Your amigo,
Sam

June 23, 1998

[TYPED]

Sam

Did I tell you I was very touched by yr letter. Well first I was surprised to get a letter but over and above that—all the stuff you were saying about anxiety, fear, guilt etc. and how that had been the atmosphere growing up and how you felt the undercurrent of it most of the time but turned away from it through activity and so on. I guess I was touched by the openness of the letter and also by the awareness implied by what you were saying. I really appreciate letters like that.

I'm reading Kerouac's letters again (this whole other side of him) and I just discovered that there's a character in *On the Road* named Sam Shepard— at least it was in one of the versions of the book before he sat down and rolled off that last speed version in three weeks. Anyway I came across the Sam Shepard piece in reading some of the letters. I was reading the book of his you sent me last year. *Old Angel Midnight.* ("Eternally I accuse you of being as craven a shit as Frank ever planked on that Leo butcher board so's mice could be crying safe in the arms of Jesus—the Little Christ!")

Every once in a while I get the urge to cut loose like that in my own way. I love the "feel" of it. It lifts me above life it seems. It struck me today what a wacky thing this fascination with Kerouac has been all my life and it's never run dry. I read him over and over, silent and aloud and in fact I'm re-reading Gerald Nicosia's great bio on Jack. It all gives me juice and hope not to mention joy. There are so many aspects that stimulate me about him; prose/poetry, friendships, fascinations, romanticism, impracticality, love of writing, journeys, addictions. I remember a talk we had up here when you were telling me about a realization you had about yourself and Beckett. These are interesting things. I don't meet too many people (anyone) who can relate to this, so this is just one of the ways I value yr friendship. [. . .]

Also just bought a book that certainly reminds me of you called *highway—America's Endless Dream*. Great photographs of old gas stations and road houses and small town main streets, Okies on the road, old motels and road signs, and text about the history of the highway in America. ("They come as close as anything we have to a central national space. They are a national promenade. America's main street and a medium which grows the carnival of individual life and enterprise.")

Yours,
John.

July 9, 1998

[HANDWRITTEN]

Sam

[. . .] Just got stopped in the hall (of the spa) by this guy Jerry who's 41, telling me about the Asian girl he can't get out of his mind & it's driving him crazy because he's married. He doesn't realize how common it is. [. . .] I was really lucky to have Scarlett in my 40's who thought it was normal for guys to try and fuck everything that moved. I told the guy if he could hang on until he was 50 he'd be ok. (Small consolation) I could feel for him—but I couldn't help him [. . .] Anyway, most people just want you to *Listen* to their woes, not solve them. [. . .]

God is a fiction like Winnie the Pooh, exercise is bad for you and you should do what ever you feel like doing. (These are heavily influenced by you.) And this is aside from my 59 rules. Here's what I learned from you:

1. Have 3 bites and push your plates away
2. Women are pets (except the one you love)
3. Eat whenever the fuck you feel like it, even if it's 5 min. before dinner
4. Try to get someone else to wash your underwear
5. Keep driving even if you forget where you're going
6. Never stay more than 30 seconds once you realize you don't want to be there.
7. Spend all your money & then get some more.

And from Scarlett I learned
1. The futility of always making choices
2. Unconditional love (the value of)
3. The value of kindness, gentleness and listening and silence
4. Spend all your money & then get some more.

You and Scarlett are the only two people I ever learned anything from in my adult life—(I mean aside from the work, ideas etc. of course) Usually I influence *other* people. But in my childhood my father taught me:

1. The value of a good cigar
2. How to eat fast.
3. Never look in your rear view mirror.
4. The joy of a hot bath.

My mother taught me

1. Women should bring me food
2. Women should love me unconditionally
3. Women should play bridge when not otherwise occupied
4. Women should forgive everything I do as long as I'm happy and warm enough.

These were my earliest influences. [. . .]

Every Wed, Thurs & Fri, Scarlett and I drive over to Calistoga to the spa resort and spend about three hours floating around on mats in the big heated (98°) outdoor pool. We hook the mats up together and then let them float wherever they will just talking & laughing, telling stories and even naps. Then we stretch out in big soft deck chairs & eat lunch & read aloud before driving home for an afternoon movie. And we do that every week—one of the perquisites of this here job.

4th of July evening we strolled the quiet streets of Healdsburg with Webster, going down to the big high school field and turned the dog loose while we walked around the track watching the sun set and the fireworks starting to go off. So as you can see—most of our times are solitary and peaceful. In the early mornings I write, and again late at night. Sat thru Tues I massage at the spa and still at seven every AM Scarlett & I head down for coffee to The Flying goat. Each man designs his life must be. Working of course takes up a lot of time away from home, away from Scarlett and away from writing but I like the work and really do want to become better and better at massage. I study now from Videos & try out new techniques on clients but not as much as I could. Certainly not as much as a man possessed. I always wanted to be a man possessed—one of those "he worked day and night on it without respite" kind of guys. The kind of guy who eats, talks, and sleeps his subject.

But I could never become that way except sometimes on speed. You have more interests than anyone I've ever known; horses, cattle, writing, reading, farming, gambling, drawing, music, hunting, fishing (how come they don't include fishing along with hunting?) and a million more things and seem to be completely absorbed in them all. I remember when I used to ride up from Marin up to Sonoma and you'd get pissed because I'd always fall asleep. You were so interested in everything up there, the farms, the houses, the fences, the little restaurants, old country people—I just couldn't get it. It bored me witless. It still does and now I'm living in Sonoma. But I've carved out a private personal life for myself at least. Maybe that's why you always said you though our friendship was "strange." But it never struck me as so. [. . .]

August 17, 1998—Minnesota

[HANDWRITTEN]

John—

Remarkable time now. Can't quite put my finger on it. Surrounded by death yet this persistent sense of the tremendous on-going force of life. Jessica's mother died & of course, this was a huge shock to her—she was so devoted to her & closer than any mother-daughter I've ever known. Then her Aunt died—another woman she was extremely close to—(her father's sister). Then the next door neighbor died—a man I'd got to know a little bit over the backyard fence. Then, almost immediately Jessica's niece shows up from Mexico with her little half Mexican baby boy & moves into Jessica's brother's house (right next door). This little boy is quite amazing—full of life, good natured—always giggling & my little son Walker has taken a real shine to him—so the 2 of them are scrambling all over the house, playing games & laughing. Walker has a new parrot that screams all day & his yellow lab, 'Pine,' who's always crashing around the place. Hannah has a new cello which she diligently practices on every day—so there's Bach & Mozart music wafting through the house. Shura is getting all keyed up to go off to college so she's watching videotapes of these little isolated liberal arts schools off in the hinterlands of Vermont & Massachusetts—images of blonde, liberally-minded girls & boys romping through the snow banks, dancing to African music, performing science experiments. Life not only 'goes on,' it's absolutely unstoppable!

—This is one of those stop & start letters. I'm picking this up again about a week later. I'm in a little cafe out in River Falls, Wisconsin. I'm in a booth across from a long table, full of old farmers (ironically). They're all talking about football—The Green Bay Packers & Kansas City Chiefs. This happens to be the town where the Chiefs hold their summer practice.

—Another jump—I'm in my cabin, out at the farm.[1] Big thunderstorm just blew through & dumped buckets of rain. Now it's clearing but still overcast & damp. Crickets are all creaking in the tall wet grass—sounds like it should

---

1. Shepard's note: River Falls, Wisconsin.

be the middle of the night. I just finished sitting for 40 minutes. I'm having a hard time lately making it through a solid hour because of the pain in my lower back & hips. Age is creeping inexorably in. I'm only just now beginning to see the first glimpse of what it truly means to be between two natures. I must admit this had always remained an intellectual notion for me for many years. Now I can really feel it. The incredible weakness of my wish & how it is always swallowed up by this adversary of my imagined self—the picture of who I am. This greedy one, never satisfied, always hungry for something 'more,' something different, something else, something elsewhere. My inclination always is to do battle with this part of myself—to 'get rid' of it; to smother it; cast it out somehow but never to simply 'see' it. Very difficult. I don't find it easy at all to accept. It's hugely seductive &, in fact, such a major part of me I don't see how I could live without it. Maybe this is the beginning of understanding 'sacrifice.' I don't know. At times I feel I'm right on the cutting edge of a whole new understanding & right in that moment I see I'm unwilling to take the leap. Scared maybe; afraid to lose the very aspect of this false self that keeps me in prison. Weird perdicament.

I'm sitting in Wisconsin surrounded by cattle, horses, crickets, chainsaws—the wind is blowing & I'm thinking of you—& Scarlett of course—& Healdsburg—& Jesse—& your silly dog.

More later, Yr Amigo
Sam

Sam

   Just finished the latest thick hardcover bio of Kerouac
Fantastic. It gets me every time. I have every bio on him a
it's all there - the speed, the traveling, the sex, the wri
and the increadable friendships between these young men. Of
course there was so much I didn't know when I first got int
Kerouac in '58. The fact that he was bi-sexual, anti-semeti
an alcoholic. Wonderful. But his books and the books about
jesus, I can't tell you the emotional effect they have on n
don't understand it but there's everything in there that I
my life to be. It was like I took his books like road maps
myself. And of course I wasn't alone - I mean he was travel
with Neal in the 40's so the effect he had on generations i
50's and 60's was amazing and under rated. He was scorned i
time and died compleatly broke and in painful misery. Looki
back from this point I feel pretty satisfied that I accompl
what I dreamed about when I was still in highschool - and n
The drugs, the travel, the friendships, the simple joy of j
daily being alive.

   This is to let you know I got your letter today and rea
to Scarlett. It sounds like it's been a terribly difficult
for Jessica and I feel for her. I had just gotten a call fr
Sharron that HER mother is dying. You and I went through th
I expect there's more to come. Life and death are certainly
ends you get when you pick the stick up.

   Reading yr letter where you talk about the adversary of
imagined self swallowing up your wish...never satisfied, al
hungry, always something more etc. Interesting because the
morning yr letter arrived we were talking about you down at
coffee shop (me and Scarlett) and I don't know why but I su
heard myself say, "Well I think Sam's suffering has always
from trying to be authentic. That's what it seems to me he
always been striving for - authentic cowboy, authentic lord
the manor, authentic sportsman etc. and yet always feeling
an impostor, surrounding himself with 'the real ones' but n
being able to climb inside their skin. He himself is 'a rea
but he doesn't realize which one that is. The whole thing h
do with the mind. With a different mind set not caught up v
an image of 'becoming', he could perform the same activitie
be at peace. Everything that needs to be seen, is in the m.

   Well, that all jumped out of me BEFORE I got your lette
morning and I don't know - I really haven't seen you for th
15 years so I don't know where all that came from. Excuse n
it doesn't ring a bell. I think we used to be good influenc
each other even when we were being bad influences, it was c
All those discussions, reflections, heart to hearts etc. Bu
were living a different life then, busy being twenty somet.
and thirty something and fourty something.

   I thought of us right through the Cassiday/Kerouac sec
the book - when they were in their early twenties and were
tremendous influences on each other. But by the time they
their fourties, they had almost no contact with each other
their lives and outlooks had gone in different directions.
when it was happening, man, it was happening.

August 22, 1998

[TYPED]

Sam

Just finished the latest thick hardcover bio of Kerouac—Fantastic. It gets me every time. I have every bio on him and it's all there—the speed, the traveling, the sex, the writing, and the incredible friendships between these young men. Of course there was so much I didn't know when I first got into Kerouac in '58. The fact that he was bi-sexual, anti-semitic and an alcoholic. Wonderful. But his books and the books about him—jesus, I can't tell you the emotional effect they have on me. I don't understand it but there's everything in there that I wanted my life to be. It was like I took his books like road maps for myself. And of course I wasn't alone—I mean he was traveling with Neal in the 40's so the effect he had on generations in the 50's and 60's was amazing and under rated. He was scorned in his time and died completely broke and in painful misery. Looking back from this point I feel pretty satisfied that I accomplished what I dreamed about when I was still in high school—and more. The drugs, the travel, the friendships, the simple joy of just daily being alive.

This is to let you know I got your letter today and read it to Scarlett. It sounds like it's been a terribly difficult time for Jessica and I feel for her. I had just gotten a call from Sharon that HER mother is dying. You and I went through that and I expect there's more to come. Life and death are certainly two ends you get when you pick the stick up.

Reading yr letter where you talk about the adversary of your imagined self swallowing up your wish . . . never satisfied, always hungry, always something more etc. Interesting because the morning yr letter arrived we were talking about you down at the coffee shop (me and Scarlett) and I don't know why but I suddenly heard myself say, "Well I think Sam's suffering has always come from trying to be authentic. That's what it seems to me he's always been striving for—authentic cowboy, authentic lord of the manor, authentic sportsman etc. and yet always feeling like an impostor, surrounding himself with 'the real ones' but never being able to climb inside their skin. He himself is 'a real one' but he doesn't realize which one that is. The whole thing has to do with the mind. With a different mindset not caught up with an image of 'becoming,' he could perform the same activities and be at peace. Everything that needs to be seen, is in the mind."

Well, that all jumped out of me BEFORE I got your letter this morning and I don't know—I really haven't seen you for the last 15 years so I don't know where all that came from. Excuse me if it doesn't ring a bell. I think we used to be good influences on each other even when we were being bad influences, it was good. All those discussions, reflections, heart to hearts etc. But we were living a different life then, busy being twenty something and thirty something and forty something.

I thought of us right through the Cassady/Kerouac section of the book— when they were in their early twenties and were tremendous influences on each other. But by the time they were in their forties, they had almost no contact with each other and their lives and outlooks had gone in different directions. But when it was happening, man, it was happening. [. . .]

yr man in the west and forever friend
Johnny

January 16, 1999

Dear John—

I'm sitting here beside my daughter, Hannah, who's just turned 13 & is a long, elegant string of water with grayish green eyes & a nose like her Grandma. She's been playing the cello since she was 4 years old, back in Virginia & is now practicing her tenor cleff. ('Chanson Triste'—French for sad song). She's in the 9th Grade Orchestra at her Jr. High School & she's only in 7th so she's a smarty-pants. Outside it's suddenly a glorious, Spring-like morning—46° & the snow is melting; water pouring off the roof in long ribbons—sun shining on everything. Me & Jessica, Hannah & the dogs took a long walk this morning—you don't know what a joy it is to be able to feel your fingers & toes again without gloves—after weeks of below zero temperatures. Jessie's gone off to Rome again to finish up her film[1] (10 days) then she's back & we'll all be together for quite a spell. All these separations due to our work in the movies & theatre are really difficult but we keep managing to hold it all together somehow. I guess it beats working 9 to 5 in an office.

Last nite we watched Terry Malick's new film *A Thin Red Line*. Kept thinking about you & me driving around with Terry that time when we were doing *Days of Heaven* & he was asking us about Milarepa.[2] I believe we were stoned, as usual. Don't know if you've seen his latest but it's a long meandering very contemplative film on the horrors of war & beauties of nature—many absolutely brilliant elements in it—but somehow dissatisfying as a movie. Amazing though that the guy keeps persisting in making totally unique films that seem to completely ignore the commercial marketplace. Maybe he'll wait another 20 years to come out with his next one.

Now it's coming dusk & the sky is layered with strips of apricot & purple as the sun goes down. From my window upstairs I'm looking out on black silhouettes of giant oaks, still clinging to crusty leaves. It's very quiet because Walker is off at a friend's house watching football & not crashing around the house with his dogs. The sidewalks below are

1. Lange was in Rome to film *Titus* (1999; directed by Julie Taymor and costarring Anthony Hopkins).
2. Jetsun Milarepa (c. 1052–c. 1135) was a Tibetan yogi and poet.

banked with snow; the aquarium is gurgling in Shura's room; a local police siren far off—as our old friend Beckett would say: "Something is taking its course." I know exactly what he meant, somehow—sometimes I can feel it—an actual presence—God, if you will.

I remain, all ears—

Your compadre,
Sam

February 3, 1999

Amigo John,

(This letter will reflect, more or less, the fractured, conflicted, rampant roaming nature of my associative state of mind.)

Burning Questions of the Day:

#1.—What exactly is this mysterious, elusive quality called "seeing"?

#2.—What is the *resistance* to seeing?

#3.—What does it mean to see the resistance?

#4.—What needs to be given up in order to see this resistance?

#5.—What is the true nature of sacrifice, sincerity & genuine being effort?

Case in point: Last nite I'm sitting in the T.V. room—(me, Jessica & the kids) watching a program on the Lost Continent of Atlantis. A whole string of scholars & authorities on the subject (mostly women; college professors, archaeologists etc.) are giving their opinions in interviews. Many "very smart" speculations & I'm taking it all in; stretched out with a glass of orange juice (yesterday was my two-year anniversary incidentally of no-booze, not one single drop) & I'm more or less enjoying myself when out of the blue Shura says to me, "Why do you always snicker & laugh at everyone? Why are you so cynical?"

"Me? Snicker & laugh? Cynical? Me?"

"Yes," she says. Then Jessica says "Yes, it's true. You laugh at everyone."

"I do?" I say.

"Yes, you do."

I don't change my posture. I suddenly "see" my posture: Arms cocked behind my head, legs stretched out & crossed in an attitude of total arrogance & disdain. I feel a terrible sudden tension across my stomach as the reaction sets in & the recognition that this is indeed a true aspect of my character—cynical, arrogant & self-righteous. I keep looking. I don't change anything. I don't speak. I just watch & I swallow whole the almost unbearable

with a glass of orange juice (yesterday
was my two-year anniversary
incidentally of no-booze, not one
single drop) & I'm more or less
enjoying myself when out of the blue
Shuna says to me, "Why do you always
snicker & laugh at everyone? Why are
you so cynical?"

"Me? Snicker & laugh? Cynical
me?"

"Yes," she says. Then Jessica say,
"Yes, it's true. You laugh at everyone."

"I do?" I say.

"Yes, you do."

I don't change my posture. I
suddenly "see" my posture. Arm
cocked behind my head, legs
stretched out & crossed in an
attitude of total arrogance &
disdain. I feel a terrible sudden
tension across my stomach as the
reaction sets in & the recognition
that this is indeed a true aspect of
my character - cynical, arrogant &
self-righteous. I keep looking.
I don't change anything. I don't
speak. I just watch & I swallow
whole the almost unbearable internal
pain & humiliation of the moment.

internal pain & humiliation of the moment. How could I be this way? How is it possible? After all these years; all this time & so-called effort? I'm just an arrogant self-righteous old prick watching T.V. & snickering.

Enjoyed your observations of Dennis. Somehow I feel a weird kinship with him & his self-deprecating. Must have been something to do with father-son relationships & childhood brandings that continue to haunt us.

I'm up in the cabin at my little ranch now, looking out over the snowy valley. A wasp is crossing the windowsill very slowly. Outside it's about 10°, very still & beautiful but cold. The fire's snapping in my fireplace. A few flies have come to life in the warmth of the cabin & buzz senselessly against the glass. I'm meeting Walker at 4:00 this afternoon to play racquetball—(not quite as quick with the backhand as I used to be). Must get down off the mountain now & head back to town through the little village of River Falls—"Home of Karen Bye," Olympic Gold Medal Winner in Ice Hockey.

Que Via Bien!
—Sam

March 3, 1999

[HANDWRITTEN]

John,

Just read that Castaneda died, a year ago in April. Never even heard about it. I met him once in San Francisco—small, unassuming guy; kind of pudgy with a bright red handkerchief around his neck. I asked him about fear & he said the best advice he'd ever heard was from one of our Presidents: ("Nothing to fear but fear itself.") I also asked him if he knew Lord Pentland, which I know he did but he denied it without even so much as a twinkle of recognition in his eye. In this article on his death (some local college rag), the writer says he was out at dinner with Carlos where a woman asked him how she could have a 'spiritual life.' Castaneda told her every evening she should sit down in a chair & realize that one day her husband & her children would die in no particular order & on no particular day. If she did this every day she would have a spiritual life.

Thanks for the recent batch of photos. I put the picture of the white Chevy up in my room. Some kind of emblem of our stoned wandering days. Spring is trying to break through the ice here but still cold in the mornings. We'll be going down to Mexico soon for our annual Spring Break:—fishing, swimming, long walks on the beach—it's always a magical time for us. Tonight we're having a big Birthday dinner for Shura, who's turning eighteen & going off to college next year. Last I remember she was crawling up the stairs in some Hollywood Hotel to discover me, a total stranger, sleeping beside her mother. Life is a series of shocks & it's hard to believe that's true for everyone on earth.

Latest development on the theatre front: Looks like Sean Penn & Nick Nolte might do my new play (brothers again—what a surprise!).[1] I've set it up for Fall of the year 2000—at The Magic Theatre in San Francisco—talk about full-circle. So there might be a possibility of seeing you & Jesse & Scarlett more than once every few years. It's a ways off yet so anything could happen.

1. Shepard's note: *The Late Henry Moss.*

Glad you like *All the Pretty Horses* so much. Actually, I think it's one of the best books I've ever read but I was reluctant to go overboard about it because I didn't want to turn you off it. I couldn't stop reading it & wished it would never end. Can't say that about too many things I've come across over the years. The only other Western I've read that could compete with it was *The Searchers* by Alan Le May—the book that John Ford made into a mediocre movie with John Wayne. *The Searchers* is a real piece of work & I'm sure Cormac McCarthy had to have been influenced by it. That was another one I couldn't put down. Now that I'm on this tangent I might as well list *True Grit* by our old friend Charlie Portis—remember the stoned afternoon we went on a frantic hunt for all of Charlie Portis's books—we assaulted the library in San Anselmo or San Rafael right at closing hour & I remembered the stunned look on the librarian's face as we stood outside bashing on the glass doors demanding entry—we were out of our minds!

I'll try *The Crossing* since you like it so much. The other one I ½ read by McCarthy was *Blood Meridian*. Incredible piece of work but terrifying in its violence—couldn't make it through, although some of the narrative on Old Mexico absolutely takes your breath away. The guy's some kind of genius I think.

I'll stop rambling for now. Hope this finds you in fine fettle.

Que Via Bien,
Sam

(Estudio Español con nueva vigor. Quiero hablar como un Mexicano. Le had lido usted Neruda alguna vez in Español? Es estupendo!

Hasta Luego amigo

SAM SHEPARD

John,

<u>My favorite ice-cream</u>: Coffee Almond Fudge by "Starbuck"

<u>My favorite recent movie</u>: 'Cookie's Fortune' by Bob Altman

<u>My favorite recent reading</u>: 'Don Quijote' by Cervantes

<u>My favorite thing to do</u>: Stroll through the pasture with cows & calves

<u>My 2nd favorite thing to do</u>: chain saw oak firewood in the forest

<u>My favorite periodical</u>: 'The Thoroughbred Times'

<u>Thing I'm most looking forward to</u>: Opening day of fishing

<u>My most persistant day-dream</u>: breeding a Grade I Stakes horse

<u>Another thing I love</u>: Golf

<u>One pet you should never own</u>: A parrot (of any kind)

    Sometimes lists are better than writing — more fun — but then they get boring — so does writing. I would like to be burning up with writing, but I'm not. Other things are more fun. Fun is important, I guess. It feels good to have fun. Did you ever consider the possibility of losing your mind entirely? Maybe we have. More later — if it comes. (Read Beckett's 'First Love' — amazing!)

        Yr. Amigo, Sam

April 17, 1999

[HANDWRITTEN ON SAM SHEPARD STATIONERY]

John,

My favorite ice-cream: Coffee Almond Fudge by "Starbuck"
My favorite recent movie: *Cookie's Fortune* by Bob Altman
My favorite recent reading: *Don Quixote* by Cervantes
My favorite thing to do: stroll through the pasture with cows & calves
My second favorite thing to do: chainsaw oak firewood in the forest
My favorite periodical: *The Thoroughbred Times*
Thing I'm most looking forward to: Opening day of fishing
My most persistent day-dream: breeding a Grade I stakes horse
Another thing I love: Golf
One pet you should never own: A parrot (of any kind)

   Sometimes lists are better than writing—more fun—but then they get boring—so does writing. I would like to be burning up with writing, but I'm not. Other things are more fun. Fun is important, I guess. It feels good to have fun. Did you ever consider the possibility of losing your mind entirely? Maybe we have. More later—if it comes. (Read Beckett's "First Love"—amazing!)

Yr. Amigo,
Sam

May 5, 1999

John,

Many things have happened—a storm of things. Events both inner &
outer. I actually feel quite mad (as the English would put it)—but I keep
referring back to Pentland on almost a daily basis & it's a huge help—in
fact just about the only real help I can find. It's so sobering to come across
things in his book like: "It is better *not* to be thinking about the Work most
of the time, better to consciously accept to be what you are, to be conscious
of what you are, instead of reacting to the noise by thinking of quietness or
something, to consciously be the noisy thought-ridden people we are." Wow!
Thanks, L.P. Or, how about this one: "We are afraid to go far enough to
admit to ourselves the truth of what many people have said: that life is meaningless, that there is no hope." Unbelievable! I've been trying an enormously
useful thing lately—to relax the face. Quite incredible what an immediate
impression it brings. You've probably tried this at some point but I never
did—all those years in "the Work."

Got off on a new book about Lewis & Clark called *Undaunted Courage* by
Stephen E. Ambrose. Very exciting—less than 200 years ago hardly any white
men knew what lay West of the Mississippi. Imagine—*no roads*—just trails
made by the trappers, deer, Indians. These guys make a little iron framed
boat that weighs 44 pounds, loaded down with their gear & they take off up
the Missouri River into totally uncharted territory. Now that's a road trip!
You can skip a lot of the preliminary stuff about their preparation (although
it's all great) & jump straight to the chase—which begins on page 133. It's
great stuff & written in a totally straight-forward narrative with no frills.

My best to Scarlett.

Warm Regards,
Samuel

June 15, 1999—Minnesota

[HANDWRITTEN]

Dear John,

I'm writing this from inside my little 7' × 7' Coleman tent. It's pelting rain outside & I'm dry as toast. We're camped out on the river for Walker's 12th Birthday—me & five boys. They're all in another tent about 50 feet away—screaming & giggling as the rain beats down. We did some fishing then I cooked them all cheeseburgers, beans & hot dogs—marshmallows & Hershey bars for dessert. It's quite amazing hanging out with adolescent boys. They're all totally insane, selfish & hysterical. A lot like adults but more demonstrative about it. One conversation they had on the boat—someone asked Walker who he'd eat first if they had to kill someone to survive. He looked around at everyone then, quite calmly, he said—"my Dad." So there you have it. After supper they played baseball with a marshmallow for a ball & a tree limb for a bat. Very Huck Finn. The river's flowing by like a wide silvery sheet, peppered by the rain. The sun has almost set & one bird is still chattering from the Maple trees, as though hoping it might clear up. My tent is very cozy & dry with a Coleman lantern hanging from the center, glowing pale white. No mosquitoes have snuck in yet. I just saw Walker's yellow lab trot across the campground with a dead fish in her mouth. She's very self-sufficient. A couple of small boats drift by with their running lights on, glowing red & green. I've always loved rivers & this one is particularly beautiful—the St. Croix, which is a main tributary of the Mississippi. Hard to believe the Mississippi actually begins in Minnesota. (No more long place-names with double letters).

6/20/99—This is an on-going type of letter. Lots of activities here lately. We just finished with a big 'Open-House' deal for Shura's High School graduation. Days of preparation with Jessica cooking all kinds of dishes then about a hundred people descending on the house, carrying paper plates around & being very social. I've actually found a way to deal with these situations, after all these years. (You know how I hate parties). I've discovered that if I just dissolve all concern for myself; any kind of investment in my own opinions (the "me" versus "them" syndrome), that I'm actually able to just allow things to happen & watch. It's a lot less stressful than having to all the time be trying to support this notion of "me."

Thanks for the material on Bodhicitta.[1] I read it all & found some useful stuff. My biggest question lately is where to find this 'quietness of mind' that everyone talks about in these books. All I find is noise, chaos & constant, unrelenting associations. When I sit I can sometimes find some small territory of quiet but immediately it goes into insane chatter when I get up & move into the activities of the day. I actually feel plagued by it—as though tormented by demons & devils. I think I actually know the experience of 'Saṃsāra.' Intellectually I understand the soundness of just watching; making the effort to be the "watcher"; "seeing"; "being here now"; "the present is all that matters" etc., etc. But the reality is that what I "see" is myself being taken constantly by any old thing—being totally absorbed, lost, asleep & quite profoundly removed from any sense of well-being or peace of mind. All I can say for myself is that I haven't had a drink in 2 years & 4 months—I haven't beaten my wife or kids—I haven't killed any dogs or cheated on my friends. I'm just a fucked up guy from Duarte, trying to make it through.

Hope this finds you well. My warmest regards to Scarlett.

Yr. Amigo,
Sam

1. In Buddhism, the concept of "bodhicitta"
   refers to the "awakening mind" or the
   "enlightened mind."

June 18, 1999

[TYPED]

Dear Sam

I seem to have cut most of my friends out from under me, except you and you're in Minnafuckingsota. Now all I got is acquaintances. But it's my choice and I'm not complaining. In fact, things are going along very well. I'm re-reading my library and now that I've finished my book, typing up all the old notebooks and transcribing all the old tapes in order to put together a kind of journal of remaining material. The notebooks are mostly the stoned writings from the past, in fact the first notebook is dated 1975 which puts us in that house in Corte Madera up on the hill. That was the year we stayed out New Years Eve and the women got mad. That was the house where Pinto ate the couch and Jesse was five and Michael Douglass came over and Dylan called about Rolling Thunder.

Interesting what was going through my mind then. A lot of the material of course is very Gurdjieff oriented with lots of "Work" terminology and references to G. and Ouspensky etc. [. . .]

Then in the most recent notebook I've got stuff like:

June 1999

It's true, you do have to make an effort and it is unnatural. You're just beginning to work out that muscle in a new way so you start very slowly and the task seems impossible and artificial and uncomfortable but eventually it becomes who you are and all the rest disappears. Mindfulness. Vigilance. Something in me is watching the mind and what that something is, I think, is consciousness. Awareness controls the mind. It disciplines it because the mind is like a disturbed child, like a mad man sitting bent over in his cell. The mind creates all sorts of problems that trigger feelings and cause one to suffer needlessly and the reason I say needlessly is because it can be otherwise by disciplining the mind. It's as though the mind was a newspaper. If you look at the daily newspaper you'll see the undisciplined mind creating all sorts of mischief, worry, anxiety, greed, anger, fear, desire. That's a product of the undisciplined mind. But a mind that's disciplined serves its proper function and can be made to live more harmoniously with the rest of the organism. Of course you can think of disciplining the mind like sending your kid to military camp but that would be the mind speaking. To discipline the mind is a good thing and everyone benefits.

I'm the president of all the separate parts of myself. All their personalities, flaws and gifts are all in me. I recognize their traits in myself and I'm the president of all that and it's time to start thinking seriously of putting bugging devices in the various offices. [. . .]

This is a typical day for me; a man of 58 walking up a trail on the side of a mountain holding a leash and talking to himself as the sun sets in the valley of the wine country. Behind him is his large black dog. They're taking a walk after dinner. And everyone who sees him thinks he's just taking the dog out. They don't realize he's living his life.

Well, this is some kind of funny letter. Keep in touch.

yr pal
John

Except for a brief postcard, John's letters from the summer of 1999 until January 2002 have been lost.

July 29, 1999

John,

Thanks for yr. card. Here's my thoughts on getting your book into print: First of all there's only one guy I can think of at Knopf–Random House who would be open enough to look at your book & see it straight on—for what it is. We could try him—see what his reaction is & then go from there. I need to know some specifics first though before I call him & see if he'd look at it:

Do you have a complete finished manuscript?

How many pages is it in full?

Is it arranged in volumes or all under one cover?

How's the spelling coming along?

Would you consider working with an editor if this guy finds some of the material appealing & some not?

Let me know about all of this & we'll make a move.

Are you sure you want to get published? (That's not a trick question.)

All the best,
Sam

October 14, 1999

[HANDWRITTEN]

John,

Got your last just as I returned from Oklahoma, having been on a four day cattle drive down there with my "brother-in-law," Dan. (I know this sounds too typical but true nonetheless). I've got a friend down there with a 6,000 acre ranch & every morning we were in the saddle at the crack of dawn covering miles of dew coated grasslands with deer popping out of the brush, coyotes running for cover & black cows with their calves trying their best to out-run us. I think I did more riding in 4 days than I have in the past two years. Sore & dog tired but exhilarating at the end of the day—then sitting around campfires listening to men tell stories of women as they slide deeper & deeper into that all too familiar drunken slur of the profoundly disappointed.

Jessica's off in L.A. visiting the Dalai Lama (some teaching session), so when I got in late last night the kids were all asleep & the house felt very empty & that old haunted feeling of aloneness crept in along with all the accompanying thoughts of self-pity & in the morning now still this terrible feeling of disconnectedness, lack of purpose & all the negative shit.

Lo & behold—another day! Jessie comes back full of awe & wonder at the Dalai Lama session. Great to see her—everything falls into place & I even laugh at my yesterday "self" who was on the verge of suicide. We've been having glorious Fall weather here with chilly mornings warming up into the 70's, golden leaves blowing across the little town streets. We took a walk with the dogs down on the railroad tracks while the kids slept.

Talked to son Jesse on the phone who described you & Scarlett & Dennis' departure for New Mexico with your rental truck packed to the gills & Dennis following along behind.[1] Sounds like a story. Hope you all arrived safe & sound & have discovered a quiet little coffee shop by now. Let me know how you're doing down there. I may come & visit. I love that part of the country &, like I said, we could always take a dip into Old Mexico for enchiladas & re-fried beans.

I'll write more later.

1. In October 1999, Johnny and Scarlett, in search of a cheaper place to live, moved from California to Deming, New Mexico.

Your Amigo,
Sam

11/23/99

SAM SHEPARD
(coming to the end of his short stationary)

John,

Here's one of my favorite Saroyan collections. I've had it for years & can't even remember where I picked it up. Maybe you've read it already - but just in case. After I read that little story of his you sent me I realized suddenly how similar your approach is to his - the flights of fancy right in the midst of the most down-to-earth descriptions. The sense of mortality all the time & the infatuation with turning the everyday into a kind of heroic act. I've always loved Saroyan & think he's totally unique yet still in that American Strain of vagabond minstrels like Kerouac & Dos Passos etc. I think you also belong in there somewhere &, although Rosenthal didn't want to go the distance into publishing I don't think you should turn away from the possibility. I know you say you don't care two hoots about getting published but I've never met a writer yet who didn't secretly harbor the desire to see his words in print. Here's what I think you should do: (I'm going to give you advise now, not because I think I know ⟶

more about writing than you do but because I (2) think I know more about how to get people to pay attention to it.) Somebody — I think it was Yates said that, "writing is the social act of a solitary man." & I believe that's very true. There's a need to get something across & I think you're made of exactly that same stuff that wants to move something through words across to other people. So, no more talk about writing diaries so your grandchildren will have something to pass the time away when you're long gone. You don't have any Grandchildren anyway so who are you kidding? Here's what you have to do: Take a lesson from Saroyan — each one of these little vignettes is framed & structured & clearly laid out. They all have the taste of real experience, real people, real place & time. Within that framework he waxes philosophical, he gets cute, he gets funny, he gets tough, he gets emotional & it's all done, seemingly without effort in the First Person.! This, I guess, is where they come up with this hackneyed coinage. "the voice of the writer".

November 23, 1999

(coming to the end of his short stationery)

John,

    Here's one of my favorite Saroyan collections. I've had it for years & can't even remember where I picked it up. Maybe you've read it already—but just in case. After I read that little story of his you sent me I realized suddenly how similar your approach is to his—the flights of fancy right in the midst of the most down-to-earth descriptions; the sense of mortality all the time & the infatuation with turning the everyday into a kind of heroic act. I've always loved Saroyan & think he's totally unique yet still in that American strain of vagabond minstrels like Kerouac & Dos Passos et al. I think you also belong in there somewhere &, although Rosenthal didn't want to go the distance into publishing I don't think you should turn away from the possibility. I know you say you don't care two hoots about getting published but I've never met a writer yet who didn't secretly harbor the desire to see his words in print. Here's what I think you should do: (I'm going to give you advice now, not because I think I know more about writing than you do but because I think I know more about how to get people to pay attention to it.) Some-body—I think it was Yeats said that; "writing is the social act of a solitary man." & I believe that's very true. There's a need to get something across & I think you're made of exactly that same stuff that wants to move something through words across to other people. So, no more talk about writing diaries so your grandchildren will have something to pass the time away when you're long gone. You don't have any grandchildren anyway so who are you kidding?

Here's what you have to do: Take a lesson from Saroyan—each one of these little vignettes is framed & structured & clearly laid out. They all have the taste of real experience real people, real place & time. Within that structure he waxes philosophical, he gets cute, he gets funny, he gets tough, he gets emotional & it's all done, seemingly without effort in the *First Person*! This, I guess, is where they come up with this hackneyed coinage: "the voice of the writer." All right, it might be corny & old hat but ultimately I think it's true. There's a "voice" to Beckett, a "voice" to Kerouac, a voice to every single one of them who's worth their salt. There's a voice to Johnny Dark but you keep running away from it into all these other voices of other people who aren't nearly as interesting. There's areas in your stuff (particularly the letters) where the voice is loud & clear. All I'm saying is find that & stick to that & get a real handle on it & turn it into something that other people can get ahold of & say 'Yes, I know that! I've experienced that! This is incredible!'—The same stuff we say when we come across writing that just explodes off the page. I think there's a lot of material in your book already that could be pulled out & worked on & shaped into something truly great but you can't leave it buried in there, laying next to long dialogues between 2 stoned guys cracking lame jokes. Nobody wants to wade through the cute stuff in order to eventually dig up something really worthwhile & I don't think you can wait for someone to come along & do your editing for you. You gotta get in there & pull it out & work at it or else go on & get busy with new stuff. If none of this makes any sense then just rip it up—but it seems to me you've got all your ducks in a row now—the move to Deming, your own house & time, precious time to get down to writing. I know this sounds like some kind of ½ time pep talk but you really ought to give yourself a shot at being a writer. Why not? Just tell yourself you're a writer & get down to it; work at it not with an eye to how disposable it is or how little you care if anybody ever reads it but with an effort toward communicating the real aliveness of your own experience—that's an extraordinary thing—why not move it across to other people so they can get a taste of it? Enough of this for now. I hope you take this for what it's meant to be & that's simply encouragement toward finding what you already have. More later.

Your old amigo—
Sam

November 29, 1999

[TYPED]

John,

Just got this great old manual portable that was given to me by Jessica's sister's husband (guess my brother-in-law). He found it in a basement somewhere and it's in mint condition. You wouldn't believe this thing. It's called a "voss," made in West Germany probably back in the forties or fifties. Art Deco design with two tone deep burgundy base and cream colored top. It's like a little Buick. I love this thing! I never have gotten used to these new fangled electric jobs. This is the kind of typewriter I learned to type on. You can really strike it and roll right along. (The left margin seems to be slipping slightly but otherwise it's a beaut.)

Hope you got the Saroyan and apologies for all the ardent advice. After I sent it I felt foolish and realized you probably really don't give a shit about any of it anyway. Why not just have fun writing whatever comes into your head without any concern for where it's going or who it's for? I doubt I've ever written like that so who am I to advise someone who does?

Just finished another made-for-t.v. film with Anne Heche and got back in time for Thanksgiving.[1] Shura came home from College weighing about eighty pounds less and in love with some guy she met out there in Vermont. She looks great and happy and makes you say: "Ah Youth!" every time you talk to her. We had a huge turkey dinner with all Jessie's relatives.

Still working on my play in preparation for production at the Magic Theatre next Fall.[2] Now you won't even be there. I was looking forward to maybe hanging out a little. Might be a chance I can get down there to Deming en route somehow.

Hope everything is good with you and Scarlett in your new digs. Talk to you soon.

All Regards,
Sam

1. *One Kill* (2000; directed by Christopher Menaul and costarring Shepard, Heche, and Eric Stoltz).
2. Shepard's note: *The Late Henry Moss.*

December 3, 1999

John,

Thanks for your letter—(a real stunner, by the way; maybe one of your all-time classic best). I was going around for days after sending you that rather corny "advice" letter, regretting it and wondering if maybe you were going to take offense to it and go pouting off into the New Mexican sunset and I'd never hear from you again. It's clear to me now that we have these two, very different, streets of thought about writing: For you it's a way of life and for me it's just a craft, like building a good boat or maybe making a chair. I actually envy your attitude about it but have never been able to take it on like that. I just got confused when you told me you wanted to get your book published and went into the practical side of things which has to do with relating your writing to other people. Now that we've cleared that up let's move along.

I'm deep in the throes of re-writing my new play; getting it ready for next season. Actually I started this thing ten years ago; abandoned it and took it up again. It's come together pretty well and I love the process of re-writing, (something I used to hate). It's amazing to continue to look into the same dialogue, same characters, same situation over a long period of time and to see how your attitude toward it keeps changing. How you swing in sympathy toward one character then fall out of love and swing to another; how your focus on what's important keeps shifting—where the true values of the piece lay. The best though is suddenly discovering new territory, something hidden that reveals itself and takes on a new life of its own. Maybe you never really get to the bottom of a piece of writing and could continue to re-write for the rest of your life. I don't know.

Hope all is well with you and Scarlett and Webster. More later.

Sam

January 26, 2000

[TYPED]

John,

Sorry to hear of your and Scarlett's bad health. Hope everything's on the mend. I sent you off that typewriter I told you about over the phone. It should arrive there by Friday (maybe even before this letter). It's nothing fancy but should serve your purpose until you can get something more up to date.

Just got back from N.Y. where they were working on another production of *True West* with a couple of funny and interesting new actors.[1] Amazing to see a twenty something year old play have a brand new life. It will be my second production on The Great White Way! It turned bitter cold in N.Y. with wind chills below zero; the wind just cutting you like a knife off the river. I remember that wind from way back in the sixties, having just arrived from a little desert town in California. I had a trench coat and motorcycle boots and a shaved head and just about froze my ass off. I'm like you—I hate the cold and winter. Jessica was there with me for a few days and we had a great time just hanging out, having room service, went to a Broadway play and felt like a couple with no children again. Then she left and I fell into a deep depression—got the lonesome, self-pitying blues again. Went to a sitting at the N.Y. house and Lady Pentland led it, looking extremely old and somewhat frail but still with that elegant grace she always seemed to carry with her. I was really looking forward to this sitting since I hadn't been in a group situation for months. I had been sitting regularly every day at home but I thought, somehow, this would really boost my intention. Almost immediately I fell into a very deep state of dreaming and then snapping out of it whenever Lady Pentland's voice came through. I remember Mr. Tilley saying years ago that we don't realize the extraordinary power of sleep and, at the time, I assumed I knew exactly what he was talking about. Now it all takes on a brand new meaning. It's hard to admit to oneself that it's the ego that's mostly interested in this whole idea of consciousness and awakening.

1. Shepard's note: John C. Reilly and Phillip Seymour Hoffman. Editor's note: The production, directed by Matthew Warchus, was notable in that the two actors alternated the parts of Austin and Lee every few days.

Anyhow, I left New York and hit the road in my Chevy Tahoe, heading east on the Pennsylvania Turnpike and fell deeper and deeper into this sense of aloneness and estrangement; wondering (like you were saying) how in the world I keep cutting myself off from everything and everyone; even the ones closest and dearest to me. I don't know what it is. The repetition of driving for days by myself, talking to no one but waitresses (only to order food), or toll booth attendants or motel desk clerks and winding up at The Quality Inn with tiny bars of soap and wondering how I've managed to totally isolate myself like this. I remember my Dad once saying to me down in New Mexico; "You know, I could die down here and nobody'd even know it." So there must be some weird heritage to this thing, although it's so much a part of me now that I suspect it will always be there. Thank God, I've got the family, the kids and Jessica. The best I can do I guess is just try to maintain some kind of balance between the scary isolated times and the warmth of being with the family.

Now I'm back home and it's still cold but good to be here and getting up early to get the kids off to school. Still working on my new play—down to the last crumby five pages and still hitting the same sort of conundrum about how to end the thing. I hate endings! Been reading a weird book called: *The Madman and the Professor* about the origins of the Oxford English Dictionary and this strange collaboration between an American Civil War doctor who murdered someone in England; a total crazy who had illusions of Irish midgets trying to crawl through the floorboards of his room and carrying him off to perform lewd acts with Polynesian women and a Cambridge professor who carries on a long dialogue through the mail about the origin and meaning of words, never realizing that the man he's been writing to is in jail for murder.[2] Very strange and haunting kind of tale (true story). Also, interviews with Harry Crews, one of my favorite Southern writers. I'm trying a new book by Phillip Roth called *The Human Stain*—not bad so far although he's a bit too intellectual and calculated for my money.

Must get back to my play now. It's white snow outside with a few long, dagger-like icicles dripping past my window. I can hardly wait for spring and Mexico and fishing and calves hitting the ground! Meanwhile—ever onward through the dream and the shocking presence of things as they are. Here's hoping your days are now healthy and sunny down there.

Fond Regards to you and yours,
Sam

2. *The Professor and the Madman: A Tale of Murder, Insanity, and the Making of the "Oxford English Dictionary"* (1998) by Simon Winchester.

January 30, 2000

[TYPED]

John,

Last night I finished my play.[1] Strange feeling. I hadn't even planned on coming to the end of it, it just suddenly happened and there I was sort of dumbstruck and relieved. Anyhow, it's a long one—168 pages, three acts and I just hope it doesn't bore the hell out of everyone. Now I have to plunge back into the short story collection and finish that before my May deadline.[2] Not real inspired to do that just yet.

Been doing a lot of reading lately—don't know just how that came about but it seems one thing leads to another and before you know it you've got five or six books laid out in front of you. One I'm really into right now is Larry McMurtry's latest book of essays called: *Walter Benjamin at the Dairy Queen*—really great little pieces of nostalgia and recollection of his West Texas childhood plus many great intellectual leaps of the imagination through time, past and present, linking American history with European Literature and the whole tradition of storytelling, both oral and written. How many things do you come across where Comanche Indians, James Joyce, Faulkner, Lewis and Clark, Walter Prescott Webb, cattle ranching and Hollywood are all linked together in wonderful looping concepts that seem to imbue a sense of lostness in time and tremendous wonder at the terrible speed of History and our puny place in the midst of it? He's a great essayist. Don't know if you remember his *In a Narrow Grave*? One of my favorites. There are some sections in this book where he just talks about the sky or a highway or a hill in the middle of nowhere. Great. Also reading Graham Greene's *The Power and the Glory* about a persecuted Mexican whiskey priest. Fabulous storyteller, but I know you're familiar with him. I went to him because of this interview book with Harry Crews who keeps raving about Graham Greene being simply the best storyteller in the world.

Now I'm off to wean calves with my son, Walker who's going to operate the gates. It's warmed up to about thirty degrees (a real heat wave for here). It's Super Bowl Sunday and Walker's having

1. Shepard's note: *The Late Henry Moss.*
2. The story collection *Great Dream of Heaven* (2002).

a bunch of boys over to watch the game with hot dogs and potato chips. Hannah's not into football at all so she's practicing her cello. I'll write more later. (Hope you got the typewriter!)

All the best,
Sam

February 6, 2000

[TYPED]

John,

   Glad you got the machine and hope you figure it out. I think I came across a replacement ribbon for the corrector so I'll send that on to you too. Hannah went off to Quebec on a school field trip to study French. Her first big trip away from home (for four days). I think she was much more cool about it than her parents. Sometimes these kids seem like clones of ancient wisepeople born into the hands of adolescent parents. I don't know how we wound up with them. Jessica took off for London the same day so me and Walker are home alone watching "Action" movies like *Alcatraz* and *Armageddon* (which Walker thinks is totally awesome!). I still can't believe the kids are still buying into the whole 'hero' deal but it must be some universal myth or something. It's great hanging out with just Walker sometimes. He had a basketball game this morning so there I was sitting on the floor of the gym yelling "Go! Go! Shoot! Pass!" and getting totally identified with the heat of competition along with all the other Midwestern parents. Then we went and had cheeseburgers at McDonald's (one of his mother's pet taboos) then off to play indoor golf at this totally science fiction looking white inflatable dome. Outside it's about ten degrees and you walk in and get hit with this blast of hot humid air and there's nine holes of pitch and putt golf with real green grass and sand traps and people playing in T-Shirts and shorts. Only in Minnesota! After that we hit the monster sporting goods store with miles of fishing gear, canoes, skis, all kinds of outdoor gear. I was looking for a very specific piece of luggage (in my mind) but wound up completely in conflict about which piece to buy. I'm taking off Wednesday for Vancouver to do a small role in Sean Penn's next film (he's directing) and I need something to carry books and papers in.[1] I didn't get it. Then next we had Mexican dinner at a place called 'Acapulco' with maps of Mexico on the wall where we pinpointed the town we always go to down there and started dreaming about fishing in ninety degree Caribbean heat. February here is a bitch because, by now, you've really had it with the winter and you know there's only about a month of it left before Spring hits but you have to tough it out.

---

1. *The Pledge* (2001), with Jack Nicholson, Patricia Clarkson, and Benicio Del Toro.

I hope you can get ahold of Larry McMurtry's new book and read the chapter on his quadruple by-pass heart surgery (I think it's Chapter Ten).[2] It's quite amazing I think and revealing the whole question of how to handle our mortality. I don't worry myself about it as much as I did when I was nineteen but it still seems like the only real inspiration toward 'work' of any kind. Been re-reading *Views from the Real World* (now there's a title I could never feel comfortable with).[3] Some of it seems brand new and other sections seem just like they always did. I don't know if I'm able to practice with it in the same way I find I can with Pentland's book. Maybe it's the familiarity with the voice. I don't know. Also reading lots of Graham Greene and remain astounded at his ability to handle so many characters, atmospheres, story lines. The man was an awesome writer!

Now that I'm finished with my play I have to face this new prospect of finishing all this short fiction that I signed up for with the publisher—(One of those many "I's" filled with confidence, later to be humiliated by not being able to come up with the goods.) I've heard of other writers endlessly postponing their due-dates and now I'm in their shoes. Anyhow, I'm taking the train out to Vancouver and I'm counting on some miracle of inspiration which trains always seem to bring to me. The French writer, Blaise Cendrars went through a time when he never got off trains until he finished his manuscript. He'd just keep taking trains all over the country for months, not caring what their destination was, just so he could write. Probably not a family man.

It's getting late here so I'll quit for now. The dogs are in, the canary's covered and there's not a sound outside but the wind.

Adios, tu amigo,
Sam

2. *Walter Benjamin at the Dairy Queen: Reflections at Sixty and Beyond* (1999).
3. *Views from the Real World: Early Talks of Gurdjieff as Recollected by His Pupils* (1973).

February 10, 2000—amtrak

John,

I'm on the train ("The Empire Builder") headed for Portland, Oregon. It's the crack of dawn & we're stopped in Minot, No. Dakota. Solid snow outside—not a living soul to be seen out there except for a rail worker in overalls knocking ice off the train wheels. Skinny curls of smoke hovering over chimneys like they were frozen in the air. Cattle with snow on their backs just standing numbly waiting for hay. Had my breakfast already—very cheerful, peppy crew of people, although Amtrak will never begin to compare to the old Santa Fe days when huge black waiters ambled up & down the aisles in white uniforms & all the silverware was real silver & you had to write out your order on a slip, because the waiters couldn't read or write. I remember taking the train from L.A. to Chicago with my Great Aunt when I was a little kid back in the early fifties (might've even been late 40's)—can't believe I'm now one of those who's actually experienced the passing of an era. Still I feel emotionally like a little boy inside—sad to confess but true. I don't believe my inner self has grown an inch in all this time. Still the same un-nameable fears & anxieties; lostness & all that harbored in the body of a 56 year old man.

Reading *Views from the Real World* again after not looking at it for many, many years. Quite amazing to find the dead simplicity & practicality of so much of what G. recommended. Going over the whole breakdown of The Cart—The Horse—The Driver & The Passenger again.

Just before I left Minnesota I sat for an hour &, in miraculous moments, actually came in contact with this "finer energy" that's so often spoken of. Then, almost immediately upon getting up, seeing & feeling the inevitable return of the churning, yearning, crazy mind with all its lunatic baggage & the reaction to it almost verging on despair & then sliding into terrible anxiety about leaving—even though it's only for about ten days & going by train not a plane—but almost to the point of some emotional break-down with my bags on my shoulders, at the door, saying good-bye to Jessie & the kids—just trembling inside—I don't know why. I can't imagine what those World War ll pilots were made of who went off in planes, trying to shoot people down in the sky. How could a human being endure that? I'm a stone coward at heart.

Still standing in the station at Minot, South Dakota. The Conductor's voice has announced there will be a delay since all the pipes in the dining car have frozen during the night & flooded the kitchen. The heat is busted in the sleeping car & new brake shoes are being installed on the rear car. There will be a morning movie being shown 'for your convenience' in the Lounge Car. The movie is called *Dick*. "We hope you enjoy your delay in Minot."

Stopover in the middle of the night in Whitefish, Montana—very fancy, chalet-style train station where all the skiers head up to Kalispell to hob-nob with the stars. The air is fresh & crisp here & smells like pines. I get to talking with one of the Sleeper Car Attendants on the frozen platform—a little hunched-over grey headed man with bugged-out eyes named "Sam." He's a Viet-Nam Vet who was shot down in a helicopter over Saigon. All his buddies were killed. He was the only survivor. Now he's been working on the train for over twenty years & loves it. Never gets tired of it. He says this stop in Whitefish used to be his favorite because they gave all the train employees 50% off at the lodge & skiing was free but now the movie stars have moved in & ruined it, he says,—jacked all the prices up.

So now I'm closing in on Seattle; foggy mountains—some of the rivers still open & free of ice—snow clogged in everywhere. It's still winter. Here's a piece of a poem I've always loved called "Goodbye Iowa" by a Montana guy named Richard Hugo:

> *"And now you are alone. The waitress*
> *will never see you again. You often pretend*
> *you don't remember people you do. You joke back*
> *spasms of shame from a night long ago,*
> *splintered glass. Bewildering blue swirl*
> *of police. Light in your eyes. Hard questions.*
> *Your car is cruising. You cross with ease*
> *at 80 the state line & the state you are entering*
> *always treated you well."*

I like that. Simple.

Here's another piece by the same guy.[1]

---

1. "Degrees of Gray in Phillipsburg."

> *"The car that brought you here still runs.*
> *The money you buy lunch with,*
> *no matter where it's mined, is silver*
> *and the girl who serves your food*
> *is slender and her red hair lights the wall."*

I love that—"red hair lights the wall"—fantastic!

He's always writing about waitresses so I thought you'd appreciate that weakness.

2/19/00

Now, I'm on the leg back from Seattle to St. Paul—the train winding along the shore of Puget Sound—astoundingly beautiful country with the rosey sun setting behind snow-capped mountains & the flat sea lapping right up next to the train tracks. People picnicking along the shore, waving at the train; little kids running & leaping across the grass toward us. Why do people love trains? I've never met anyone who actually disliked trains.

Finished up shooting my part & it's more than just being a powerful movie star or a great actor. Like, for instance, Al Pacino doesn't fall into the 'Roguish Man' profile, neither does Robert De Niro—in fact it's hard to find anyone nowadays that even comes close to Nicholson in that way. Just one of those passing ideas I'll never write but fun to think about. Sean turns out to be a pretty decent director with a good eye & of course it's always a blessing to work with someone who understands what acting's all about. He does probably the best imitation of Marlon Brando I've ever seen.

Now, I'm back home in Stillwater and I find yet another mint-condition antique portable typewriter that Dan has left me to try, so here I am trying it and liking it very much. Maybe I'll open a shop of old portables. I can't tell you how grateful I am to be back in the bosom of my little family. I think I'm getting very soft with age. I love being back in my little room with three desks and typewriters all around and books and old ashtrays and lamps—my nest. There's a giant stack of mail here with, I notice, many letters from you. You've been a busy man! Haven't had a chance yet to go through them all; but will shortly.

Ran into a guy named Michael Fitzgerald whose father, it turns out, translated the definitive *Odyssey* by Homer so I went out and got a copy and it's quite astounding.[2] I've never had the courage to plow through it before but this version really sings with all the primitive grandeur of an epic poem. It's a monster and now I see why it's so much referred to by modern writers as one of their source inspirations.

I don't know exactly how to end this thing—it just keeps rambling but I suppose I should attempt to bring it to a close. Always good to hear from you. I keep thinking of those lines by Beckett: "I can't go on. I'll go on." What else can we do??

My fondest regards to Scarlett and your New Mexico sunny life down there. Keep taking those baths. Be talking to you soon.

Hasta Luego,
Sam

2. Robert Fitzgerald published a
   renowned verse translation of
   the *Odyssey* (1961).

February 24, 2000

[TYPED]

John,

I'm suffering a luxury of riches here with all these alternative typewriters—switching back and forth. This one is the little Hermes portable which is very light and smooth but tends to slide around the desk more than the Voss.

Last couple of days have been very mysterious and foggy with the temperature rising to almost fifty (which is a heat wave here for this time of year). Me & Jessica rise early, in the dark to get the kid's lunches ready, their breakfast, then I drive them both to school (two different schools) then I come back and Jessie makes soft boiled eggs, we read the mail, listen to the canary sing, have coffee, sometimes go down to town for breakfast but mostly we hang out in the house. We have our seventeenth anniversary coming up (St. Patrick's Day). Hard to believe there's been that much water under the bridge but here we are, still together and much more tolerant of each other's differences. Still in love and sort of stunned that we've managed to raise kids, maintain a family, have two separate careers moving all over the world and still together!

I empathize with your struggle with dope but don't exactly know what to say about it. I'm not even sure if you regard it as a struggle. For me, it just came down to a kind of terrible emotional crash where I knew I had to turn something around in myself or suffer horrible consequences. Some of those consequences I was already under the influence of and it began to really bear down on me in a way I couldn't handle any more. I came very close to destroying just about everything that really meant something to me—my relationship with Jessica, my kids most of all. I couldn't believe the amount of self-destruction I was capable of and I became so isolated and removed from everyone that I thought I might as well take a look at this alcoholic situation to see if it really applied to me. I still couldn't believe I was alcoholic when I entered the meetings for the *second* time in New York. I kept drinking through about the first week of meetings and then, slowly something began to bend—I guess it was my pride more than anything. I had a

our physical self and the psychological part takes over. That's t
ough one for me because it all has to do with this thing of loneli
nd the inability to have easy relationships with other people.   I
he very reason I started drinking in the first place- THE BAR, the
Nightlife"; the excitement of meeting strange women; the "Adventur
his whole notion that there's something out there I'm missing out
nd booze was definitely the ticket that opened the door. The fals
ourage that drinking gave me allowed me to indulge any idiocy that
ame along with never any thought of having to pay for it down the
lso, there was the "romance" with the bottle- I was a writer, I ha
license to drink. All writers drink, even great ones. I was a "
uy". I could take it. I didn't give a shit what anybody thought
 didn't really give a shit what I did to other people in the way o
buse or denial. I was my own guy! I'm amazed I lived through it
ctually: blackouts on the road doing ninety miles an hour, winding
p sleeping in ditches; fist fights with Marines; hangovers that we
n through half the day and were only remedied by more booze, stran
omen who could have been carrying anything; pool games til the cr
f dawn with Italian Mafioso types where I lost hundreds of dollars
errible fights with ones I loved; the shakes, vomiting, shitting m
ants on the street- Sounds like fun, huh? From the outside one m
ay well, sure, it was probably time for you to take stock of yours
ut I never saw the least little part of it. I thought the world w
ucked up and I was just reacting like some kind of underground her

Anyhow, the long and short of it is I know that you and I are
omewhat similar in the area of our difficulty to get along with ot
eople and the world at large- this isolation thing. It may be one
f the reasons we've maintained such a friendship over the years.
o one else will dain to talk to us! I think the personality type
hat we both carry (I don't know the name of it or the category it
ight fall into on anybody's chart) is particularly prone to addict
f one kind or another. I know there have been times I would do
nything to get out of this feeling of being completely cut off. B
e're both lucky in that we've found amazing women in this life; we
tumbled our way across actual esoteric knowledge and had the good
ortune to meet men like Pentland; we still get a kick out of strin
ords together and concocting images and feel the importance of try
o attempt to get down something of our experience through time and
hose blessings seem to more and more out-weigh the temporary tranc

hard time seeing myself in the same exact bag as my old man, who I swore I would never resemble. In a way, the decision to stop drinking was the easiest part—of course you go through about a three month stretch where you body has to de-tox and get rid of all the poison you've built up and through that time there's a lot of craving and self-pity but then the "need" for booze kind of leaves your physical self and the psychological part takes over. That's the tough one for me because it all has to do with this thing of loneliness and the inability to have easy relationships with other people. It's the very reason I started drinking in the first place—THE BAR, the "Nightlife"; the excitement of meeting strange women; the "Adventure"—this whole notion that there's something out there I'm missing out on and booze was definitely the ticket that opened the door. The false courage that drinking gave me allowed me to indulge any idiocy that came along with never any thought of having to pay for it down the road. Also, there was the "romance" with the bottle—I was a writer, I had a license to drink. All writers drink, even great ones. I was a "tough guy." I could take it. I didn't give a shit what anybody thought and I didn't really give a shit what I did to other people in the way of abuse or denial. I was my own guy! I'm amazed I lived through it actually: blackouts on the road doing ninety miles an hour, winding up sleeping in ditches; fist fights with Marines; hangovers that went on through half the day and were only remedied by more booze, strange women who could have been carrying anything; pool games til the crack of dawn with Italian Mafioso types where I lost hundreds of dollars, terrible fights with the ones I loved; the shakes, vomiting, shitting my pants on the street—Sounds like fun, huh? From the outside one might say well, sure, it was probably time for you to take stock of yourself but I never saw the least little part of it. I thought the world was fucked up and I was just reacting like some kind of underground hero.

Anyhow, the long and short of it is I know that you and I are somewhat similar in the area of our difficulty to get along with other people and the world at large—this isolation thing. It may be one of the reasons we've maintained such a friendship over the years. No one else will dain to talk to us! I think the personality type that we both carry (I don't know the name of it or the category it might fall into on anybody's chart) is particularly prone to addiction of one kind or another. I know there have been times I would do anything to get out of this feeling of being completely cut off. But we're both lucky in that we've found amazing women in this life; we've stumbled our way across actual esoteric knowledge and had the good fortune to meet men like Pentland; we still get a kick out of stringing words together and concocting images and feel the importance of trying to attempt to get down something of our experience through time and those blessings seem to more and more out-weigh the temporary trances of being smashed and carried away with images of myself as some kind of fascinating fellow. I don't think too much about booze anymore but when I was up there in Vancouver doing the film and every night going out to dinner with all these actors and movie people around—Sean Penn, Nicholson et al; and everyone was drinking and telling stories and carrying on—I thought—the "thought" crossed through my mind of how easy it would be to just order a little shot of bourbon straight-up and knock it back and feel that warm glow of confidence and giddiness and stupid arrogance again and just have a grand old time sitting around ogling girls and telling lies and letting all the bullshit fly but then something else came in that flat knew that if I did that I would be long gone down the lost road again. I'm not saying I'm on the "found" road now but I can tell the difference between a dead-end and an open highway. It's very clear. And I don't even know exactly how I came to it but I think I had to come to that very severe bottom end before I ever considered the alternative. I'm three years sober now but there's still always the possibility that the maniac could leap up one day and decide to have a "little drink." Who knows? It'll probably always be there. And I could say, "Well, I've been a very good boy for three years and I actually deserve a little drink. What the hell!" And there I'd be—right back where I started. I was looking at the Aphorisms in the back of *Views from the Real World* the other day and happened to stick on this one: "If you already know it is bad and do it, you commit a sin difficult to redress." Of course, words like "bad" and "sin" don't sit real easy with any of us anymore but somewhere we know exactly what he's talking about and somewhere we might even begin to taste the beginnings of a conscience—"woe is me!."

I'm off to New York soon but I'll write some more and you do the same. Regards to Scarlett and the big dog. Hope things stay sunny down there.

Que via bien!
Sam

March 28, 2000

[TYPED]

John,

    First off, let me explain the little enclosure is *not* dope but a genuine Cuban cigar smuggled in from Mexico. I rarely smoke cigars but I tried one of these little wonders and the first thing I thought was, 'John would really enjoy this,' so here it is. Very smooth. (Don't forget to snip the closed end before you light up. But you probably already know this.) Needless to say we just returned from another amazing journey down to Tulum in the Yucatan— same place we've been going each Spring Break with the kids for the last five years now. Each time seems to have its own particular resonance but this time was truly spectacular. We arrived the night of the full moon and down there it rises gigantic and bright orange like the sun and casts a shimmering golden path clear across the flat black Caribbean Ocean. Palm trees rustle in the sea breeze like hula dancers; Grackles and parrots scream out from the jungle; Iguanas make this weird chirping sound almost like a squirrel; battalions of Pelicans come gliding down the beach in search of fish and in the mornings the sun brings you straight to your feet at exactly 6: A.M. The miracle of airplane travel is still something I can't quite get over. I have this handy drug called Xanax now (I think it's the same thing you might have been taking for your anxiety attacks)—it really works! I almost feel cocky now about climbing on board and nestling into one of those blue seats with the little pillow and the blanket all laid out for you. Still, it absolutely blows me away that one minute you can be standing in Minneapolis with a sweatshirt and jacket on in thirty degree temperatures, not a leaf on a tree and then three hours later you disembark to the sounds of Spanish, black-eyed Indian people and the sun cooking the back of your neck like a barbeque. We rented a ridiculously tiny Jap car with wheels that look like they came off a tricycle and barreled ass down the highway for an hour to the tip of Quintana Roo. Stayed in a little fancier place than we're used to, run by a French couple who speak so many languages it makes your head swim. (I'm finally getting a pretty rudimentary handle on Spanish where I can read it and hear fairly well and speak enough to get along in most situations. One thing I didn't understand for a long time is that while English has only six possible tenses for the verb, Spanish has fourteen! No wonder it's more "colorful," as they say.) Me and Walker caught more fish in two days fishing than we did all summer in Minnesota. Fish like you wouldn't believe. Everything down there is exotically painted with stripes and dots and splashes of color—the fish, the birds, the houses—even the taxis. I taught Walker and Hannah how to body-surf the waves and they really got into it. They asked me where I learned to do that and I reminded them that I grew up in California. They care very little about my past and seem totally uninterested in any of my vague stories. Just as well. I don't care much about it anymore either. I guess I exhausted too much of it in writing plays about it. Incidentally, I finally have a smash hit production on Broad-way of *True West*—(only twenty some years after it was written). Two very hot young actors in it who swap roles every three nights. The sucker is sold out and got the best, across-the-board reviews I've ever had in my life. I'm in a state of shock. It's already broke the box-office record sales for the theatre it's in. I remember way back when we did *True West* in San Francisco and you came to the opening night party stoned in sunglasses and something else weird you were wearing or saying and everyone was slightly bewildered by you and I thought what a cool thing it was to have a mysterious friend like this that nobody could figure out. "He's your father in law?" they would whisper and I would try to explain the convoluted relationship we had with Scarlett and O-Lan and Jesse and it still seemed to befuddle them. I can re-member an aura though coming from people that almost smelled like jealou-sy and/or paranoia, I don't know which. Oh, while we're reminiscing, I don't know if I told you that John Lion died very suddenly of a heart attack.[1] He was about our age I guess. I remember him too as being someone like the Mr. Jones in the Dylan song. Nice enough guy but I always felt uneasy around him, like he wanted to get "in" on something that in reality didn't even exist. I guess I'm rambling now. I am rambling now. Now I'm rambling. (I've been conjugating Spanish verbs too long.) Great book I'm reading now which you've probably already covered, being a Graham Greene fan, called *The Heart of the Matter*. Don't know why this guy isn't universally recognized as one of the monsters of modern fiction. He comes up with absolutely chiseled thoughts like . . . "the most enviable possession a man can own—a happy death." Or . . . "lack of faith helps one to see more clearly than faith." Or . . . "It's a mistake to mix up the ideas

1. Lion, the founder and longtime artistic director of the Magic Theatre in San Francisco, died August 1, 1999.

of happiness and love." Or, here's a killer . . . "the stigmata of loneliness." Splendid! I'm supposed to be working on short stories now but have found myself diving into yet another play. I did a film of *Hamlet* set in contemporary New York but with all the original Shakespeare language in tact and it came out very powerful.[2] I play Hamlet's ghost of a father and I'd never tried Shakespeare before. Quite something to tackle that language. But what I understood through the film for the first time was how Hamlet is totally destined to fulfill this revenge. He has no choice in the matter. And I started for some reason or another to think about a female version of Hamlet—not exactly the same play but based on the essential working principal of it which is this animal compulsion toward revenge. I don't know why that fascinates me but it does. I don't believe in revenge or anything like it but the idea that someone can be driven toward a terrible act just because they are born into the predicament of it. I was thinking like in the case of modern children who find themselves with one parent only and begin to harbor a grudge against the absent one that carries through their whole life. Anyhow, that's what I'm beginning to tackle and I'll probably quit if it turns out to be not much fun.

It's night now, back in the chilly Midwest. Walker's practicing piano downstairs, Jessie's reading and Hannah is doing her homework. All very cozy. I'll sign off for now but hope everything is well with you all down in New Mexico. Needless to say I miss seeing and talking with you but—one of these good old days—

Vamos a ver,
Sam

2. This film version of *Hamlet* (2000) was directed by Michael Almereyda and starred Ethan Hawke, Kyle MacLachlan, and Diane Venora.

June 1, 2000

[TYPED]

John,

   Tried calling you several times on the road but no answer. Just got back
from Chicago—my uncle Buzz died down there and I went down for the
service. Very strange returning to the little town where my mother and
father were raised—west of Chicago, now suburbs surrounded by swarming
highways full of a zillion cars. The population impact on this country is just
astounding—the way it's transformed what used to be rural America into an
anonymous maze of maniacs seemingly with no connection whatsoever to
each other or themselves. Then there's the extended family of my father's
side (Buzz was my dad's younger brother—there were five brothers all born
on a wheat farm in McHenry Illinois). There I am standing in a humid little
funeral home in the "village" of Glen Ellyn, Illinois in my blue suit hugging
my aunt Nancy (wife of Buzz) and all these family members start coming
up to me, most of whom I barely recognize and some I've never even seen
before. There's these two Phillipino kids with tattoos and ear rings, teen-
agers who turn out to be the children of Buzz's adopted son, Dan. Dan went
into the service and got stationed in the Philippines where he began spending afternoons, out of boredom, at the local women's dart throwing contests.
You can imagine a big strapping American kid (Dan's about six foot four and
weighs two hundred pounds) suddenly in the midst of Phillipino women
throwing darts. He gets smitten by one particular girl who happens to be
the Women's Phillipino Dart Champion and he can't take his eyes off her.
In the middle of the contest he sends her a note up on the platform where
she's in the middle of the contest. The note says: "Look out in the audience.
The tallest guy in the crowd would like to meet you for a drink." So she
turns and spots him. Then it's her turn to throw the dart and she misses and
takes second place in the contest. Needless to say, they meet for the drink,
get married and proceed to have these two teen-agers who are now standing
in front of me, introducing themselves as my second cousins or something.
Then there's this ancient guy with a lump on the side of his face who comes
up to me with these rheumy runny eyes and right off the bat tells me that my

Grandfather, Sam (father of Buzz and my Dad) once spit right in his eye. I ask him how that came about and he laughs one of those laughs that turns into a bronchial spasm, coughing and hacking his way until his throat clears and he tells me he was in the back seat of a Model A Ford with my Grandfather driving and drinking from a whiskey bottle when Grandpa Sam suddenly let loose a lunger out the window that came back and hit him square in the eye. He never forgot that, he says. Then there's Mike, the son of Dick—another brother of my Dad's (the one with the amputated leg that I based the character in *Buried Child* after) who brings me a framed photograph of my father during World War II, crouched in front of his B-24 bomber with a whole group of other pilots. There's my Dad, grinning out at the camera, maybe twenty three years old, young, handsome, full of himself—looking like one of those Spencer Tracy, Clark Gable war movie heroes. Mike knows more about my Dad's war career than I do. He knows the name and number of his outfit; the dates of his missions over Italy and Rumania; the number of missions; how many bombs they dropped—it's amazing. He tells me the main objective of my Dad's bomber unit was to knock out all the oil and petroleum fields in Rumania because that was the Nazi's main source of fuel. They flew those huge cumbersome B-24's flat out, only two hundred feet above ground surface so they wouldn't be detected by Ray-Dar and dropped thousands of bombs then returned to Italy. No wonder he became an alcoholic! I find a chair next to my uncle Dick (father of Mike who just handed me the photograph—I hope you're following this). Dick is now 74 but looks fifty at the most; bald head, big hooked nose with darting bright blue eyes; massive hands and shoulders but because of the polio and his amputated leg very slight from the waist down, almost emaciated. There's a vitality about him that's hard to resist. I remember him when I was about nineteen and had long hippie hair and a bad attitude—He trapped me in the kitchen of my Grandma's house and pinned me up against the refrigerator with one of his crutches (the pants leg from his missing limb was waving around like a flag), his blue eyes bore into me with that same maniacal intensity that my old man had and he said to me, "Don't you ever forget that you are living in the greatest goddamn country in the world!" These were back in the flag burning, Viet Nam days. Now he's much milder, almost meek and he leans over to me in his chair and calls me "Steve" because that's what he always called me when I was a kid. "Steve," he says, "I know you wanted to go over and pay a visit to Scottie—" (Now this is Uncle Scott, the very youngest brother of my father's—only about eight years older than me.)—"but I talked to Scottie this morning and he told me, under no circumstances did he want anyone coming over to the house." "Okay," I say, "that's fine." Dick goes on—"He's got the damn depression stuff. He's on all kinds of medication plus the diabetes. And he just had that bad car crash, you know." "That's fine," I say, "I'll see him another time." The lie comes out of me. I haven't seen uncle Scott in about six years but I thought, since I was down here anyway, I'd pay him a visit. In a way I'm relieved.

The afternoon drones on and the room is filled to the walls with people. Already, I've been here two hours and the service hasn't started yet. The humidity is rising, everyone is sweating and all the windows are closed up tight as a drum. An ancient black woman (the only black person in the crowd) comes over and introduces herself as Sadie. She tells me Buzz was one of her best friends in the whole world. She tells me she had a son who was a college all-star football player at Oklahoma State, back in the sixties. Sadie had an old car that was always giving her trouble and on the eve of her son's homecoming football game in Oklahoma, her car failed her. Buzz found out about it and drove Sadie all the way out to Oklahoma so she wouldn't miss her boy's football game. All these stories amaze me in their simplicity. There it is—life in the raw. Then a tall, elegant gray headed lady comes up and tells me she was Buzz's first sweetheart. She also confesses she was the best looking girl in all of DuPage County. She chuckles to me out the side of her mouth in recognition of her present age. She says she used to double-date with Buzz and my mother and father and, one time, Sam (my dad) and his brother (Buzz) came out to their farm in the same model A to pick my mother and her up to go on a date but they also had my uncle Dick along with them. There was no room inside the coupe so the two girls decided they'd ride on the fenders of the car while the men drove. (Those were the days!) So off they went through the cornfields with the girl's skirts flapping in the wind. "Look!," she says to me, and hikes her dress up to her knee revealing an old gnarly red scar. "See that? That's from the burn I got off the engine of that old Ford. That's it, right there." And so it goes. Story after story and there's no way I can do any of them justice in the re-telling.

Anyhow I'm back home now and kind of stunned from it all. More than anything it left me with this passage-of-time thing that almost seems too sad to even look square in the eye. Then there's the return to the recognition of the preciousness of the moment and still, a kind of horrible sense of futility

1980

Sam Sr. in front of his homemade
beer-top curtain. New Mex.

"You tell my son when you
see him that he owes me a couple
of hours of yard work from when
he was a kid. I could never get
him to do that yard work. I had
a hell of a time with him on that."

that everything is just passing me by. All my kids are almost grown now (some of them already are). I look at pictures of them when they were little and I can't fathom the passage that's already taken place. "Something is taking its course." And that's all there is to it.

Hope everything is roses down there in the Land of Enchantment. Best to you and yours.

Sam

August 22, 2000—Calgary, Alberta

[TYPED]

John,

One of the huge difficulties I find in writing letters (and maybe this has always been the case) is the overwhelming feeling that there is absolutely no way in hell of ever getting everything down and what you do manage to get down is only a tiny sampler of the whole experience. I'm back into Graham Greene again (his collected stories) and stunned totally by his ability to go so cleanly and directly to the heart of the matter—the core event—the 'burning center,' as Frank O'Connor put it. I've read a lot of modern stuff lately—like for instance Denis Johnson who has an amazing ability to dazzle you with language and structure and yet the whole thing winds up being about people and characters who are just plain old fuck-ups and malcontents. Also reading Dante's *Inferno*—on the other end of the spectrum. Surprised to find out that gluttony is a far more serious offense against God than those who succumbed to the temptations of the flesh. I like a writer named Tim O'Brien who wrote something called "The Things They Carried." It's very late now and I'm rambling. Just returned from the barley fields outside Calgary shooting a sequence of scenes all day for fourteen hours, clear into sundown; driving a team of four Belgian horses pulling an old McCormick hay binder—harvest scene, similar to *Days of Heaven*, in fact this whole thing is so reminiscent of *Days of Heaven* it shocks me sometimes.[1] Same place— twenty four years later. Twenty four years ago Terry Malick came to visit me up there at the 'Flying Y' when we were running around in the mud feeding Reena Yates' forty some head of boarding horses and asked me to do that film. I can remember all the thoughts and feeling that ran through me then. I remember thinking—"The movies! I can make lots of money and I won't have to ever again apply for a Guggenheim Grant or a Rockefeller Grant or a Ford Grant or a National Endowment Grant or write a play on commission for Joe Papp just to get a crumby five thousand so I can pay the fucking rent to some whacked out landlord."[2] I remember that

1. Shepard was filming *After the Harvest* (2001), a television movie directed by Jeremy Podeswa.
2. Joseph Papp (1921–1991) founded the Public Theater in New York.

was definitely a motive. And it wound up I made a total of six thousand bucks off that film! I remember also the feeling that I was about to enter a whole new world and that world was somewhat scary in its connectedness to the public and the fear of becoming maybe 'famous' and how I might lose something of myself as a writer and all kinds of confusing psychological frictions—all based on some notion of 'self,' without really realizing that I had no sense of 'self,' that I had absolutely no clue who I really was or what I was trying to accomplish, and I had a kid—a young boy (Jesse was six then) and I loved him in a way I couldn't begin to explain. And then there was the whole bunch of us—you, me, Scarlett, Kristy, O-Lan, Jesse—an extraordinary little galaxy of people who'd come together and we were actually just starting out on a life of our own, having been thrown together by circumstances none of us could have foreseen and The Work was going on and Lord Pentland and then all of a sudden I go off and do a movie, in Canada of all places! What kind of madness was that? There are these monumental turning points in a life that cannot be denied. Circumstances. Choices. A fork in the road. Whatever you want to call them. Things come up in which you could go one way or the other and no matter which turn you make your life is forever, irrevocably changed. The decision to do *Days of Heaven* was one of those moments where the consequences (good and bad) keep ringing out until you die. A life in the movies. Or, more accurately a life in and out of the movies. The "movies"! If it hadn't been for the movies I wouldn't have met Jessica. If it hadn't been for the movies I wouldn't be living in Minnesota raising more kids. If it hadn't been for the movies I wouldn't be here right now in this place doing yet another movie. (It just occurred to me the term "movies" has to do with movement, action. I guess I knew that all along but rarely associate that meaning when I use the word. A dark room where a bunch of strangers sit down and watch huge images of other strangers who somehow seem more familiar than the people they know in life.) Anyhow, here I am now in this wonderful little town in the far northern reaches of Canada. Calgary feels like some kind of blueprint for what towns might be like sometime in the future, after the holocaust and the fires and the famines and whatever else might lie ahead—in other words, after the world's settled down again and people are trying to figure out how they all might live together in a society. It's a totally modern city set out in the middle of a prairie. There's every possible race of people here, all kinds of languages cascading through the air. There's a fabulous little river called 'The Bow' that meanders through the entire city and a bike trail that seems to go forever. In fact, the guy at the bike shop told me you could actually travel one hundred miles by bike just following the river out into the country and back again. Needless to say, I bought a bike—first day here and every chance I get with time off from the set I just get on the sucker and take off. What turns me on about a bike is not the exercise or the speed—in fact, I enjoy going as slow as possible mostly unless there's some terrific downhill slopes where you can coast along with enough momentum to carry you back up the other side. I've done some adjustments to the handle bars where I can sometimes sit almost upright and just barely cruise along. (Remember all the diddling you did with the handlebars on your first Jap motorcycle in Mill Valley until you finally figured out you wanted a Harley?) Today, for instance, I only had one scene to shoot out on the prairie—very short and easy where I galloped my horse over a stretch of land to where my "children" are working on a fence line. I pull the horse up to a sliding stop and yell at them to get to work (I play a mean guy.) then I gallop back off again. Simple. It's my only scene of the day and I'm done. The sun is shining out across the wheat fields clear to the Rocky Mountains in the distance. Everything is absolutely golden. The driver takes me back into the city and dumps me at the hotel. I ask the attendant guy at the door—a young man in a green uniform and cap—to get my bike out of the storage room. He brings it to me, walking it my way across the lobby floor. I jump on it, tip the guy a buck and I'm on my way! It's like instant happiness, just gliding through people walking to and from the park. All kinds of people but not the huge throngs like you get in New York or major cities in the U.S. Women with strollers and babies, roller skaters, kids darting in and out of fountains, old couples with walkers, and as you glide along the people begin to thin out so there's just a kind of gentle stream of joggers, Koreans eating lunch on the riverbank, and casual strollers out to take the air. Now I'm cruising right alongside the river and it suddenly strikes me how similar in a way a bike feels to being in a canoe. They're both almost silent and they both give you the sensation that you're being carried along by a momentum that's able to be initiated with very little effort. Just a slight turn of the pedal can carry you quite a ways before you have to apply another stroke of the leg. Just one dip of the paddle and you glide along with the current. Another part I love about the bike is the passing by of things which isn't quite the same as when you're walking and definitely not the same as when you're driving. It's the exposure of your body I think—having the body completely out in the open where all the sensations are hitting you and the air is pouring across you. I guess that's the thrill of the motorcycle too but I prefer the silence of the bike and the slow pace, slow enough where you're almost a part of things and yet slightly distanced. I make my way across a bridge, looking down at some kids throwing stones into the river—a girl in barefeet smoking, two guys fishing. The water is rushing below me in green swirls opening out into flattened pools where you can see clear to the stoney bottom. Some guy on skates is in front of me on the bridge being pulled along by a maniac Golden Retriever on a leash. The kind of dog that doesn't have a clue—crazy eyes, its tongue lolling out the side of its mouth, charging ahead into people with the guy trying desperately to hold his balance on the skates. I pedal quick and get around them before they have a chance to wreck. Once across the river I head into a different part of town that looks much older and without the downtown tourist frills of the hotel area. There's a couple of drunk Indians (the old cliché but there they are) rolling a cigarette between them. A young Japanese girl waiting for a bus. Fewer people and more abandoned looking streets. I stop at a place called "Billy's News" and buy a Racing Form. It's been more than a week since I've seen a Racing Form and I'm thrilled to find one right here in Billy's News. I fold the Form up and stuff it into my belt and ride on, turning back toward the river. The river pulls me. Why is that? It's true. Water or something. The movement of water. You can smell it as you get closer. Smells like fish and green weeds and the birds are swooping down toward it. All kinds of ducks and gulls and hawks and crows and little bitty sparrows. They race along through the trees and dive down to get a drink then swoop back up in flocks like one fluid animal all in synch. Now I'm heading out into a more remote stretch where you can still feel the city around you but it's further away and you can't see cars anymore, just hear their whooshing from the highway and you can't see tall buildings, just simple town houses and back porches now and then or the hint of a neighborhood down some alley and the bike path isn't smooth anymore, it's got ruts and rocks in it and rain holes and all the fancy crushed red clay they laid on it back in town has now disappeared entirely so that you're really crunching along and not smoothly sailing like before. Still, it's great to now be out where there's hardly anybody else—one pair of very old ladies sitting side by side on an iron bench smiling at the river holding hands with a blanket stretched across their laps. It looks like it might be a regular rendezvous for them. Big willow trees shade the path and black squirrels scutter across carrying nuts in their mouths. I suddenly realize I'm absolutely content to just be here on this ride without a care in the world. I can't remember how long it's been when I could truly say that. There's usually always something hovering inside—some plan, some scheme, some worry, some doubt, some guilt, some past of one shape or another. Nostalgia's a big one. Going back to some time in your mind. That must be part of the curse of age. Indulging in the past more and more until it consumes the present. Like for instance, I start thinking of the two of us riding around Mill Valley on bikes back in the seventies—we were in our thirties and we'd get bombed on weed, jump on our bikes and cruise down through the back streets in the middle of the night having long convoluted conversations then convulsing into laughter to the point where we couldn't pedal anymore and we'd just stand there on some street like 'Maple' or 'Olive' or something, straddling our bikes and laughing so hard I thought my insides were turning to knots. What was so fucking funny?? Those were truly high times and I remember thinking at the time that this was something completely unique and amazing—two "grown" men able to essentially have a relationship like two kids, like two boys out of time with the rest of the world. And nothing much else made any real sense—not even the Work really because my whole relationship to the Work at that time was one of the "bad boy" trying to shape up to my imagination of the 'Conscious Ones'—the real adults, which is exactly what my whole relationship to my father was like and my relationship to school and my relationship to the whole fucking world. I never really outgrew that horrible sense of not cutting the mustard, of being always 'out of the loop' with people and things around me, so I began to live entirely inside the imagination. I had long dialogues with myself as a kid where I was a professional golfer, for instance, being interviewed by CBS after winning the Masters or I was a famous horse trainer or a famous Veterinarian or something always "Famous." I wanted to be "famous" for something. I wanted everything turned around where I was the one revered and instilling a sense of awe in other people, where other people wanted to know me and I held a certain sway over them, a certain power, a deep mystery. Low and behold it all came true much faster than I'd ever dreamed and suddenly I was caught in the little nightmare of my own making.

This has gone on way too long and all of a sudden I'm really bored with it and have to cut it off. I'm due for work in fifteen minutes. Today we shoot the fire sequence. More later. Love to Scarlett and Godspeed!

Your Amigo,
Sam

November 19, 2000

John—Been meaning to write but there's so much to tell it's overwhelming. Having a rough spell right now but you know how that comes & goes. Thinking I might come down & visit you later in month.

All the Best
—Sam

NEAL CASSADY & JACK KEROUAC
San Francisco   1952
Photo by Carolyn Cassady

January 12, 2001

[TYPED]

John—

   Back home and still reeling from the amazing avalanche of experiences over the past year. I think you and Scarlett may have the absolute right approach: never leave your cozy little home and your warm baths and your big fuzzy dog because life will just bash you over the head out there. I remember leaving Deming and feeling very lonely and driving out into that long stretch of highway with nothing around and suddenly my cell phone ringing and it was Jessica calling from London! I was so amazed to be talking to her over all that distance. Right afterward I called you and then I headed on to Santa Fe where I thought I might spend a leisurely day and do some writing but, instead, I went out that night to an old restaurant me and Jessie used to go to called the Pink Adobe and asked if the owner was around—a great old Louisiana woman named Rosalie but it turns out she had died last summer, which kind of shocked me and just when I heard this news I turned toward one wall of the restaurant and saw a picture of Jessica and my son Walker on the wall from when they had visited a year or so ago and then I went staggering out of the place and the moon was full and everything was so reminiscent and nostalgic of the time me and Jess had lived there and the air was full of that wonderful smell of burning pine—so I decided I would get good and drunk. I hadn't had that thought in over three and a half years—totally dry—not one single drip of liquor and now, suddenly, I know without a doubt that I am going off with the full intention of getting absolutely smashed. I know exactly what bar I am going to and exactly what kind of booze I'm going to indulge in—red Cabernet from Healdsburg, California where my other son lives. The bar is completely on the other side of town, way up on Canyon Road and it's a Sunday night and no one is on the streets at all and I'm walking and there's that great New Mexican mountain chill in the air. It's only about forty degrees and having gotten used to Minnesota winters it feels like nothing and with my new reamed out heart artery I feel almost invincible anyway so I walk the whole distance, find the bar where some fat guy is singing old Dylan songs and I order my big glass of red wine. Sitting there at the bar and looking down the row of slightly pathetic middle-aged ex-hippie types who are obvious regulars the whole aching despair of bar life comes flooding back and I can't believe I'm actually back in this situation—this old familiar situation of drinking alone with strangers. I finish my wine and leave and start walking back down the hill into town again—back toward the plaza. I walk for miles and miles, wondering if maybe I've gotten disoriented and forgotten the way but then I keep checking for landmarks and realize I'm on the same road me and Jessica used to bicycle down every morning with Shura strapped to the back of her mother's bike like some little papoose—she was about three years old then and we would go to this little coffee shop connected to the La Fonda Hotel and have breakfast. Then I go diving further into the past and remember when you and I had met each other in the lobby of the La Fonda after a night of debauchery with two women and no sleep and I keep right on associating into the inevitable memories of my Dad being a custodian at the La Fonda and then, before I know exactly what's going on with myself I'm there inside the La Fonda at the bar ordering another glass of red wine! There's a whole group of English tourists sitting in one corner of the place ordering German beer. They're very organized and even go about getting drunk in an orderly fashion. I finish this second large glass of red wine and go out into the lobby and start wandering around staring at all the great photographs of early Santa Fe days, some dating back to the very early 1800's—views of the plaza with muddy streets and burros and Indians and Mexicans and soldiers and all the great mix of races and the marketplace and traders from all over—none of them with even the slightest clue that the whole place would one day be invaded by Hollywood and millionaires and that the biggest commodity would be art and Indian jewelry. I head out into the street and find yet another bar, another hotel, another big glass of red wine and finally manage to get myself good and sloshed. Now, I got to the plaza or rather, try to walk through the plaza on my way back to the hotel where I'm staying. There's still not a soul on the street. One low-rider car—a silver Chevy which I'm actually surprised to see—I thought all the low-riders had moved up to Española. The plaza is completely decked out in Christmas lights—everything is wrapped and draped in lights: the trees, the band shell, the bank, the Governor's Palace, the iron fences surrounding the snow covered lawn—red, green, blue, white; blinking on and off. I get to the very center of the plaza and start turning in circles for some reason and staring up through the barren trees, very drunk, seeing the big moon overhead—something like one of those early bad foreign films with sub-titles and I start feeling very sorry for myself and conjure up all this stuff about my father and the play I just finished in San Francisco which deals with his death and all that stuff and the whole thing just becomes a god-awful drunken mess of emotional indulgence in the past!!![1] At one point I'm crying out to the moon and the heavens in a drunken wail, thinking there's no one around and all of a sudden I see someone walking straight towards me across the plaza—not a cop, just a person but It's so shocking to see another human being—and this is part of what I was trying to tell you down there in Deming in the coffee shop—how it sometimes feels as though I am absolutely unaware of anyone else existing in this life that I wonder to what extent I am cut off from other people—how far have I removed myself into this totally ridiculous state of isolation???

Having survived those bad Santa Fe blues I make it back up into the cold country. Soon as you cross into Missouri and Kansas you begin to feel the chill. Everything turns gray and soon snow begins to appear in patches out in the corn fields of Iowa and Nebraska. I come home to an empty house. Not even the dogs are there. I don't know what I was expecting but the emptiness gets to me a little. I have to rattle around in this big old house for three days before the plane takes off for London. Then I start going through all the old airplane anxieties—(sometimes I feel just like I'm in a Woody Allen film or something).

On the day, I drive myself out to the airport, take my Xanax pill and climb on board the huge DC-30 or whatever it is. It has seats set in pairs; six across with two aisles. The drug starts setting in and I'm in that courageous "could give a flying shit" mood and start chatting it up with the guy next to me who turns out to be some representative of an Energy Resources company who flies about three times a week back and forth to Europe, trying to convince middle European countries like Latvia to clean up their act and invest in American know how and ingenuity. Finally, he gets bored or tired or something and turns out his little overhead light, plunks his seat back, turns his butt toward me and goes to sleep. There's this total stranger sleeping right next to me! It's like summer camp or something. I can't sleep of course so I turn on the little armchair T.V. set that accompanies every seat and it has a color map of the world and the oceans and everything and there's a little white replica image of our plane in flight with a red dotted line showing our projected course of travel (twenty nine thousand some feet above the

1. According to Shepard, the play is The Late Henry Moss.

earth!), over Labrador and Newfoundland, then trekking out over the vast icey expanse of the Atlantic Ocean and on to jolly old England. I still can't quite fathom it, even on this wonder drug I can't get used to the idea that I'm up here so far above the earth with a whole bunch of people I don't know, making our way over thousands of miles and everybody's acting like they're in some big old fancy restaurant or something! Maybe I was born in the wrong century. I watch the progress of our little white replica plane on the t.v. screen. Every now and then it scoots a millimeter or so forward along the projected route, so that now we appear to be directly over Michigan, heading toward Ontario, Canada. I start trying to calculate the time it would take me to drive from Minneapolis to Canada and then compare that to the amount of time the plane's been in the air and I begin to feel pretty good about how smart I am to be flying rather than driving. Of course I don't take into account that you can't actually drive to England.

The plane lands at Heathrow Airport, England about six and a half hours after take off in St. Paul/Minneapolis and I haven't slept at all but don't feel much of anything except relief that we've made it! Jessica's Cockney driver is there to meet me in his black Rover car. He's a short, stocky little man who used to play rugby or soccer and he grabs my bag and throws it in the "boot" of his car and we take off for London. It's very early in the morning and the airport is miles from London itself. The weather is extremely gray and gloomy; drizzling rain and Ben the driver tells me that it's been like this for a solid month—no sun and rain every single day. The ground outside looks absolutely saturated; mud everywhere, crows huddled up in bare trees, sheep dripping wet. Finally, we hit the outskirts of London; rows and rows of bleak brick housing units, little red telephone kiosks on the corners and slowly the morning traffic begins to converge on us until we are in the middle of a major world Metropolis in full swing. Ben finally pulls the car up in front of a white three story apartment building on a quiet street and I see Walker peeking out of the window at me and then running for the door. He's the first one I meet as I go trotting up the front stairs and then Hannah and Jessica and suddenly it feels like everything is exactly in place and this is where I'm supposed to be and it's all perfect.

For the next three weeks we go on Jessica's theatre schedule—sort of like Rock and Roll stars—sleeping until eleven or twelve in the morning; not going to bed until at least 3:00 A.M.; staying up late watching old movies, drinking tea and eating English biscuits. Then, we all stroll down to the local little café and have breakfast and coffee and take walks across Primrose Park or up to Hampstead Heath (where I used to live with O-Lan back in 1971 and Jesse was a one year old infant) or we take a cab over to the Tate Gallery or go stare at William Blake's totally amazing visionary drawings of angels and devils and whatever other bizarre fucked up Christian mythology he had going in his eighteenth century little mind. Or, maybe we go to a bookstore or do just whatever we feel like and have dinner in some Thai restaurant and then drop Jessica off at the theatre where she goes in the stage door in a back alley of the West End, right next door to a strip-tease lap dancing place and she gets her wig on and her make up and gets all dressed up in her turn of the century Elizabethan gear and goes out on stage in front of fifteen hundred people and plays the role of Mary Tyrone in O'Neill's *Long Day's Journey Into Night* while me and the kids go back home and watch t.v. or read or play chess or play music or go to a movie or something. That's about it.

Now, I'm back again in Minnesota with the kids back in school. Jessie won't be done with the play over there until early March. It's going to be a long spell but then we get to go off to Mexico and our favorite beach. Just laying around in the sun, swimming and fishing and eating. It will be great!

Looks like I've signed up for that Ridley Scott flick—*Black Hawk Down*, so I'll be taking another plane to North Africa in May or June then the whole family's going to meet me over there and we're going to Spain for a couple weeks. I've always wanted to see Spain.

Hope the two of you are doing well. All best regards to Webster!

Your amigo,
Sam

February 5, 2001

[TYPED]

John,

    I've stumbled on a brand new way to get myself to write. (I'm sure you don't have this problem but I keep getting lazier and lazier and would almost do anything but sit down and write.) I've gathered up all my old tattered notebooks, some going back several years, and I'm going through all of them, page by page, and whenever I come across anything that seems even the least bit interesting, even if it's only a sentence—I type it out and then go on to the next one. So now what I have is a whole stack (about fifteen or so) of stuff that I then go through each day and work a little bit on. It's great because now, rather than sitting there staring into the same dull couple of pages that seem to go absolutely nowhere, I can now just go on to the next thing and see if that triggers something. Pretty soon I've actually created the illusion of being a writer at work and feel good about myself for a while.

    These days now are very strange and somehow new for me. I don't know exactly what's changed but I feel it has to do with this heart condition that I had attended to in California. Ever since then I've felt different—more estranged and almost under water. I can't put my finger on it. Also this deep winter up here and being without Jessica for so long is kind of trying some-times. [. . .]

Con muy amable,
Sam

August 4, 2001

[TYPED]

John,

Thanks much for your more than generous notes on the stories. I'm at that weird phase in a book like this (I remember it being true of *Motel Chronicles* and *Cruising Paradise*) where you suddenly seem to have enough material where it begins to actually look like it might be a book but somehow it doesn't quite jell into a real structure yet.[1] I have a lot more work to do and your comments really help me see where to focus. I think you're absolutely right about 'Coalinga ½ Way' going first. I was reluctant to put it there out of fear it was too 'down' and I thought the other story—'Living the Sign' would be a brighter way to begin but now I see that it just doesn't have the power of 'Coalinga.' 'Remedy Man' is actually pure fiction and owes more to the memory of the 'Flying Y Ranch' than anything else. I think you're right about the boy's description of the rock in 'Berlin Wall Piece' being too sophisticated. This was one of those instances where I knew something went wrong right there but I couldn't put my finger on it. Thanks for nailing it. 'The Door to Women' I still don't know quite what to do with. I think the problem with it is that it wants to be much longer—more like a little novella, but I don't seem to be able to find the door into that (no pun intended). I'm really thrilled that you like 'It Wasn't Proust' because this was one of those that when I finished it I thought was one of the best things I'd ever done and then, after letting it sit for a long time and coming back to read it, I began to think it was just awful and boring and stupidly presented. I still have some trouble I think trying to find the precise structure for it. About the ending—I'm not sure I understand your objection to the ending: "Don't go to France," unless you think it's too point blank. For some reason it isn't the ending that bothers me so much about this story as it is the shifting from describing the environment of the place then back to the characters and their dilemma on the dock. I'm also thrilled you like 'Stout of Heart'—this is another one I'd completely lost a bead on. I don't know if you have that kind slipping of perception about something you write—as though from one reading of it to the next you go 180 degrees in your opinion of it. I think you're right about 'Foreigners'

---

1. Shepard's note: *Great Dream of Heaven.*

being just "o.k."—it doesn't seem to go anywhere and do anything other than just sit there as a 'voice.' I may just cut it altogether. It doesn't seem to fit in. I've now finished 'Great Dream of Heaven' and I'll send the completed version off to you plus one more, tentatively titled 'Silent Me'—as soon as that's done. Again, thanks so much for the great help of reading this stuff and giving your eye to it. Hope all is well. Love to Scarlett—

Con bien Amistad,
Samuel

January 21, 2002—MN.

[HANDWRITTEN]

John—

Today is Martin Luther King Day. The kids are off school. Walker's out sledding with his friends on fresh snow. Everything outside is white, bright & cold. On the deck before me is a cup of strong, hot tea, my *Ultimate Spanish* book, a biography called *Wire to Wire* about Walter Merrick—an old Oklahoma cowboy I've admired for decades; a collection of stories by an eccentric old gal named Grace Paley & the script I'm still working on with Wim—our current title is 'Phantom of the West' (working title).[1] I'm starting all over with Spanish as though I never studied it at all & it's amazing the stuff you discover, thinking you already had it stored away in your memory somewhere. I'm doing the same thing with the Pentland book—*Exchanges Within*—endless new material pops up.[2] My main obsession lately is a new mare I bought—Quarter Horse—6 years old & completely broke to reining & cutting. I've never been on the back of an animal like this. She's what you call 'push-button' sensitive & so quick & explosive it's almost scary. More than once I've lost a stirrup & been up over her neck while she's cutting a cow. I guess I'm still going in 6 directions at once & haven't 'evolved' one inch over the years. I do miss having the handy opportunity of our friendship back in the seventies but life goes on.

Thinking of you both,
Sam

1. The film became *Don't Come Knocking* (2005), directed by Wim Wenders and starring Shepard, Lange, and Tim Roth.
2. John Pentland, *Exchanges Within: Questions from Everyday Life; Selected from Gurdjieff Group Meetings with John Pentland in California, 1955–1984* (1997).

Sam

Just got yr letter. Great letter - like getting a letter from Norman (Rockwell). The writer at his desk with his tea and his books with son sledding outside in fresh Minn. snow. I had to stop and ask myself "Do I know this guy or what?"

Yesterday Scarlett and I (day after I talked to you on the phone) drove 120 miles (round trip) to Las Cruses to see Black Hawk Down. Got lost going but at least it was light. Coming bac it was dark and I got on highway 25 heading the wrong way into oncoming traffic and just at that moment a police car appeared with lights flashing, spotlight glaring, cops creeping up cautiously on both sides of the Nova, hands on guns (this is right after sitting through Black Hawk too) and the first thing the cop says to me is, "Have you been drinking sir?" And I said "No, I always drive this way." (Just popped out of my mouth) Bu I smoothed it over and the cops eventually stopped all traffic I could turn around and pointed me toward the Deming ramp. Scarlett of course, just sitting there taking it all in like th time the cops threw me up against the wall in Oakland after I tried to break into Magic's apt.

Anyway - I knew it was going to be a good film with pleanty action and of course it was. I'll see it again when it comes ou on vidio. I thought they gave you a great part - the way he kep cutting back to you throughout the picture and not just a walk- part but huge craggy closeups. And you did a fantastic job. I mean that. We both enjoyed it although Scarlett thought it was really more of a boy's movie. Good job, m'boy. Well done.

Man, but was I glad to finally get back to Deming. I don't like to drive and as you remember, I never liked to leave home unless there was a piece of ass involved and then when I left, all I wanted to do was get back to the bath. (Remember the time you tried to keep me away from home all day because of a suppri birthday?) Anyway - it made me want to read the book again. I'm glad you decided to do the part. Jeeze, what a fucked up missio: that was - and the Samalies had the high ground. We were really lucky to have avoided Viet Nam - I kept thinking.

January 25, 2002

[TYPED]

Sam

Just got yr letter. Great letter—like getting a letter from Norman (Rockwell). The writer at his desk with his tea and his books with son sledding outside in fresh Minn. snow. I had to stop and ask myself "Do I know this guy or what?"

Yesterday Scarlett and I (day after I talked to you on the phone) drove 120 miles (round trip) to Las Cruces to see *Black Hawk Down*.[1] Got lost going but at least it was light. Coming back it was dark and I got on highway 25 heading the wrong way into oncoming traffic and just at that moment a police car appeared with lights flashing, spotlight glaring, cops creeping up cautiously on both sides of the Nova, hands on guns (this is right after sitting through *Black Hawk* too) and the first thing the cop says to me is, "Have you been drinking sir?" And I said, "No, I always drive this way." (Just popped out of my mouth) But I smoothed it over and the cops eventually stopped all traffic so I could turn around and pointed me toward the Deming ramp. Scarlett of course, just sitting there taking it all in like the time the cops threw me up against the wall in Oakland after I tried to break into Magic's apt.

Anyway—I knew it was going to be a good film with plenty of action and of course it was. I'll see it again when it comes out on video. I thought they gave you a great part—the way he kept cutting back to you throughout the picture and not just a walk-on part but huge craggy closeups. And you did a fantastic job. I mean that. We both enjoyed it although Scarlett thought it was really more of a boy's movie. Good job, m'boy. Well done.

Man, but was I glad to finally get back to Deming. I don't like to drive and as you remember, I never liked to leave home unless there was a piece of ass involved and then when I left, all I wanted to do was get back to the bath. (Remember the time you tried to keep me away from home all day because of a surprise birthday?) Anyway—it made me want to read the book again.

1. *Black Hawk Down*, directed by Ridley Scott and starring Josh Hartnett, Ewan McGregor, and Tom Sizemore as well as Shepard, opened on January 18, 2002.

I'm glad you decided to do the part. Jeeze, what a fucked up mission that was—and the Somalis had the high ground. We were really lucky to have avoided Viet Nam—I kept thinking.

I know just what you mean about reading stuff all over again from the beginning (Spanish, Pentland etc.) That's what I've been doing. It's always a whole new ball game. I've thought for a long time now that you probably only need one small shelf of books. You just keep going deeper and deeper into them.

I'm sure we'll all get together again somehow. Tell Jesse to have a baby or a wedding or something so we can get dressed up in bowties and get together and celebrate something.

yrs truly and sincerely wishing you all the best I remain your obedient servant and ol' time partner in sickness and in health

Johnny

March 18, 2002

[TYPED]

Dear John,

    Thanks for the notes from St. Elmo, way back when. I looked at the
date—June 14th, 1970 and such a feeling of remorse and nostalgia coursed
through me, I could hardly believe it. There you were in San Francisco,
working for the Humane Society, attending the Work, way before me and
O-Lan and Jesse arrived and you'd been living in the Haight where we
visited you once, then Mill Valley, I guess, and you'd come back from Mexico
where Scarlett had bumped into someone who had Ouspensky's book and
then you began searching for the Work in San Francisco (a rough approxi-
mation of your history). Then we all joined up in 1974, was it? Good God!

    I'm having a gigantic depression here. Winter won't go way. Here it is,
mid-March and everything is covered in snow and ice, cold as hell. I'm full of
complaints. My whole being is one big complaint. Plus, me and Jessie aren't
getting along. Right after our nineteenth anniversary (St. Paddy's Day) and
it's like the bottom fell out on us. I don't know what happened. This Friday
we're all supposed to go down to Mexico for our annual Spring Break and
we're not even talking. I can't stand it. Been reading Beckett's short stuff
again which hasn't really helped my mood; only re-enforced a kind of ornery
curmudgeon loner attitude. I don't know what to do with myself. I'm beyond
'Eeyore' in the self-pity department. I have no friends, I feel alienated from
my own family and all of Jessica's relatives, I can't stand Minnesota—the climate, the people, the whole stupid place—and yet I don't have any idea what
to do or where to go or what the answer is. This is really the pits.

    Sorry about the whole negative drift of this—I'll have to try again later,
when the sun comes out. Here's hoping things are brighter down there in
Deming.

Yr pal,
Sam

John,

Suddenly I have this impression of us both living very strange lives off in various hinterlands of the country; you motoring across Texas in search of a lost camera having deep phil associations about yourself in relation to others- setting people straight about their lives, etc., and me, down the road with a bu of horses and old men trying to win some cutting event in souther Wisconsin of all places, being saddle sore and eating spaghetti d in a bowling alley listening to an ex-professional baseball playe from the Chicago Cubs yammer on about how now (that he's past 50) most exciting thing in the world for him is to sit on top of one these explosive cutting horses- like it's a volcano going off und neath him or something- maybe a vicarious sexual thrill, I don't It is kind of scarey to suddenly realize something about yourself a flash- to actually see it in all its gorey splendor- for instanc on this recent road trip with a crazy old 75 year old horse traine named Bob McCutcheon- hauling our horses some two hundred and fift miles down the Mississippi River (I still get a kick out of spell that word) and getting to this cutting show where I rode the hair right off my mare; rode until my hand was bleeding from pressing the saddle horn- I asked myself why in the hell I was doing such a mad thing and the answer was plain and simple and internally quite embarrassing- TO WIN! That was it. I JUST WANT TO WIN SOMETHING I don't care what it is. I just want to win. I like winning. W is fun. Losing is not fun. I always feel like a loser. I've alw my whole life felt like a loser of one kind or another and I've always wanted to WIN!! And that's all there is to it. I'd do an thing to win, win, win! So there it is.

More later,

May 7, 2002

[TYPED]

John,

    Suddenly I have this impression of us both living very strange lives off in various hinterlands of the country; you motoring across Texas in search of a lost camera having deep philosophical associations about yourself in relation to others—setting people straight about their lives, etc., and me, down the road with a bunch of horses and old men trying to win some cutting event in southern Wisconsin of all places, being saddle sore and eating spaghetti dinner in a bowling alley listening to an ex-professional baseball player from the Chicago Cubs yammer on about how now (that he's past 50) the most exciting thing in the world for him is to sit on top of one of these explosive cutting horses—like it's a volcano going off underneath him or something—maybe a vicarious sexual thrill, I don't know. It is kind of scarey to suddenly realize something about yourself in a flash—to actually see it in all its gorey splendor—for instance, on this recent road trip with a crazy old 75 year old horse trainer named Bob McCutcheon—hauling our horses some two hundred and fifty miles down the Mississippi River (I still get a kick out of spelling that word) and getting to this cutting show where I rode the hair right off my mare; rode until my hand was bleeding from pressing into the saddle horn—I asked myself why in the hell I was doing such a mad thing and the answer was plain and simple and internally quite embarrassing—TO WIN! That was it. I JUST WANT TO WIN SOMETHING!! I don't care what it is. I just want to win. I like winning. Winning is fun. Losing is not fun. I always feel like a loser. I've always, my whole life felt like a loser of one kind or another and I've always wanted to WIN!! And that's all there is to it. I'd do anything to win, win, win! So there it is.

More later,
Sam

May 9, 2002

[. . .] Just some later random thoughts about "winning." For myself—I find the experience of winning a lot more unpleasant than losing. And when other people are not involved, as in a solitary game, the idea of winning seems totally absurd. My favorite thing, I guess, is not to play the game at all. You said that it was fun to win so you probably are driven to experience the fun as well as escape from the inner feeling of being a loser. But It's always struck me that this feeling of being a loser (or at other times, feeling lost or alienated) is an experience of a profound truth and in that sense, completely positive— since we are alienated and lost, since we don't know where we come from and realize that life is this temporary gig and we have no idea what ceasing to be is all about. Why should we not feel cut off from each other or from any real meaning. It seems to me, once you can get your mind around the essential truth of being a lost and alienated loser (all of us)—the whole thing suddenly turns around into the appearance of this great positive truth toward which we've actually been striving. What else is self knowledge but that?

May 15, 2002—Minnesota

[HANDWRITTEN]

John,

Writing this on the back of yours because—guess what—I'm having breakfast in a small café & have no paper. Woke up with a great renewed feeling of inspiration—about what, I'm not sure—just the great feeling of the morning & dropping my kids off at school & the whole day in front of me & I'm thinking—why are these sensations of beginning something so exciting—beginning anything—and why do they inevitably degenerate as the day goes on. Then I get back home & get a call from the Doctor's office that the results of my stress test (for the heart) have turned up a glitch of some sort in the area where they did the procedure a year & a half ago. So, right away, fear kicks in followed by depression & all from a phone call. Anyway, thanks for the letter about winning & losing. I'm sure you're right about the truth being somewhere deeply embedded in the sensation of being a 'loser.' I've always suspected that but have never really accepted it the way you have. I tried sitting this morning & fell completely asleep—woke up with a jerk & almost fell over backwards. Now that's a loser! Anyway, thanks again for your inspired thoughts. Always good to hear from you. Love to Scarlett

—Yr Pal,
Sam

June 24, 2003

John, old man—

Sitting here in the barbershop in Stillwater, MN with the urge to write but no paper, so I'm using your letter. Figure if I wait for paper the urge will be gone—so here it is.

My old friend & collaborator, Joe Chaikin, died yesterday & I'm still kind of shocked from it. His whole life was about living with death from day to day—a chronic heart condition, dating back to when he was a baby with Scarlet Fever—given up to some kind of children's ward in Florida for hopelessly ill kids. His parents were Russian/Jewish immigrants without a dime. You probably remember him from the San Francisco days when we did *Tongues* and *Savage/Love*. Anyhow, he was very influential to me in the early days of N.Y. theatre & for many years after. A truly courageous soul, I thought—something like Scarlett in his ability to accept his fate & continue on against all odds.

My daughter, Hannah, is off in Puerto Rico with a group called 'Earth-watch,' planting mahogany trees in the rain forest. No way for her to phone us so we're assuming everything is good with her. This is her first big venture into the wide world. Hard to believe I was chasing her around in her diaper just a few years ago. Now she's an honor student, cello player & soon to go off to some fancy college in the East like 'Smith' or 'Sarah Lawrence.' I can remember chasing those kind of girls around in N.Y.,—back in the 60's. Time is a fantasy.

This Barbershop is right out of Norman Rockwell—a magazine rack with *Popular Mechanics*, *Field & Stream*, *National Geographic*; old rifles on the wall, deer antlers, a dead pheasant in flight. Vern—the older barber & owner of the show—steel gray hair, handlebar mustache, thick glasses—he has a son in the pulp wood industry who he's very proud of. We talk about the weather as he trims my hair—the rain, floods of years gone by—the rising & falling of the river. He's cut my son's hair since we first moved here in '95 & Walker was 8 years old—now he's 16 & as tall as I am. The guy in the chair next to me is talking about fishing with the younger/apprentice barber—they brag about lakes up North where the Northern Pike are so wild they just come leaping out of the water in to the boat.

The days are great now—temperatures in 80's—afternoon breezes off the river—occasional short thunderstorms. We have a screened-in porch with a climbing pink rose bush that covers one whole side—bees hovering over the blooms & the perfume of roses wafting through the screen. It's my favorite place to be in the summer. I have all my books & writing piled up in stacks around me—iced tea—a silver ash tray & macanudo cigars (which I don't inhale). I've been reading a wide variety of stuff from Suzuki to Frank Conroy to Walker Percy, whose essays are always fun to peruse. He has one entire chapter devoted to Bourbon, in fact its title is simply: 'Bourbon'—where he waxes philosophical & then gets very specific about the wonders of drinking Kentucky mash, full of recipes for the drink, the proper chair to sit in & the right time of day to enjoy its pleasures. It reminds me of Bunuel's great chapter called 'Earthly Delights' (women & booze) in his great autobiography. I remember one line out of that Bunuel book where he's in his late 80's & he's invited some of his friends to dinner & he's sitting at the table with them & he says something like: "It's wonderful so late in life to have the pleasure of dining with friends. I just wish I could see you." He, of course, had gone blind by then.

Yes—stay in touch for sure—even though my communications may be few & far between doesn't mean I don't hold our friendship deep in heart.

Love to Scarlett

Your amigo
Sam

John —

We have the greatest little porch that juts off the east side of the house, facing the St. Croix River. In summer its just about perfect. It's all screened in with a rambling rose bush climbing all over one side of it; sunflowers with huge bumble bees humming over them sway outside in the garden & a light breeze carries the sounds of motor boats & feely up from the little town of Stillwater In certain moods it's idyllic. We sit out here a lot - reading, sipping coffee, napping on the couch sometime

I've been reading a guy I never heard of before named John Fante (Always looking for writers I've never encountered & hoping to get thoroughly surprised.) This guy's very 40's terse - at times like Dashiell Hammett, H. L. Mencken but much more autobiographical. You might like him if you haven't encountered him already.

We're still half way recovering from a huge wedding we threw

July 19, 2003

John—

We have the greatest little porch that juts off the east side of the house, facing the St. Croix River. In summer it's just about perfect. It's all screened in with a rambling rose bush climbing all over one side of it; sunflowers with huge bumble bees humming over them sway outside in the garden & a light breeze carries the sounds of motor boats & Harleys up from the little town of Stillwater. In certain moods it's idyllic. We sit out here a lot—reading, sipping coffee, napping on the couch sometimes.

I've been reading a guy I never heard of before named John Fante. (Always looking for writers I've never encountered—hoping to get thoroughly surprised.) This guy's very 40's terse—at times like Dashiell Hammett, H. L. Mencken but much more autobiographical. You might like him if you haven't encountered him already.

We're still half way recovering from a huge wedding we threw up here for Shura & her husband Bruce—about a week ago. I finally bought that white suit for the occasion, which I'd always imagined would be a good look once you hit 60 or thereabouts. (Everyone in those old movies always looks great in a white suit.) Remember we had that idea of meeting up somewhere in white suits as very old men? I'm not sure how old we imagined ourselves to be but we might be fast approaching it now. Anyhow, the wedding & festivities turned out really great. The day before was the 4th of July so Jessica had rented a white yacht complete with crew in white shirts & black shorts who catered the party, carrying silver trays full of drinks & appetizers & fancy little things to nibble on. It was quite a combination of people—Bruce & his family are all from New England & quite distinct from the mainly Mid-Western folks of Shura's side; showing up in long, Puritan-looking beards & wearing little pocket-knife Leatherman kits on their belts & the women in austere long skirts with their hair in braids or piled up on their head. Jessica's family are all big, raw-boned Minnesotans & the New Englanders are like little Hobbits. We sailed out onto the river negotiating slowly through dozens of little week-end boats with families of half-drunk revelers waving American flags & shooting off firecrackers.—

(Right about here is where my letter-writing comes to some horrible abyss. I just can't seem to sustain whatever it is that's required to make the full journey. I can see how it needs all the details & innuendos to make it really come to life & somehow I just lose interest.)

Long story short—the next day was the wedding with white tents set up & tables & chairs with flowers & a tall wedding cake & the weather is in the 90's & steamy—everyone fanning themselves with the wedding programs—Hannah plays a fantastic Bach piece on her cello—the couple is hitched by a friend of Bruce & Shura's who has some affiliation with a church of some kind—their 3 month old baby is passed between them & the whole affair is very happy & generous & full of good will toward the new couple & their fresh life together. Then the eating & drinking begins. The band starts playing—everyone dancing & carrying on—my white suit is getting sweat-stained. Baryshnikov is there & I'm getting along splendidly with him—having conversations about raising Shura in New Mexico & how he's grateful to me for having helped raise her. It's odd—the tremendous velocity of time passing—it seems like New Mexico was only yesterday—horse-back riding in the moon-lite with Shura falling asleep in the saddle at age 4—just a baby—now she has a kid of her own.

Then—as the night gallops on—I'm getting pretty drunk & spot Hannah's boyfriend flirting flagrantly with one of Hannah's best friends. The next thing I know, acting on some weird impulse (this is how I always get into trouble) I march over to this doofus kid & ask him to leave the party. He blinks off into the darkness & before long the word is out that I've kicked Hannah's boyfriend out of the party—Hannah's crying—Jessica's livid, blaming it all on my alcoholic ways & I've jumped into the pool in my Armani white suit, splashing around with all the other drunken revelers & having a great old time—oblivious to the ruckus I've caused.

Next day (there's always a next day) & Jessica & Hannah have teamed up against me in some female covenant & I tell them I'm not feeling the least bit guilty—the ass-hole kid had it coming—his behavior was entirely inappropriate (of course mine was atrocious but who cares) & on top of that, I tell them, had it been a different culture—say Mexican—where the step-father of the bride & blood father of the maid-of-honor (what does all this mean) is witness to the shameful behavior of the boyfriend—the Mexican man might have shot the kid. Justifiably. Jessica & Hannah look at me stupefied, unable to follow any of my reasoning. I go off to meet Maura & Jesse at the big break-fast down at the old hotel being given by Shura's husband's father (I don't know if you can follow any of this.)[1] Anyway, Jesse & Maura are wondering why I show up at the breakfast alone—without Jessica or Hannah. This goes on & on & develops into fantasies of me going off to live by myself in Montana somewhere with only my horses. A couple days later & it's all blown over. Hannah didn't really like the guy that much anyway—Jessica seems to have seen my side of the issue & Jesse & Maura are already down the road, heading for South Dakota & points West.

—8/4/03

Now I'm here holding down the fort with the "kids" (they're 16 & 17, hardly kids anymore) while Jessica has gone off to the Congo on some UNICEF mission to save the children of Africa. She's really amazing that way. She just takes it into her head to go off & do something like that & she actually does it. She has a pale blue united nations passport & she's going right into the heart of the Congo with a bunch of French people to be an Ambassador of Good Will. Me—I can't even save my own ass let alone the downtrodden of the dark continent.

This morning I was reading in *Beginner's Mind* (a book I always return to—actually the copy you gave me years ago in Mill Valley) . . . "we love flowers and we do not care for weeds. This is true of human nature. But that we are attached to some beauty is itself Buddha's activity. That we do not care for weeds is also Buddha's activity. We should know that. If you know that, it is all right to attach to something."

I like horses—always have. I like being around them. I like traveling with them—hauling them places, competing on their backs. I like being around people who talk about horses over coffee & bacon (all right—so a lot of them are old men—I am too, now). I love days spent entirely in the company of horses & horsemen & cattle & dogs. I don't know why but these kind of days seem perfect to me. This week-end I'm going up to a little town in the middle of Minnesota called Nevis to show two of my horses in the cutting up there. It's just what I want to be doing. I'll haul about two hundred miles, unload them—put them in their stalls—spread sawdust on the ground—water & feed them—unhook my trailer then go off to have some supper at the

1. Jesse and Maura were
   married in 2007.

little café.—There's a book by Tom McGuane (who occasionally is capable of a really great sentence) called *Some Horses* which is all about his obsession with cutting horses. Some really great stuff in there.

Anyway, I'm through rambling on.
Always great to hear from you.
Wish we had more contact.
Maybe Mexico some day.
Hope all is well
Love to Scarlett

Yr Amigo,
Sam

October 21, 2003

[HANDWRITTEN]

John—

Just returned from amazing fishing trip with Walker to Montana. Maybe the most beautiful place on earth—Distant snow-capped mountains, raging rivers winding through the flat plains skirted by golden-leafed cotton woods—the land of Lewis & Clark.

We listened to *On the Road* on tape in the car, read by David Carradine, who at first, I didn't care for then slowly grew to like over the course of the book—or maybe it's just the enormous seductive quality of the writing. What a book! Still, my favorite section is where he falls in love with the skinny Mexican girl at the bus stop & goes on his extended affair with her up into the Central Valley, living with her family & picking cotton & sleeping in tents & shacks—ecstatic—'lackaday'! So many parts of the book I'd forgotten—the trip down to Mexico with the whores—the many returns to Denver & Carlo Marx—all beautiful & full of exuberance—even the sad stuff. Of course, on a smaller scale, it reminded me of our friendship & what a rare & strange thing it is to know someone in this life you feel a true kinship with & also how fast the time is pouring by & how we should try to meet up before too much longer. It could be my 60th birthday coming up that's causing all this but nevertheless it may be important to get together & just sit on a bench somewhere in Deming or Las Cruces.

I've suddenly gotten into Haiku poetry for some reason. All these years & never rally looked at it much. Found a book called *The Essential Haiku* & reading it every night[1]—I love the incredible economy of it & the visual aspect like:

> *'Winter*
> *Horse tethered*
> *snow in both stirrups'*

great stuff!

1. *The Essential Haiku: Versions of Basho, Buson, and Issa*, edited by Robert Hass (1995).

Right now we're back home in front of the fire. Getting to be a chill in the air—tail end of Indian Summer. The kids are deep into school—studying hard. Hannah will be off to college next Spring. Hard to believe. Love to Scarlett.

Your old pal,
Sam

November 16, 2003

[TYPED]

John—

Here's a copy of my new play (obviously unfinished and needing lots of work but you can get some idea of the structure, story and characters).[1] A copy of my awkward birthday poem which I read at the little dinner we had downtown on the night of the fifth.

Been reading lots of Chekhov again. Some stories like "The Kiss" and the "Bishop" are beyond belief—the uncanniness and simplicity of them. The way they just seem to tell themselves and almost lose the sense of any "author" at all.

Weather here is gray, drizzly but not too cold. Me and Jessie took a long walk this morning, across the golf course and around through town, encountering the village idiot along the way who jumped out from the cattails with a scarf around his face and holding a golf club out in front of him, making threatening gestures and asking if we were Irish. "The Irish can't be trusted!" he yelled out and then ducked back into the bushes and disappeared. His name is Buster and everyone in town knows him, in fact he grew up here and became a Golden Gloves boxer in his youth then, somehow or other, just degenerated into the Village Idiot. We see him all the time with a red scarf across his face, blue mittens and a ski cap, riding his bike.

I'll get this off to you now without too much procrastination. Hope everything's good down there in the Land of Enchantment. (I hate broken words but . . .)

Fond Regards,
Sam

---

1. *The God of Hell*, which opened at the Actors Studio Drama School Theater in New York on November 16, 2004.

Now it's not so bad this knowing

you've somehow reached ~~the~~ an alarming number

in your head when the body still _{can} manages

~~leaping~~ out beyond itself without respect

for calculated clocks and calendars or snapshots

of you, ~~████████████████~~

(dodging vicious livestock ~~&~~

rolling ass over teakettle through your teen-age years

or even piercing ideas of the whole mess breaking down

one day which it _{most} certainly will but when

we can't exactly say

Right now here is all we've got

and it's just good and lucky to be in the flow

of kinship, kindness and the human friend

and not be stuck out somewhere deep like Big Bend

in some wasted Super 8 without room service t.v.

or a chrome hot plate

it sure is damn good and lucky

4/6/03
MN

SIXTY

Sixty say the number and the mind
goes dumb with little nagging failures
like not being able to pop over barbed wire
the way you used to or swinging up
on saddle horses in one hop or
now having to crank your entire torso
one hundred eighty degrees when someone calls out
because your leathery chicken-neck has gone
way way South

Who is that calling out anyhow
who exactly is that now back there
Is that your beloved wife
your willowy [dark-haired]² daughter
your skinny son
your entire tiny family heading toward you
on the run through sheets of yellow Maple leaves
and Autumn dust

There seems to be a glassy film now
between your eye and the shimmering human shapes
one blink and it all comes clear
they are the ones you recognize
from lifetimes and lifetimes
they are the ones you know and love and live among

Now it's not so bad this knowing
you've somehow reached [an] alarming number
in your head when the body still [can] manage
[leaping] out beyond itself without respect
for calculated clocks and calendars or snapshots
of you dodging vicious livestock
rolling ass over teakettle through your teen-age years
or even piercing ideas of the whole mess breaking down
one day which it [most] certainly will but when
we can't exactly say

2. Brackets indicate handwritten insertions
into or changes to the typed poem.

Right now here is all we've got
and it's just good and lucky to be in the flow
of kinship, kindness and the human friend
and not be stuck out somewhere deep like Big Bend
in some wasted Super 8 without room service [t.v.]
or a chrome hot plate
it sure is damn good and lucky

Sam Shepard
11/5/03 MN

November 23, 2003

[TYPED]

Sam

Very pleased to get yr first draft and the poem as well—both of which I
enjoyed. I get the feeling that your plays (unlike your prose) are amazingly
similar to what takes place during a sitting. I sit down with a vague image
of tranquility, balance, attention and a quiet mind and within seconds I'm
railing against the many imagined injustices done to me or plotting out some
scenario to deal with the impending doom of a new level of destitution into
which we've been thrown or Scarlett's death in which I vacillate between
suicide and stoic acceptance; in other words your plays seem like a perfect
representation of what Krishnamurti calls "The Content of Consciousness."
And I recognize much of myself in the directions you take—because I may
be wrong but I would bet you hadn't begun with the idea of writing a play
that would end in the basement (always in the basement) with penis torture.
But I was also visualizing it on stage as I read and could catch the comic
aspects in the way the dialogue played with that repetitious rhythm you have;
squeezing all the possibilities out of a small phrase until it bleeds, as well as
the political undertones. But politics, the mid west, misplaced patriotism
and heifers aside, we're still going to end up with someone screaming bloody
murder down in the fucking inner-basement. ("Shepard has definitely come
under some new and powerful influences of late. It's been a long trip from
Icarus's Mother to *The God of Hell*.")

And by the way, I also enjoyed the poem. And talking about ". . . now
having to crank your entire torso one hundred and eighty degrees when
someone calls out . . ." I'm sitting here feeling miserable and listening to a
Schumann lullaby called The Slumber Song. I'm sitting near a window in the
sunlight typing this at 9:30 a.m. and I'm feeling miserable because I've been
stoned on dope, coke and pills for the past four days and am just now coming
down (remember me emerging from the garage at the Strawberry house after
a night on speed?) and on top of that I've done something terrible to my neck
and can't turn it at all to the left and have to walk with my head cocked all the
way to the right like Mr Caryl.[1] I don't know what caused it. [. . .]

---

1. Bill Caryl was the longtime leader of the
   St. Elmo Gurdjieff group in San Francisco.

So—here we are, two writers in their 60's sending letters, prose, plays etc. back and forth to each other and who could have imagined when we sat on the stoop on 11th st. almost thirty-six years ago. By the way—I never heard from you about the piece you asked about for *The New Yorker* or the other one I sent. Does that mean they were above comment? Below comment? Speak to me. [. . .]

Thanks again for writing. It was much appreciated.

John

April 28, 2004

[HANDWRITTEN]

John—

Thanks for your letters. Yes, it's true I did have something of a negative reaction to your falling out with Jesse.[1] It just caused a great sadness in me for a while about all the time & history people have with each other & then a sudden ending—a kind of death, in a way. But I know it will probably heal itself up with time. I hope.

I'm going through an enormously painful time right now with Jessica & finally beginning to realize all the pain I've caused her over the years. I don't know what's wrong with me. That's the hard part. I don't know why I keep returning to these horrible bouts of drinking & bad behavior. I've ruined an amazing relationship just out of a callous disregard for anyone else's feelings & the worst part of it is that I don't really know how it all happened. Anyhow, she has finally come to the end of her rope with me. The pathetic part is I don't know what to do now. I know that if I can't stop drinking I'm really finished. We've decided to soldier on for a while because of the kids. Hannah's finished high school this year & moving on to College. Walker's going to be going to a private school in New York for his next 2 years of High School. Jessie's bought herself an apartment in Manhattan & I have a farm in Kentucky. I guess it will all work itself out somehow.

Don't mean to unload a lot of shit on you but that's what's going on right now. Suddenly it's summer here—80° & a hot dry wind blowing in from the South. Still no leaves on the trees. Weird part of the world this is. Everything is changing very fast now. I just didn't see it turning in quite this way.

I'm going to be doing another film with Wim this summer. (The one we've been writing for 3 years. I think *Paris, Texas* only took 2 years to write.) Wim is his same sweet methodical self & I've grown to really admire his forthrightness over the years. He's just recovering from a severe stomach operation but apparently will be good-to-go by mid-July.

I'll have to write more later. I need to sleep. Good to hear from you & love, as always, to Scarlett.

Your friend,
Sam

1. According to Johnny, he was always having "falling-outs" with members of Scarlett's family and doesn't remember exactly what this one was about.

October 9, 2004—N.Y.

[HANDWRITTEN]

John—

Thanks for continuing to send me interesting reading material. I love the poem about the old man at the racetrack &, of course, Kerouac in Mexico. Actually, I'm sitting in the N.Y. airport right now about to fly down to Durango, Mexico to do a film with Salma Hayek & Penelope Cruz.[1] Might be interesting.

I can't even begin to tell you what kind of a whirling dervish of a life we're leading now. We've got an apartment in the West Village on Waverly right across from Washington Square Park. It's like re-visiting the 60's. Walker takes the subway every morning to school in Brooklyn, after spending his early childhood in rural Virginia & the frozen Mid-West. He's a real trooper. He's become the star of the soccer team & is beginning to dig his new school which has a lot more art & creative opportunities which he wasn't getting in Minnesota. Hannah's doing great things up at Sarah Lawrence & might rule the world before too long. She just keeps getting smarter & avidly interested in everything.

I have a break-neck schedule coming up. Just started rehearsals on my new play over on Bank St. where Joe used to live.[2] It's funny—I was thinking about Joe the other day—just walking around in his old neighborhood & stopped for a cigar in front of a young tree. Looked down & there was a bronze plaque that read: *Joseph Chaikin—1935–2003*. Still can't believe he's dead. One day, no doubt, there'll be a little plaque like that for me somewhere. Wonder what the end date will be???

After Mexico I come back to start rehearsing a play I'm going to act in.[3] Terrifying idea, but I knew it was the chance of a lifetime to do this amazing play written by an English woman. Then after that, Ed Harris is going to be directing a new production of *Fool for Love* on Broadway. I guess there's enough on my plate.

1. *Bandidas* (2006; directed by Joachim Rønning and Espen Sandberg).
2. *The God of Hell*
3. Caryl Churchill's *A Number*, which opened at the New York Theatre Workshop on December 7, 2004, was directed by James Macdonald and starred Dallas Roberts as well as Shepard.

—Now, I'm in Durango on a Sunday, sitting in a beautiful little zocalo very similar to the one in Healdsburg. The bell is ringing from the Catholic church. Pigeons fluttering about, kids shouting, people strolling in their Sunday best. Things are very slow & leisurely here—civilized—people smile as they pass you on the street. Amazing to me how fabulous old places like this seem to exist somewhere outside the insanity of the modern world, completely independent. Now you can hear the mass being chanted from the church. Little green & white striped diesel taxis go rattling by. It's easy to see how Kerouac got caught up in that familiar sense of nostalgia for a world gone by that Mexico seems to inspire.

Here I am a week later having finished the shoot with the two gorgeous women. Got to be horseback most of the time in big open country of the Sierra Madres (the same name of the mountains I grew up near in Duarte, Calif.). I asked one of the film buffs here if this is where John Huston shot *Treasure of the Sierra Madre* & the guy told me "no, actually that was shot in Bakersfield." Lots of John Wayne films shot here though, & Peckinpah's great *The Wild Bunch*. The guy was full of information. He told me Anthony Quinn was born in a boxcar during the Revolution to a Yaqui Indian woman who followed the troops as a prostitute. Durango is also the birthplace of Pancho Villa & Dolores del Rio. Fascinating stuff. I've always loved Mexico. The other night late, I went out into the central plaza & got a boot shine. One of those old fashioned shoe shines you can hardly find anymore in the States except maybe the South. The old guy had my boots looking like glass & it cost about 20 cents. While I was sitting up in the chair, with him brushing & buffing away the streets were jumping with life—little wagons set up on the corners with people cooking tortillas & grilling meat, beautiful black haired Indian faced girls strolling the streets looking for action, old bent-over men in serapes begging with tin cups, Mariachi bands playing right on the sidewalk, the fountains splashing away in the plaza where lovers lean into each other on the benches locked up in love. I remember that extraordinary feeling of being captured in love & so linked to the other person that the outside world didn't matter.

Now, back in N.Y. again, in full gear between the play I'm acting in & the one I've written across town. It's great to get out of one rehearsal & walk my way (I love walking in the city) across town via 4th St. to the West side past many familiar places from the 60's—40 some years ago. How can life be so slippery that you can't account for all the years? Went past the back side of St. Mark's Church the other day, past the very stoop in front of your old apartment where we sat & talked about theatre & writers I guess & you asked me upstairs for a spaghetti dinner with Scarlett. Had to have been 1966 or thereabouts. You had a red plaid shirt on & looked like Kerouac & I remember thinking 'I like this guy because he's not a hippy & he just talks like a guy without an agenda & no ambitions of any kind.'

I went to a funeral of an old friend the other day—uptown, very Jewish but something happened which I kind of saw coming & I think it could probably be some kind of story or movie or something. I knew if I went to this guy's funeral that I would more than likely run into his old girlfriend who I was balling back then on the side. One of those extremely sexy & totally nutso kind of women with a body that could jump-start a car (borrowed from my friend T-Bone).[4] Well, sure enough, as I'm trying to plow through the crowd of Jewish mourners with their black caps & black suits to get to the man's wife to offer my condolences—the girlfriend from the past shows up & starts tugging on my elbow, only now she looks like Cruella De Vil from *101 Dalmatians*. Her face is all wrinkled up & her body has deflated in all the places you remember lusting wildly after. She wants to know if she can share a cab downtown with me & I tell her no I have an appointment & she still won't give it up so I have to ditch her in the crowd after a hasty 'I'm sorry' to the widowed wife.

Now, here I am on a dinner break from the Tech. rehearsal of the play I'm acting in. They're already starting up with the Xmas carols in all the stores. It's winter. I'm captured here with the play until mid-January & then I'm going to take a long sabbatical—down to Kentucky. It's funny, on my walk to the East side to the theatre, I pass the open-air parking lot where my big blue truck sits in a corner against a brick wall, lifeless. I sometimes go in & ask for the key, just to warm the truck up so it doesn't die on me. I sit in the driver's seat, facing a brick wall in the city revving the engine & dreaming of the open road. I really miss it. I think maybe that's where I've felt most at home; just driving.

Mas tarde—
Yr old compadre,
Sam

4. T Bone Burnett, musician and producer.

December 14, 2004—New York City

[HANDWRITTEN]

John—

Merry Christmas! Got your extended (even for you) description of the Bruce Weber visit.[1] Must have been exciting to have people actively interested in your work even though they were invading your privacy & bringing New York City notions of success & commercialism into your cloistered lives. Also got your second letter where you characteristically want to shoot yourself in the foot, burn all your work & disappear deeper into the desert. Hope you find some happy medium. Weirdly enough, me & Jessica are going to be having dinner with Bruce & Nan on Thursday. He's coming to see the play I'm in & I hope he'll tell me something about his trip to Deming. No doubt he'll have a different perspective.

It's turned bitter cold here in the City—wind blowing from every direction—holiday madness on the streets. I can hardly wait to get back to the country again.

Been reading all kinds of new stuff—mostly poets: Machado (Spanish), Pavese (Italian), Codrescu (Romanian) & Borges (Argentina). Borges is a real discovery to me although he's been around for a century. Poetry has always intrigued & evaded me somehow even though I feel my stuff has some element of poetry in it, I've never been able to actually write what they call "verse." Always felt intimidated by it.

Jess & the kids are going down to Mexico for a week & leaving me behind (I am tied down to this play until Jan. 16). Will try to not go straight to the bottle & drink myself silly, although this season of the year always brings out the worst in me.

Hope you & Scarlett are both well & warm down in New Mexico. I've very glad for you that you're getting these books done of your photos & writing. It's great! You deserve it. If nothing else look at it as a good way to catalogue some of your material rather than keeping it in cardboard boxes.

Feliz Navidad!
(Love to Scarlett)
Sam

1. Dark's letter has been lost. The visit concerned Dark's book, *People I May Know*. Bruce Weber is a photographer and the publisher of Little Bear Press; Nan Bush is his longtime agent.

March 23, 2005—N.Y.C.

[HANDWRITTEN]

John—

Good to hear from you. Many new developments here. Out of the blue Patti Smith calls me up & wants to meet up—so we meet at Café Dante down in the West Village where Dylan used to play & I was a busboy right around the corner about a hundred years ago. Patti's as sweet as ever, somewhat haggard around the edges like all of us. She has 2 teen-age kids from a guitar player husband who drank himself to death & she's had a lot of death in her immediate family but nevertheless still maintains a great bravado about life. One of the things I always liked about her. Anyway I tell her Jessica is about to open on Broadway in Tennessee Williams' *The Glass Menagerie* & would she like to come to the opening & bring her daughter along. So, she comes & there we all are—me & my 2 kids—Walker & Hannah & Patti & her daughter & Jessica's on stage acting her heart out. Life is absolutely overwhelming. At the party later me & Patti are standing around with a plate of cookies kind of giggling like little kids & I confess to her that I'm completely confused by all this. It feels exactly the same being around her now as it did then except we've now got these grown kids. She says she knows what I mean. Now, my son Walker might be going out on a date with Patti's daughter whose name just happens to be—Jesse! Unbelievable.

Anyway, good to hear your Deming voice—great picture of you peeking out the suburban doorway. I'm re-reading all my collected history books about the West from early 1500's (Spanish invasion) to the 1890's (closing of the frontier). My absolute favorite era. Keep coming across extraordinary details & characters.

Love to Scarlett—
Talk to you soon—amigo
Sam

April 6, 2005

[HANDWRITTEN]

John—

Down in KY floating (Equine dental work) my horses, which entails tran-
quilizing them with heavy German (who else?) drugs before the vet sticks a
huge file in their mouth & rasps their teeth. The cell phone rings & its my
agent in Hollywood with news about my travel arrangements for the upcom-
ing Cannes Film Festival in France, which our movie—the one I did with
Wim last summer—has been accepted into.[1] I try to explain to her that I have
3 stoned horses on lead ropes & I'll get back to her about Cannes.

—I'm writing this on the torn second page of one of yr letters since I had the
sudden impulse to write & thought if I wait til I have decent paper I won't
feel like writing anymore. Just read your great line: "There is absolutely
nothing I wish to do except to do nothing."[2] Very liberating.

I'm sick of feeling driven all the time—The need to be busy with some
project—whether it's horses or fishing or writing or movies or fixing up the
farm or any of it. I know exactly what you mean about just standing there
watching a cat or watching a hawk circle the field & suddenly have no need
to move or "do" anything. Then the familiar relentless pull of the imagination comes back in & I'm off following some impulse or other to get something done. I've been attending sittings again at the house in N.Y. & actually come out of the last one with a genuine sense of emptiness—that is, no
thought, no wanting, no need to get on with something! It lasted about four
blocks on my walk back down 5th Ave.—then it was gone. Alas! Alack!

Anyhow, good to hear from you from the land of the once all-powerful
Comanche Nation.

Best,
Sam

1. Shepard's note: *Don't Come Knocking*.
2. The letter has been lost.

April 8, 2005

[TYPED]

Sam

Once again the financial monster that's been plaguing me all my life has reared its head. After buying this house there wasn't much left of the money my mother left me but everyone told me I should invest it and live off the interest so of course having no idea how to do that I went to a financial planner who made great promises about what she could do for me. Then she had a nervous breakdown and my account was transferred to another office in Palo Alto. It only took me about six weeks to realize these people were taking me for a ride so on the recommendation of the woman who was doing my taxes, I switched to a firm in Berkeley and again the woman inspired great confidence with promises of how she'd be able to restore my fortune but after several years the result was a loss of about nineteen thousand dollars. At this point no one had told me (and I was too dense to realize) what pariahs these people are and each firm blamed the previous one (or blamed me) for the difficulty I was in. So when we moved to Deming I switched to a firm here and within a year lost another ten thousand. Finally my boss, who had been a tax attorney and financial planner filled me in on all the horrors of turning my worldly wealth over to financial planners and warned me to get my money out as soon as possible before all my principal was gone and to protect it in CD's although the interest would only amount to about $200 a month. It is unnecessary to recount (but you can imagine) the unpleasantness of having to go to this last planner to inform him that I was closing the account—and that's where we are now. It has been amazing me lately how unknown the future is or the next moment for that matter.

Scarlett is completely unemotional about money. I'm exactly the opposite. The thought that we'll go broke fills me with terror not to mention the remorse I feel about what my ignorance in these matters has brought about. Scarlett says that as long as we're together she would be content to live in a box and I believe she's serious. And of course not knowing what the future holds—the imagination fills in all the horrifying details. It's the same old story. There seems to be a level of fear and anxiety which, once reached, can't be stifled by any philosophy. Save me from my mind.

We received a wonderful letter from Jesse all about the construction he's doing on his house complete with amusing stories of the bumbling workmen and his own involvement. I sent him 15 pages of a piece I'd written but I don't think he read it. Hard, I think, to read something by someone you know I suppose. I've never had much luck getting my friends to read my stuff although I've always appreciated your responses. Eugene usually just throws it away before reading it and Dennis always manages to lose it before he can read it. Of course there is the possibility that it's just plain bad, boring and trite—regardless of how much it pleases me to write it. I'm the last to know.

As I write this a scream comes from the kitchen. I run in and find Scarlett standing there with her mouth agape.

"What is it?"

"There's no bread in the house and this is my toast day."

I just finished re-typing a piece I wrote in Healdsburg which I hope you won't mind reading. Always good to hear from you.

John

May 28, 2005—Kentucky

[HANDWRITTEN]

John—

Yes—thanks for your letters. It's a gorgeous morning here in Kentucky.
I've got 3 days off from the film I'm shooting in So. Carolina so I came up to
the farm here for a little rest.[1] I'm really glad I have this place although each
time I'm here Jessica feels as though I'm abandoning her or something. Like
a jealous lover. I don't know. I think you're really on to something with this
happiness thing. That somehow the gauge for how we're doing in this life
has to be around happiness—otherwise what the hell's the point? [. . .]

There must be an art to aging & dying just like there is to growing up &
living. It seems overwhelmingly sad sometimes—how ill-equipped we are to
face the truth & how unprepared. It's an old terror of mine that I will wind
up totally alone, somewhat mad & dying in a motel room somewhere in
Nevada.

Looks like you've got your hands full with that giant puppy. What a great
face he has! Probably not the kind of dog you would want to be on the wrong
side of. This film I'm working on is all about dog fighting—nasty subject
but incredibly interesting to watch these dog trainers & handlers work. Of
course the Humane Society is breathing down our throats every second to
make sure there's no real abuse with these dogs. The way it works is the dog
trainer has brought about 17 Pit Bulls (some of them mixed breeds from the
pound), all of them puppies—close to a year or a little more. At this age all
they want to do is romp & play—like all puppies—but on film it looks like
fighting. Then they add all the growling & vicious sounds onto the sound
track & presto—magic of film you have the illusion of savage dogs—add the
bleeding make-up & scars & it's very convincing. The great thing is that
most of these dogs were rescued from animal shelters & turned into actors.
These trainers have them eating out of their hands—laying down playing
dead—sitting up & then standing on their hind legs—rolling over—it's totally
amazing & fun to watch. [. . .]

Anyhow, this letter was written over the 2 day week-end & now, here it
is Monday, Memorial Day & I have to get back down to So. Carolina. The

1. *Walker Payne* (2006; directed
by Matt Williams).

farm's been great though—we just put up the first crop of hay & the air has that sweet smell of fresh cut clover & orchard grass. I was walking down in the bottom field yesterday, along the river & saw this red flash jump by me out in the hay field. I stopped & backed up a little & there between the trees I could see this little red fox hunting mice—just like a dog, the way they stand frozen, ears pricked & then pounce on their prey, jumping maybe 3 feet in the air. Then I walked on a little further & there was another one— probably female doing the same thing. It would be nice to have a mate you could go hunting with. Along the river all the painted turtles were lined up on logs sun-bathing. Then when I came along they all flopped into the water like fat little frogmen from those horrible war movies I used to watch in matinees at the movies.

Well, it's time to pack up the truck & head out. Nice talking to you. Love to Scarlett.

Yr Old compadre
Sam

June 1, 2006—Kentucky.

[HANDWRITTEN]

Johnny, my Good Lad—

Sitting on my back porch in Kentucky under the fan, which is about my favorite place to be these days. It's extremely hot & humid these days but the mornings have a cool breeze & all the birds are out twittering & flitting from tree to tree. Can't believe how many varieties of birds there are. I saw Terry Malick not too long ago down in Texas & bird-watching is he & his wife's favorite pastime. Terry has always been an enigma to me but you got to love him.

Been working again on another book of stories & journals[1]—pouring thru old notebooks that go back to the early eighties & came across these notes on that road trip that me, you & Dennis took down to L.A. in '82 where we apparently stopped in San Juan Batista in a café & we're all pretty stoned. I'm having great fun making a total fiction out of us three—as stoned characters wandering around a small California town with nothing much to do except associate madly & sit in cafes. I'll send it to you when I get it hacked out. Oh, incidentally, I finally tracked down that book of Beckett's short fiction—I had no idea it had become a rare item. had to order it thru an esoteric bookstore in N.Y. & got a message on my phone that it's finally come in—so I'll send it to you when I get back to N.Y. Sorry about the delay.

Today—June 1st, is the day Jesse & Maura get their final confirmation on her pregnancy. Keeping my fingers crossed. I think Jesse will make a great Dad. It's funny—the whole idea of the "Father" has been one of my grand obsessions all these years & now here's the real-life situation of having fathered a son who has grown into becoming a father himself. It's just amazing how life works. There's a great quote from Flann O'Brien—"I am my own father & my son." I feel that way these days. The Great Wheel keeps on turning.

Been completely absorbed in a brand new book called *Mayflower* by Nathaniel Philbrick (Viking) about the Founding Fathers of Plymouth Colony of which my ancestors were a part of. A woman named Susanna Fuller White on my Dad's father's side of the family—came over on the Mayflower &

1. The book became *Day Out of Days* (2010), a collection of stories.

while it was parked in Cape Cod & they were sending out little expeditions of Pilgrims in rowboats, trying to locate the best location to start the new colony—Susanna gives birth to a boy named "Peregrin"—the first white child born in the new colony. Of course, then inevitably the whole grand scheme of forming an idyllic society separate from the Church of England & the tyrannical King Charles runs amuck when the Pilgrims encounter the Indians. It was anything *but* the ridiculous myth of Thanksgiving we've been handed down where the Indians & Pilgrims all sat happily at a long plank table eating turkey & sharing brightly colored corn. A terrible war broke out that almost devastated the entire population of native people—setting the stage for everything to come 200 years later with the greedy sweep Westward. I love these chunks of history that sometimes feel like pieces of a crazy puzzle where things begin to make sense in a perspective of warped memory & at the same time how impossible it is to feel any real link between now & events that happened 400 years ago, let alone a thousand.

I'm beginning to hunger for a sandwich so I'll quit now. Sometimes I certainly miss the old days of just walking downtown to the Book Depot & hanging out. Alas—alack!

Say hi to the little woman

Yr old pal,
Sam

November 10, 2006

[TYPED]

Sam

[...] The weather has been holding in the high seventies, low 80's and Scarlett and I have been relaxing and enjoying it as much as possible, usually in our garden or on long walks (trying to get her legs ready for New York.)

As far as writing goes—I've settled back (comfortably) into my old opinion that 1. I have no talent of any consequence for it and 2. that I've said everything I have to say or want to say, which admittedly isn't much, and so I've been content to amuse myself with some photography in small measure and some hanging out with Scarlett in great measure. It's difficult I think to keep current with oneself because nothing remains fixed and one is always changing. The danger lies in listening to the head [...]

I've also been thinking a lot about my mother; that is, memories of her keep popping up sporadically usually from the late 40's and early 50's along with a feeling of regret that I wasn't more vocal about how much I appreciated all she did for me.

As my life becomes quieter and more static there seems to be less and less to write about that would be of any interest to anyone. ie: walked the dog, sat in the garden, read aloud to Scarlett, took a bath, etc. etc.

Well, I suppose all this peace and quiet will come to a sudden end for a while once we hit New York—and I'm looking forward to it. And it will be equally good afterward to return to Deming, which is probably my equivalent of your Kentucky, from what you've written.

Take care

yr pal
John

November 14, 2006—Kentucky

[HANDWRITTEN]

John—

Always good to get your wacky letters. Sorry, I have been so remiss in writing—I'm back down here in Kentucky. Very peaceful & quiet—but alas & alack—seem to always get a lot of writing done down here. Still working on book but have now exploded into a new one act/one man play called *Kicking a Dead Horse*—which so far I'm really enjoying—that's the thing—enjoying.[1] I don't believe it's worth it to write unless you just flat out enjoy it anymore. Maybe that's what you've come to, as well. I have this great opportunity to write & direct a play at the famous Abbey Theatre in Dublin, Ireland. (William Synge's old theatre where he first did *Playboy of the Western World*). One of my favorite actors—Stephen Rea (Irish) is available to do it—so I'm plunging in—looks like sometime in mid-February. Me & Jessica are going to Rome in January & then up to Ireland. Our daughter, Hannah is going to school at the University of Ireland in Galway—so we'll be able to visit her there. I really miss her. She is a peach of a girl.

I was touched by your mention of your mother in your last—& how you regretted not being more vocal with her in appreciation for what she had done for you as a child. I feel the same about Jane &, of course, now it's too late.[2] I never understood how people could brag about having no regrets about the past. I just don't see how it could be true unless you're some kind of Zen master or Saint or lived in a closet (even then you might have some—regrets, that is)

Returning to Beckett again & again with renewed awe & admiration. Read *Krapp's Last Tape* again & couldn't believe it was less than 20 pages long & yet leaves you with the impression of an EPIC poem. Also dipped into *Beowulf* (speaking of epic) in a new translation by the Irish poet Seamus Heaney—some kind of genius scholarly intellect whose introduction to the translation is as fascinating as the work itself.

1. *Kicking a Dead Horse*, directed by Shepard and starring Stephen Rea, played at the Abbey Theatre, Dublin, in March–April 2007 and again that September.
2. Shepard's mother, Jane Elaine (Schook) Rogers, 1917–1994.

he had done for you as a child. I feel the same
about Jane &, of course, now it's too late. — I never understood how people could brag
about having no regrets about the past.
I just don't see how it could be true unless
you're some kind of Zen master or Saint, or
lived in a closet (even then you might have
some — regrets, that is)

Returning to Beckett again & again
with renewed awe & admiration. Read
'Krapp's Last Tape' again & couldn't believe
it was less than 20 pages long & yet leaves
you with the impression of an EPIC poem.
Also dipped into 'Beowulf' (speaking of
epic) in a new translation by the Irish
poet Seamus Heaney — some kind of genius
scholarly intellect whose introduction to
the translation is as fascinating as the work
itself.

Jesse sent me some of his new stories
which are quite impressive even though he
told me he's become disenchanted with the
short story form. Maybe just something he's going
through. It was great to see him recently
though a bit scary to see him as a full
grown man.

Looking forward to you guys in December.

Jesse sent me some of his new stories which are quite impressive even though he told me he's become disenchanted with the short story form. Maybe just something he's going through. It was great to see him recently although a bit scarey to see him as a full grown man.

Looking forward to you guys in December. See you at the TRAIN!

As always,
Sam

January 7, 2007—Kentucky

[HANDWRITTEN]

Dear John,

Sitting here by the fire in Kentucky on a grayish wet day & happened to notice a book laying randomly on a table—*The Dog of the South* by our old friend Charlie Portis & remembered that mad day in San Rafael years ago when, stoned of course, we absolutely had to have a copy of that book in our possession. It became a matter of life & death as we rushed over to the library in the white Nova only to discover they were about to close for the day & we began begging & pleading with the librarian how desperate our situation was—how far we'd traveled to get there—how we needed to have that book as though it were our last drink of water. Then, of course, the poor fellow let us in, we located the book, checked it out then, as I remember, neither one of us managed to read more than about five pages of the damn thing & we were on to the next mad caper—stealing bathrobes or something like that. Those were indeed rare & cherished days full of a wild sense of being alive but not having a clue why or what or how.

Glad to hear (thru Jesse) that you made it back safe & sound to your little Deming haven. It was great to see you in N.Y. although it seemed very brief & somewhat frantic—trying to fit in all your meetings over those few days. Hope it wasn't too stressful on Scarlett. I may have a chance to come down & see you toward the last week in January—I'm going to be in Texas & I'll try to get over there. Let me know if you ever acquire a new phone # or write me a note if you're going to be there then. I expect you will be.

I've finished revisions on my new play that I'm going to be doing in Ireland & getting excited about going over there to direct it.[1] We start rehearsals Feb. 7 & open Mar. 15. I'll be able to visit with my daughter, Hannah, who's going to College in Galway & then I'll go to London where Jessie is doing *Glass Menagerie* in the West End. Til then I'm just hanging out on the farm reading *Undaunted Courage* again—(about Lewis & Clark), taking long walks with 'Pine' & cooking big pots of split pea soup.

Hope all is well with you both [. . .]

Much deep affection,
Sam

1. *Kicking a Dead Horse*

June 2, 2007

[TYPED]

Sam

Went to work this morning which is supposed to be my day off but the boss is on vacation and they asked me to come in for a few hours.[1] I daydream in the car on my way remembering my first night on the AIDS ward at San Francisco General Hospital. I went there with Roy who showed me the ropes and then I went from room to room massaging the feet and legs and backs of AIDS patients who were all on oxygen; thin, frail, dying. I had the strangest feeling of belonging. It was all very familiar for some reason. I thought I might like to make my living as a massage therapist. Then Irene called me about massaging a dying homosexual Cancer patient in San Francisco. She said she thought it was a job for a heterosexual because of the patient's parents. I had never thought of myself as a heterosexual before. [. . .]

---

1. In Deming, Johnny took a job in the deli at a Peppers Supermarket.

June 9, 2007

[TYPED]

John,

[...] I'm sitting here on my farm in Kentucky, convalescing after having nearly every tooth in my head pulled out by a gorgeous blonde dentist who looks sort of like a very intelligent Kim Novak. I knew this was coming and had been procrastinating for months but decided I ought to get it done before work piled up on me again. So, I've set the whole month of June aside for this endeavor and, so far, it's not much fun. On the second day my whole face swelled up like I'd gone ten rounds with Mike Tyson—black and blue bags under my eyes, puffed out jaws and cheeks and a thumping head-ache to go along with it. You get the picture. Waking up at the crack of dawn then taking pain killers, falling back asleep and having very disturbing dreams about all my children. They keep appearing to me at different ages; like this morning it was Walker at the age of maybe five years old in N.Y.C. and completely independent, walking home by himself—me trying to find him in the city, not being able to catch up—him hiding behind dark glasses—that kind of stuff. Then, at one point, it seemed to be Jesse and not Walker at all. Then Walker appears, strolling up my gravel driveway and suddenly he turns into Hannah. I don't know. Then I wake up and the sun is shining, birds are singing, I stumble downstairs, make coffee, gather all my stuff together on the table—I have lots of stuff now—glasses, pens, notebooks, poetry books, small cigars, cell phone, etc., etc., and, balancing all this plus the cup of coffee, I make my way outside to the stone patio where Pine greets me, all wagging and panting and always ready for something I'm not sure what, but at least she's glad to see me. I sit at my table surrounded by books, ash tray, typewriter—I guess I'm quite the recluse now and, the scarey thing is, it feels natural. Sometimes I'll talk to Jessica on the phone and she's in the fucking city, which I absolutely can't stand anymore and she's got the Grandkids and is very busy with all kinds of big city doings like museums and parks and exhibitions and meetings and seems happy enough to be consumed by that all the time but all I want to do anymore is just sit on my back porch, sip coffee and stare at the birds. Anyway, it's a beautiful day and the sun is blaring down on me right now.

I've gone back into one of my poetry-reading spurts where I can't get enough of certain writers like: Vallejo, Pavese, Cendrars, Machado, O'Hara. That's all I read now and still I find the poem to be the toughest form, except for possibly writing a song. I don't know why. I would love to be able to write a whole bookfull of story poems like Pavese but when I read his stuff I realize it was something he found that absolutely fit him for who he was and I guess you don't have a lot of choice about something like that.

I'm re-writing my play *Kicking a Dead Horse*, which is the one we did in Ireland with Stephen Rea and going back there in the fall to re-stage it in the main stage at the Abbey Theatre. I can't believe I'm working in the National Theatre of Ireland, founded by W.B. Yeats, William Synge, Bernard Shaw, et al. It's amazing to me. We were trying to bring the production to New York but now Stephen, my actor, feels like the three-quarter situation with the audience at the Public Theatre is not going to work for him and we may have to cancel and find a different theatre. Anyway—these are all some of my little dilemmas these days. Not bad for an old fart.

I'm looking forward to the Wedding festivities and the long trip out there. Haven't driven across the entire country for a while, but I always get excited about the prospects for some reason. I guess I kind of grew up in cars my whole life. Driving. I'll go up to Minnesota, on my way, and spend about a week with Jessica and, hopefully, one of the kids. They've all got jobs for the summer so I don't know if they can get away.

Today is Belmont Day (part of the Triple Crown) and I've been invited to a little gathering over at one of the Thoroughbred farms to watch the big race. Not sure if I'll volunteer myself for that unless the swelling in my face recedes some. It's funny the different forms one's vanity takes. I can't imagine what it must be like to look at my face right now. Meanwhile, I'm hiding out on the farm.

Hope everything is well with you and Scarlett. Always good to hear from you.

Yr old amigo,
Sam

August 2007

[TYPED]

Sam

Finally just finished reading yr play which I think is the best written piece (play) of yours I've read tho admittedly I haven't read them all. Hysterically funny and beautiful prose speeches.[1] Overall feeling—as with the other plays I've read—one of chaos, hopelessness, frustration, despair and loneliness (particularly loneliness.) However not anger this time as was in other pieces and violence subdued. And it always amazes me—this aspect of yr psychological experience since it seems that those traits have somehow always been absent from our particular relationship and in fact most of my memories of you, that is, our time together, has been one of lightness, laughter and joyful banter yet when you write. . . It's probably the difference between "events" and "states" one being inner and the other outer.

Nevertheless a beautiful piece of work. Made me laugh out loud. I could picture it. Should be a great success I'd imagine and God knows what existential meaning people will read into the thing. Thanks for sharing it with me. Most enjoyable. Enviable. Makes my writing seem like Mickey Mouse at the best—(actually last thing I ever wrote was about Mutt and Jeff.) Maybe I'll write again someday but what's the point? Without drugs I have no interest. Smoking in California this last time was the first time I smoked in about a year and I suffered afterward for two days. I went through the wedding up to the dinner absolutely straight but couldn't hook into the event and began feeling guilty so I smoked with Kristy behind the barn to generate some excitement and ended up raving about who knows what nonsense to my neighbor at the dinner table. But even with that—the drinking and the smoking didn't really "take me out of myself" which was what I had been wishing for I guess and what seemed to be behind that was the feeling that I was dull. Difficult to walk "The Middle Way" when I've spent most of my life racing after the extremes but the extremes don't seem to make it anymore. Not easy to keep current with oneself, is it?

Hope you are well. You have a lovely family—and yr a fine lad.

yr pal
John

1. Dark's note: *Kicking a Dead Horse.*

and the headed back to the
border and home to Deming

August 25, 2007—Kentucky

[HANDWRITTEN]

Dear John

Many thanks for the photos of the wedding. Great moments revealed between people that, normally, just fly by. Particularly interesting to see Hannah & her sister Shura & how Hannah watches her with this piercing sort of awe-struck observation. Also, Walker in all his innocence. I sent a lot of the pictures off to the kids & kept the Jesse/Maura shots which are very beautiful.

I've been drinking way too much & too often. Can't seem to ever learn the lesson of it, whatever that is—other than total abstinence. Total anything never seems to work. Like making a New Year's resolution you know is bound to be broken sooner or later. Your little tale about your wandering dreams thru Germany etc., not knowing 'where' in Germany, what town or who you're looking for exactly, I found very moving & close to my own sense of lostness & 'homelessness'—we're two pathetic old fellows actually.[1] Maybe that's why we seem to get along so well—some sense of deep kinship I don't know.

I'm turning back to Beckett again after going off on my 'Lewis & Clark' journals & plains Indians accounts of the final days of the 19th century in the U.S.A.—back when the 'U.S.A.' was generally considered to be east of the Missouri river & everything West was the big bad frontier. Can't believe it was a mere 200 year ago—or less.

But back to Beckett—just listen to Beckett—there's nobody like him & never will be:

"I don't know when I died. It always seemed to me I died old, about ninety years old, & what years, & that my body bore it out, from head to foot. But this evening, alone in my icy bed, I have the feeling I'll be older than the day, the night, when the sky with all its lights fell upon me, the same I had so often gazed on since my first stumblings on the distant earth."[2]

He blows you away in a single paragraph. A voice from the dead; the living dead in his icy

1. Johnny's letter has been lost.
2. Samuel Beckett's short story "The Calmative," from *Stories and Texts for Nothing* (1954).

bed: My friend Rudy Wurlitzer—(I think you might remember him visiting us in Mill Valley with Robert Frank—on a road trip to visit some guy in New Mexico who was photographing lightning out on the plains)—anyway, Rudy told me that Beckett destroyed him as a writer because when he first encountered him he knew he could never measure up to him.[3] I feel the opposite—to me he's pure inspiration toward the unknown—the possibilities seem endless when I read him & have nothing to do with hoping to compete. You just take for granted that he's in a completely different league. [. . .]

I'm enjoying my last few days on the farm in Kentucky before I have to go off to Europe again Sept. 1. First to the Venice Film Festival (the Jesse James movie is being screened there) then back to Dublin to do *Kicking a Dead Horse* again.[4] Thanks for your comments on it. Glad you liked it. I'm still attached to it somehow, which is very unusual for me. Normally, once it's done I'm ready to move on to something new but I'm looking forward to working on it again. Maybe it's the relationship with Stephen Rea (the actor). We've known each other over a long span of time & it's easy for us to come to certain agreements that don't seem so possible with actors you hardly know at all.

I feel very unclear about all my unfinished writing now. (And there's a lot of it. Two unfinished plays & this endless book of prose & journals & stories etc.) I don't know where any of it is going or exactly why I should pursue it. That's another thing about Beckett—he wrote & continued to write until the very end—in spite of his conviction that the entire thing was futile.

Well, I have to go turn my horse out to pasture. He's been tied to a fence, drying off in the sun after I gave him a bath this morning, after riding. Great to still get up on a horse & go off into the woods for an hour or two without seeing humans. Deer, wild turkey, turtles splashing into the pond on our approach; hawks circling—one of those perfect summer days with powder blue skies & puffy clouds. I miss people sometimes—but I get over it. Hope all is well with you & Scarlett. Happy Birthday to Scarlett. I forgot to send her a card—damn!

With great fondness,
Sam

3. Rudy Wurlitzer (b. 1937) is an American novelist (*Nog, Flats, Quake*) and screenwriter (*Two-Lane Blacktop, Walker, Little Buddha*). Robert Frank is a noted American photographer and filmmaker.

4. The film is *The Assassination of Jesse James by the Coward Robert Ford* (2007; directed by Andrew Dominik and starring Brad Pitt and Casey Affleck as well as Shepard).

November 5, 2007

[TYPED]

Sam

A letter on yr birthday.

I'm glad you got a chance to see where I work. I like the job quite a bit. Today I had to make three Ruben sandwiches. It was a busy day and I make a mean Ruben. [. . .]

And the women are all so interesting. They all speak Spanish and gossip about each other and laugh and argue. Everyone is doing the best they can, living their own particular drama; Liddia is talking about Anna behind her back and people are talking about how Liddia talks about Anna since Anna is on parole for drug violations and Carol sends people home for the smallest infraction of the dress code even though Carol hasn't any more authority than anyone else and meanwhile Antonia is wandering around in some kind of Mexican haze with people yelling orders, getting in each other's way, waiting impatiently for scale time, waiting in line for the slicer and then having to clean off the remains of the last person's cut (and praying it's not Muenster cheese or Cajun Chicken) and then just when you think you're out of the woods, a woman wants a foot long sandwich of Prosciutto. And the customers . . . all sorts of people; Mormons dressed in square dancing overalls, plaid shirts and cowboy hats, Mexican field hands covered in dirt, women cops, women soldiers, firemen, city workers, sheriffs in cowboy hats, old ladies with walkers, obese teenagers, drooling idiots—everyone absolutely perfectly attired for the role in which they've been cast and meanwhile we're running out of plastic bags and we're running out of mustard, and we're running out of plastic gloves and there are six people and two scales and one of the scales has just run out of tickets thank you very much and everyone is moving at top speed making hot sandwiches and then at one o'clock it's time to clean the grill which for some is like the Devil showing up in their bedroom and saying, "Your time has come."

The grill has been going since five in the morning making burritos and piles of potatoes and ground beef all caked and baked black and crispy which puts me in mind of Kerouac's description of an old diner grill ("Grill is ancient and dark and emits an odor which is really succulent, like you would expect from the black hide of an old ham . . .") [. . .]

Later,
Johnny

March 2008

[TYPED]

Sam

Took a long walk this morning and got to thinking about myself and who I am (didn't get anywhere with that) and how I was bought (adopted) in 1942 at about a year old for $6000 the way you buy a puppy. You give them the money they give you the dog and now here I am 67 without a clue to not only who I am but where I came from although It really doesn't seem to matter much although it's strange I never had kids what with all the fucking and being married twice and I don't think I've ever used a rubber in my life. But we don't really have much of a say about things. I was talking to Scarlett about the body the other day, how the heart is beating and the blood is pumping and the lungs and moving in and out and the colon is doing its work etc.—machines in the real sense of the word. And then of course psychologically we simply react and are the slave of our desires and passions and so on. I mean I didn't decide to have the nature or the personality I have. It seems to have come with the package. [. . .]

John

March 8, 2008

[HANDWRITTEN]

Dear John—

Back to KY after almost 2 mos. In New Mexico doing that film then returning to N.Y. & Jessica & kids & Grand kids & Birthday celebrations in Providence, Rhode Island & now here—only to arrive in midst of 'ides of March' snow storm—freezing, snow blowing north to south but wonderful to be back in this little lost house in the middle of nowhere.[1] I Love it!

I think yr Deli Diaries are great & you should continue—beautiful stuff, although I know you do your best to convince yourself you're not a writer & nothing you do in that regard has any value. You're completely nuts! It's better stuff than almost anything I've read. [. . .]

I've enclosed most of my new play which I'll do in Dublin again with two of the absolute best actors over there—Stephen Rea (again) & Sean McGinley—probably in the Spring.[2] It's still unfinished but there's enough of it there to give you an idea. Hope you like it. [. . .]

I have the feeling this letter has now taken on a slightly hysterical aura. Must be the time of night, booze & my growing sense of mortality—although I recently had a complete physical—(EKG—heart—colon—blood pressure—& the organ that produces semen that gives men such nightmares as they progress in age p → prostate.) Everything A-Okay. But still you know, down the road, something's going to get you. It's Just a Matter of Time. Glad to hear you're still holding up strong at the Mexican Deli.

All my love to Scarlett & yr fine self.

Your old amigo,
Sam

---

1. The film is *Felon* (2008; directed by Ric Roman Waugh and starring Stephen Dorff and Val Kilmer).
2. Shepard's note: *Ages of the Moon.*

March 2008

[TYPED]

Sam

[...] before reading the play: Thanks for the play.[1] This is the play I've been waiting for—the two-old-guys-on-a-porch-play. What's the matter, you didn't want to finish the two prospectors play? I'm going to read both parts of this play aloud to Scarlett tonight—Ames and Byron should rival Scrooge and The Ghost of Christmas Present, one of the great two character acts in the Biz. And I know—I just know that somewhere in the middle someone is going to have his brains blown out or some chick will be taken in the cellar and have a shotgun shoved into mouth or someone's home will be wrecked, you're such a sick sonofabitch, and after we've been lulled into a false sense of security by yr boyish charm and ready wit.

As for the Deli Diaries—I realized after I sent you that excerpt that not only wasn't I the writer I always thought I was but I wasn't even the person I always thought I was and that I wrote like the worst woman writer for the worst woman's Daily magazine, so I decided to unburden myself from an identification with which I no longer feel any attraction and throw 50 years of writing away. However Scarlett got wind of the plan and there was an altercation at the dumpster. The binders of writing are now in several green plastic garbage bags in the back adobe building (no floor, no ceiling) in the same way my 5th grade drawings ended up in my Grandmother's attic in a trunk with my yo yo and soldiers. It's out of the house and I feel like a man who's just picked his nose.

later after reading the play: It's funny because I was just listening to some of those taped conversations going all the way back to the ranch. You can hear the difference the years have made on our voices. Well these two characters, Ames and Byron are talking to each other in the same way as we talked to each other except with Byron and Ames, it's just you talking to yourself. I love the sudden flashes of self knowledge, the bit about women and the moon—you just want the rest of the play to stay on that level but no! Shepard dips and dives and swivels. It reminded me how not so wonderful I am or

1. Dark's note: *Ages of the Moon.*

ever was. It's not enough for a man to be a miracle simply by being alive. He wants to be wonderful as well. I think that's probably why I joined The Work. I wanted to be even more wonderful than I already thought I was. Because I have trouble facing my own degree of wonderfulness.

And the great piece about seeing the age on the face of a friend and for the moment, being taken aback by its mortal implications. In that moment two friends are acknowledging each other's mortality, which is a pretty cool thing to be doing—and yet they have to maintain a certain masculine stance lest they turn into a pair of screaming hoooomo-sexuals right then and there on the porch. And you pull it off beautifully. Everything that's wide and expansive about you is in this play. Everything's that's narrow and prejudiced is in this play. Everything witty and hip and mistrustful is in this play. Everything tender and violent is there too. And you did this in your sunset years. I'm impressed. Every line, all I could think of was getting to the next line because I couldn't wait to hear what the other guy was going to say. It even had a dash of Laurel and Hardy and Crosby and Hope in it. (But here Shepard the myth writer swivels again as one of his characters suddenly reveals to his best friend that his wife is dead and not only that but that he's been carrying her dead body around on his back all over town revisiting the places they'd been to together. "One of Shepard's saving graces is that he knows enough to end on a minor note.")

I loved every bit of it. I held back from fear of feeling the grief and suffering Byron must have felt not wanting to let go of her—how much he loved her. It scared the shit out of me. Maybe I'm just a pipsqueak after all. In any case, well done, m'boy. It's a lovely thing and I had a ball reading it aloud.

yr pal
John

Sam signing his latest manuscript
(book of prose) which he gave me
to read.   2008

Spring 2008

Sam

Trying to think of how to start this thing. Where are they now? There was this pretty little girl who lived on the first floor of the apartment in Jersey City where I grew up. I lived on the fifth floor in another wing of the apartment. This was around 1945 or so. When I was eight she was ten and we used to play hide and seek in her house when no one was home and end up in parents' closet kissing. A year before that we had shown each other our genitals. We took long walks together thru the city when we were 11 and 13. Fifty three years later I learned that that little girl grew up, moved to Boston and became a divorced mother of two lesbians and one Jewish lawyer. She herself was an artist who decorated bridges with old shoes and constructed arches of willow branches deep in the middle of the woods and covered the walls of rooms with aluminum foil and the ceilings with egg cartons. That's how that little girl ended up. The little boy ended up at the age of 67 working in a Mexican Deli somewhere near the Mexican border. And now our parents are dead and all our uncles and aunts are dead and the place where I grew up is lost to me forever and my time is running out. Soon I won't be able to watch the words slip from under my pen. All of this will be lost. How am I supposed to behave in the face of something like that? The fact is, I just don't think we're very important. We're certainly not as important as we think we are. Our ceaseless feelings, our relentless thoughts . . . who gives a shit. Not important to the Galaxy.

Wait a second—not important?? You mean nobody cares what I think or what I feel? You mean I'm going through all this suffering alone and no one gives a shit?

Time doesn't flash by. It's much quicker than that. For all intents and purposes, there is no present. The present is gone before you realize it's taken place and there you are with Penny in the tar paper shack feeling funny. And there you are at the Cherry Lane Theatre talking to Joyce.[1] And there you are crocked out of your mind on LSD in the middle of some Connecticut

1. The actress Joyce Aaron, Shepard's girlfriend at the time.

woods. This was the real present once upon a time for you, fraught with feeling, emotions, teeming with thoughts all of which nobody really cared much about. People just don't give a shit. Well yes, but I feel that a person should . . . (We don't give a shit.)

However I do have this thought on the subject . . . (Nobody give a shit.)

All the blabbering and blubbering we've done and are doing and will do . . . nobody gives a shit, not on this planet or any other. And look—there you are in France talking French with a dumb American accent. And look, there you are visiting Mr Tilly for the first time dressed like some sort of Rolling Stone vagrant. And look, there you are telling me about the relationship between the clown and the announcer in a Rodeo. "Yeah and they have little dogs riding Burros and they have Burros that beg and Burros that roll over on their backs." And there's the two of us with yet another idea; a book of biographies of famous people's fathers; an idea that survived vigorously for nearly a half an hour. Or the idea about a book of people's worst fears. We take random samplings over a ten year period and collect over a billion fears from all over the world and call it a billion fears. And there you are down in Kentucky floating yr horses. And there you are sitting with Patti in the Cafe Dante. And there you are in the Minnesota cabin by the lake passing through life sagas with just a dash of melancholy. And there you are nervously waiting at the train station in Albuquerque and suddenly—there you are celebrating your 60th birthday in Minnesota and not stuck in some godforsaken wilderness somewhere or holed up in some remote Motel without room service and nothing to cook on but an old chrome hot plate. And no one gives a shit. [. . .]

The rest of the day went like this. Scarlett slept on the couch. I lay down on the bed next to my Anatolian Shepherd whose snoring made it difficult for me to fall asleep. Then I woke up, took a pain pill, smoked a joint and went out to run several errands. When I came back Scarlett was still asleep on the couch. I took another hot bath. No one gives a shit.

yr pal
John

5/7/08

K.

Dear John,

Although it's true, I'll agree with you — [who] gives a shit; I'll persist in the [vein] [of] Beckett — 'I can't go on — I'll go on' etc. —

I have nothing better to do or as Patti [said] to me once 'Aw hell let's just all ~~fuck~~ [kill] ourselves' — I, like that one too. What else [are we] going to do? No one said it better [than] Shakespeare — ('To be, or not —) that pretty [much hit] the nail on the head. But you must [have] [to] stop perpetually plunging into ho[t] [bubbl]y baths every time the going gets a [little] tough — I would have thought you [had grown] [out] out of that by now. Here's a quote for [you] [fr]om a book I'm reading called 'Blue Highways' [it] sounds remarkably like a quote from the Wo[rk] isn't.

'I begin with this broken truth that I a[m]. I start from the entire broken man — entire bu[t] not whole. Then I work to become empty. An[d] whole. In looking for ways to God, I find pa[rt] of myself coming together. In that union, I find regeneration.'

Brother Patrick Duffy —
(Trappist monk in Georgia —
formerly a Brooklyn cop who
delivered 13 babies in the ba[ck]
of his squad car, trying to get [t]

May 7, 2008—Kentucky

[HANDWRITTEN]

Dear John,

Although it's true, I'll agree with you, 'no one gives a shit', I'll persist in
the vein of Beckett: 'I can't go on—I'll go on' etc.—Why? I have nothing better to do or as Patti said to me once 'Aw hell let's just all go kill ourselves'—I
like that one too. What else are you going to do? No one said it better than
Shakespeare—('To be or not'—) that pretty much hits the nail on the head.
But you must find a way to stop perpetually plunging into hot bubbly baths
every time the going gets a little tough. I would have thought you'd grown out
of that by now. Here's a quote for you from a book I'm reading called *Blue
Highways* which sounds remarkably like a quote from the 'Work' but it isn't.

'I begin with the broken truth that I am. I start from the entire broken man—
entire but not whole. Then I work to become empty. And whole. In looking
for ways to God, I find parts of myself coming together. In that union, I find
regeneration.'

BROTHER PATRICK DUFFY—(Trappist monk in Georgia—formerly a
Brooklyn cop who delivered 13 babies in the back of his squad car,
trying to get the mothers to the hospital)[1]

So, anyhow, I continue to write because basically that's all I've found I can
really do & it doesn't much matter whether anyone gives a shit or not. Right
now I'm working on a journal in my book about the weird trip you, me &
Dennis took down to L.A. where Dennis went off to a strip joint & you went
to some Japanese restaurant and caused one of the waitresses, fresh off the
boat, to fall in love with you.[2] Of course, I've greatly embellished the events &
circumstances but it's kind of fun careening around inside these 3 characters
& inventing stuff of certain known de-
tails & then just letting them go down
the road. It starts in San Juan Batista
where the tall mission chapel tower is

1. *Blue Highways: A Journey into America,*
   by William Least Heat-Moon (1982).
2. These stories became the four "Highway
   152" sections in *Day Out of Days.*

that Alfred Hitchcock shot *Vertigo* in & ends at the Tropicana motel in Los Angeles. There's no story—just these 3 guys careening down the road.

Came across a crazy Chilean writer named Roberto Bolaño who's unlike anyone I ever encountered. Kind of a strange mix of Borges & early 60's art movies. You probably wouldn't like him. Re-reading the Beckett trilogy & can't believe the stuff I missed. Soon I'll be up in New York again re-doing the play I did in Dublin (*Kicking a Dead Horse*). Not looking forward to summer in N.Y.—but there you have it. Re-read Borges' astounding story 'The South' from his collection—*Ficciones*—he crams more into 8 pages than most novelists can in 500. I continue to be amazed by his constructions—for instance: "Blind to all fault, destiny can be ruthless at one's slightest distraction." Who comes up with that?

My dog is snoring on the horse blanket on the back porch (KY.), the rains have subsided & all the birds are carrying on with their various songs. Why do birds have various songs? Their colors are incredible—like little jewels hopping around on my stone wall pecking at the seed I've laid out: Gold-finches, Cardinals, Bluebirds, Indigo Grosbeaks, White Bellied Nuthatch, Woodpeckers, Blue Jays, Red-Wing Blackbirds, Chickadees, Grackles, Cowbirds, Mourning Dove, chipping Sparrows. It's a paradise! I must get to work. I've been averaging about 5 pages a day on my book—chipping away. Working on a story now where this character runs into an old girlfriend in a Holiday Inn lobby in Indianapolis after not seeing her for 40 years.[3] So far it's rolling along. I'll send you a copy when the whole thing's finished. (Maybe never.)

Anyway, good to hear from you & much love to Scarlett.

Yr old amigo,
Sam

3. "Indianapolis" in *Day Out of Days*.

Summer 2008

[TYPED]

Sam
   [. . .] I've been hitting the dope pretty heavily these past few weeks and on top of that I've become addicted to Scarlett's pain pills. I don't know what they are but they feel as if they have codeine in them. They wire me up which, combined with the dope has me raring to go at work. I need to get off both which I'm hoping to getting to do the next two days which are my days off because I'm sorely depleted. Coming down is terrible. Of course I started writing as soon as I started getting high—that's part of that energy which ordinarily I don't have. I've been having a blast moving words around, breaking sentences, laying some of Pentland's talks out in broken lines, changing a word here and there for clarity. It makes what he's saying much more understandable to me. Here's a sample:

> *When I say*
> *I'm trying to "do,"*
> *I may be accepting*
> *or admitting to the fact*
> *that there is an ego,*
> *a subjective*
> *very often emotional person*
> *which is trying*
> *to get what it wants out of things [. . .]*[1]

I wonder if that was part of Burroughs interest when he was doing his cut-up experiments with prose.
   Everything fine here although my health could be better but what can I expect with all the drugs etc. Very hot. 100 or more every day. Scarlett is well. We're both looking forward to Jesse and Maura's visit in Aug. Always interesting to see what's become of the lad . . . goodness, he's pushing 40.

John
P.S. If you want an absolutely fantastic read, with great prose and adventure (like *Black Hawk Down*) read *Deliverance* by James Dickey.

---

1. Dark's note: from Pentland's *Exchanges Within*.

July 17, 2008

[HANDWRITTEN]

Dear John,

Just now got back to my KY sanctuary from a month ½ of hyper-tensive work getting my play mounted in N.Y. (*Kicking a Dead Horse*). You'd think, since we'd already done it twice in Ireland that it would be no sweat doing it here but it was very taxing. Anyhow, it's opened & I'm free of it for a while, thank God. It's just great to be out of the city & back on the farm. No dodging taxicabs, skateboards, Chinese on bikes; just birds, cattle & horses.

Got all yr letters, photos, Bukowski, etc. Especially dug the James Dickey *Deliverance* piece where he's trying to shoot the guy with a bow & arrow.— Fantastically gripping. the kind of writing you know had to be done by a man who has shot a bow & arrows before & studied every aspect of it—(like *Zen in the Art of Archery*) [. . .]

Funny, your messing around with verse & poem configurations—breaking up the lines etc. like you did with Pentland stuff, because in one letter you sent me a while back about that thing I wrote for Bill Hart's death—you said "why do you want to break up the lines like that?" You said, "I prefer my lines un-broken." So, being always easily influenced, I went through my entire book & changed everything I'd written in verse-style back to prose-style &, I must say, it works better that way. But here you are now breaking up the fucking lines like e .e. cummings or something. I can't keep up! It is surprising though how well that Pentland stuff works, in verse. When you think about it, though, he was a bit of a poet himself.

Here's an odd note on the remnants of the 'work' in one's life. I was walking down the street in N.Y. and (as often happens in N.Y.) this total stranger walks up to me & says, 'Hi, I'm a friend of John Grosman's, Remember me?' No, I said, I don't remember you or this fellow Grosman. Who exactly are you? "Oh, don't you remember? The 'work.' Sitting. Paul Reynard.[1] The 'Institute' on 65th St.?" I said, no I don't remember any of it. And I walked away, much to his utter dismay. But, it was true. It all seemed like some vague dream. What was I doing back then? What was I thinking? I have no clue. I haven't read a 'Work'—related book in years. I've stopped sitting. Now & then I have some notion about being in the present but the whole thing

---

1. Paul Reynard was co-president of the
   Gurdjieff Foundation of New York.

seems to have gone up in smoke. Maybe I'll die in hell. Who knows. More & more, these days, I'm addicted to writing. I have a book bag I carry everywhere that must be 100 lbs.: Beckett, Rulfo, Camus, Cendrars, Borges, Malcolm Lowry, Cortázar, Parese, Richard Hugo, Bolaño, Kleist, *The Journals of Lewis & Clark*, the *Iliad*, Machado, the *Encyclopedia of the Civil War*—I can't do without this stuff—*The Conquest of Mexico*—Cortez and Montezuma—what am I going to do? [. . .]

So, here I am, back on my porch; birds singing, traffic far off on the Interstate, dew on the morning grass. Guess I'll work on my book. I'll try to send you a copy when I have it more gathered up. Love to Scarlett.

Yr Old Amigo,
Sam

September 24, 2008—Kentucky

[HANDWRITTEN]

John,

   Feeling somewhat melancholy but peaceful. Brilliant afternoon on my
favorite stone porch—hot breeze coming out of the south, leaves starting
to fall; just a hint of autumn in the air. Got your last letter & good to hear
you have the situation with Scarlett in hand. It was great talking to her on
the phone. I've decided it's not so great living so much of the time alone &
I've told Jessica that I think we should find a way to spend most of our time
together. I've also told her I'm not going to live in N.Y. city anymore & so
the compromise for her seems to be someplace up-state N.Y.—in order to be
close to Shura's two little girls. I'll go along with that. When you know you
have a destiny with someone, why put it off? We were meant to live together
for the rest of our lives & that's now become more important than horses
& farms & fishing & New Mexico & Kentucky & running up & down the
American road like a chicken with his head cut off.

   Turns out I never had a vision of my future like you describe. I had no
clue where I was going to wind up or with who. Most of my life, I now realize, has been consumed by flight. I guess, initially, from the nightmare of my
father's wrath which I never understood & still don't. In some ways, working
on this new book has actually shown me aspects of myself I'd never really
seen before. The frantic futility of constantly searching for a new place; a new
life, a new partner. As though change itself were some kind of elixir.

   This new book has got me in a kind of spell now. It's turned into something totally unexpected. I don't know if I'll ever finish it actually. It just
keeps unraveling. But now, rather than gleaning material out of all my
notebooks, I seem to be in some kind of conversation with the book where
one of the characters (like the amputated head for instance) pops up & has
something to say. So I write it down & sift it into the pages. Then the 'Kid'
puts his 2 cents worth in—then the son & the father. It goes on like that. Oh
well—it's something to do with this agonizing time on earth.

   Hope everything is picking up with Scarlett. Keep in touch.

Yr old pal,
Sam

October 1, 2008

[TYPED]

Sam

Got yr letter about spending more time with Jessica and moving to up-state New York. I've written three replys and thrown them away. I guess it's not the kind of letter I can reply to. It's the kind of thing I guess one has to wait and see what happens. You have your own nature to deal with. Is this going to be another actual phase, I wonder? I can see now why they kept on in The Work about not drawing conclusions but rather to just see what happens.

It's been a trip having Scarlett jr[1] and Jesse here—especially for someone who's not crazy about having other people around (and now O-Lan and Kristy are going to be coming out in a week) [. . .] They've all been incredibly helpful. I must be difficult for them. Jesse says that everyone knows to tip toe around me. Jesse has certainly developed into a real Calif. liberal. And Scarlett jr. is like some smart, naïve, revved-up 17 yr old with a thousand impractical plans (even though she's 24). They were both a tremendous help with Scarlett.

We're about to leave for the hospital and the heart stint and all that that implies—whatever they may be. By the time you read this a thousand more things will have occurred.

I appreciated yr letter. Yr friendship means a lot to me. Good luck with whatever the next phase turns out to be. Down the road.

yr pal
John

---

1. Kristy's daughter.

January 15, 2009—Thurs. (Thor's Day) Kentucky

[HANDWRITTEN]

Dear John,

  Got yr latest missive and again apologies for not remembering yr birthday. I don't know why I can't remember anyone's birthday. Not my mother
or father, sister, children etc. Jessica's I remember for some reason—but
nobody else. Then, as I'm rolling down the road (soon to be an affair of the
past) I suddenly remember I've also forgotten my daughter Hannah's birthday—which is/was Jan. 11. So I frantically call her on this twisting Kentucky
country road & apologize but she just laughs hysterically & I realize I've
become the crazy old coot of a father who always forgets her birthday plus
now also gets arrested for drunk driving with his loopy mug-shot all over
CNN & *People* Magazine.[1] Great! A laughingstock—at my age when I should
be revered & honored. Incidentally, I found your latest mug-shot (the photo
you sent me) absolutely profound & oddly moving. A man facing things as
they are—in the dark—or semi-light of his bedroom or bathroom or wherever he's mounted the camera for the purpose of the self-portrait. Brilliant
bravery, I thought. Although, my absolute favorite attitude in photographic
portraits is Beckett's. The raw face, without pretense—something I've found
impossible when facing the camera. I like Georgia O'Keefe's portraits too but
then I wonder about someone who obviously loves being photographed so
much that they become iconographic—if you know what I mean.

  It was a lovely morning, this morning although un-godly cold—8°—but
the sky pale blue & layered with pink drifting clouds. The kind of morning
makes you damn glad you're in the country & not New York City. This place
has become quite the little sanctuary for me—especially in times like these
when the media loves parading your vagaries all over the country & your
old-lady won't talk to you & your children begin to wonder just how insane
their father might have become & you get to find out exactly how many good
friends you actually have. I bundled
up, with gloves & a quilted vest,
climbed the 4-rail fence & began
chopping ice out of the water tank

1. On January 3, 2009, Shepard was arrested
   for DUI in Normal, Illinois. He writes about
   the experience in the "Normal (Highway
   39 South)" section of *Day Out of Days*.

for the horses—all of them lined up, waiting for a drink, breath steaming out their nostrils. (Remember us taking turns feeding, those cold mornings at the 'Flying Y'? You might call them our "hay days.") I continue to be stunned by the unforeseen turns in life. I had the most ridiculous fantasy life as a kid—thinking I'd grow up to be a veterinarian with a flashy station wagon & a flashy blonde wife, raising German Shepherds in some fancy suburb. It was all based on the stupid social hierarchy I saw going on in High School in So. California. I actually aspired to a respectable position in society. Thank God that didn't come true. I mean, I guess a writer is one of the best things you could possibly be because no one has a clue how to characterize you. What is a writer? I have been lucky beyond reason—yet still bewildered.

Now it's time to return to New York & I'm not looking forward to it, although, the next stop is Dublin & rehearsals for the play—which I am looking forward to.[2] I got a long-distance call from the director the other day describing the rehearsal room & the 2 actors preparing for their first day & I got a picture of it in my head & I thought, this is incredible! Somewhere on the north side of Dublin—across the river Liffey, where Joyce & Beckett & Yeats used to stroll there's a small dark room on the 2nd floor of a Protestant church where 2 actors are sitting down at a table to read my new play. How amazing is that? Somehow, miraculously, I'm connected to a lineage of literature in the 21st century. "Something is taking its course." Love to Scarlett & I'll send you both a postcard from the Emerald Isle.

Yr enduring friend,
Sam

2. *Ages of the Moon*

January 25, 2009

[TYPED]

Sam

Thanks for your big letter just prior to your going to Ireland. Always great to hear from you. What a blessing it's been having a great friend such as yourself—in fact your very self. My life would have been a lot poorer and a lot duller if I had never met you. [. . .]

I just re-read yr story abt the time me you and Dennis went to L.A. You were right. It was pre-Jessica but only pre-living-with-Jessica. You were still in Mill Valley but losing yr mind because of going back and forth between Jessica and O-Lan. You hadn't made the break yet. So the plan was we were going to go to L.A. and I said let's take Dennis along for some laughs and you said O.K. We were all supposed to get stoned on the ride down so I scored some dope, the morning came to leave, Dennis came over and off we went. It must have been cold because I have a picture of you guys bundled up, head covered, eyes covered, Dennis with his head down on the back of the front seat. I remember thinking, "These guys are nervous about something—they're all covered up." But apparently something had gone amiss with you and Jessica because when we got in the car it was clear you were depressed. We hit the road and I broke out a joint but you turned it down which meant that just me and Dennis were going to be stoned and you were going to be cold fucking sober so it was a little tense and of course you weren't saying what was wrong. Men never communicate. We got about halfway down and stopped at this restaurant just as in your story and of course I had my tape recorder with me and wanted to tape some conversations, but you got pissed off and snapped "hey, we're trying to have a conversation here!" So I got up and went outside to cool off. It didn't amount to much. By the time we got to L.A. things had lightened up. I don't remember what we did except there was that foot race between you and Dennis on the way to the museum and I think we visited Jessica on the set of some movie. I remember we went into a studio where they were shooting and you and Dennis went up to her between takes but I waited in the back because I didn't feel she liked me and I remember some girl sat down with me and we started talking. Then that night back at the hotel we saw on T.V. that a great storm had hit the Bay area and when we called home, Scarlett said that the basement had been completely flooded and they had brought all the animals into the house. Dennis and I flew home and ended up for some reason at Val's house in S.F. They said the bridge was going to be closed because of high winds and sure enough we couldn't find a taxi that would go over to Marin but finally we found a Mexican gypsy cab that would take us and we made it home. That varying emotional state we were all in at the beginning of the trip would account for a lot of your story's perspective. It all seems so real when I think about it (and probably when you wrote about it) and at the same time so long ago, as tho it all happened to somebody else. And that somebody was me.

Now I'm sitting at my desk in the 21st century and the dog is drinking from the toilet. [. . .]

yr pal
John

February 8, 2009

Sam

Scarlett began hemorrhaging yesterday through her nose and because of blood thinners, it hasn't stopped bleeding 24 hrs later tho I took her twice to the ER and they shot a wad of something up her nose. Trouble is just when it starts to harden (the blood) she rubs her nose & it starts it running again. We spent the night in the ER but are home now. Her oxygen tube therefore has to go in her mouth. I didn't know what to do. The doctor suggests driving to Las Cruces to have it cauterized. Blood everywhere. Another fucking hospital? But what could I come up with?

Meanwhile Scarlett jr. who went back to Calif in December was bad-mouthing me to Kristy and Kristy called in the middle of all this to thrash it out with me. I explained what was happening to Scarlett and she said "Give her something to make her sleep and keep her hands away from her nose" then she said "I have to get off the phone because I'm in my car and there's a cop behind me and I don't have a phone-head set."

Well maybe that was the solution. So I gave her a whole Xanax and she went out like a light.

Now I'm sitting in a chair by the couch where she's sleeping to make sure that she doesn't touch her face in her sleep. I have a furious headache and I can barely leave the room for fear she'll start it bleeding again. So I'm reading a bio of Tolstoy and practicing the guitar (from music). I just told them at work I wouldn't be in tomorrow because I have to watch her. My world has suddenly become even smaller than it was before—me in this chair keeping a vigil & Scarlett breathing heavily on the couch. Bad as it is it's not as bad as what we went through in Arizona in Dec with the double stomach aneurysm.

I just took two Excedrin. I really think I've come to the end of smoking dope. The last couple of days both my arms and hands have been numb and I got worried about my heart. But I can't afford to check it out now being the sole care giver & provider for Scarlett & the dog. I guess writing this makes me feel less alone. So does reading Tolstoy. I get to see what I'm made of and I've come close to losing it a few times but have pulled myself together. Not

to the end of smoking dope.
The last couple of days both
my arms and hands have
been numb and I got
worried about my heart. But
I can't afford to check it out
now being the sole care giver
+ provider for Scarlett + the
dog. I guess writing this
makes me feel less alone. So
does reading Tolstoy. I get to
see what I'm made of and I've
come close to losing it a few times
but have pulled myself together.
Not as strong as I thought I was
I guess. I'm just hoping the
blood will clot now that she's
knocked out. As you can imagine
the doctor scene here is less
than ideal.

Sorry this isn't more up beat.
Probably will feel better when
the Excedrin kicks in. Hope
yr time in Ireland was
fruitful and that things are good
on the home front.

Johnny

as strong as I thought I was I guess. I'm just hoping the blood will clot now that she's knocked out. As you can imagine the doctor scene here is less than ideal.

Sorry this isn't more upbeat. Probably will feel better when the Excedrin kicks in. Hope yr time in Ireland was fruitful and that things are good on the home front.

Johnny

February 9

Sam

. . . although that's probably not the correct date. Scarlett slept on the livingroom couch last night which I had covered with towels against her wetting it in her sleep since she was drugged. I had tried to tape the oxygen tube in her mouth but the tape kept coming off and all night I was worried as I slept on and off in the livingroom chair, that her nose would begin hemorrhaging again. What would I do if it didn't clot? And the next day she was due in dialysis & the day after that at the family doctor for a blood test & the day after that in dialysis & the day after that in Las Cruces about moving her catheter. Then there was shopping to do, the dog to feed & care for, the house to clean, meals to prepare not to mention going to my job—which incidentally I'm not going to today because I have to watch Scarlett & see she doesn't begin bleeding again. I have no Kentucky to run to. This is my Kentucky. [. . .]

yr faithful friend,
John

February 11, 2009—Kentucky

John—

Just got in the door here in Kentucky—from the howling wind (60 m.p.h. according to radio)—middle of night—drove 350 miles from Normal, Ill— (scene of my infamous D.U.I. & the courtroom). Showed up out there a day early to meet my attorney—great old guy with a gray beard named Hal Jennings—been a lawyer there in Normal for 46 years—knows everyone in town, which is reason I hired him. Chain smokes green Pall Malls & uses old Mid-Western phrases like: "Peachy dances" & "You don't know me from a load of turnips." Stayed forty miles north west of Normal in a town called 'Peoria' so press wouldn't sniff me out. Great town on Illinois river—Lincoln gave several speeches there on slavery & the 'Negro perdicament'—also home of Ronald Reagan & wonderful turn of century buildings made out of red sandstone with turrets on the top & lights blinking for low-flying aircraft (back in the day). Day before my court appearance for the terrible offense of driving blind drunk (which I've been doing for 50 years & just now got caught)—beautiful bright sunny day—strolling the streets of a town I've never been in. Then, later, meet my attorney at the 'Mark Twain' hotel where the manager lets us have a booth to ourselves in the back & 'Hal' (lawyer) sets his brief-case down & outlines the exact procedure of what we'll be going thru in court the next day: what he'll ask me—how I should respond— what not to say—how to behave as though I'm the nicest, most polite citizen on earth & how I've learned my lesson & never ever again will I even think about stepping into a vehicle of any kind having had even a swallow of beer.

Next morning, I meet him ('Hal') at a Barnes and Noble on the outskirts of Normal (it kind of rhymes) & the first thing I do is excuse myself, go in the Men's Room & take a big nervous dump while Hal fiddles with his papers & files through his brief-case notes. Then he drives me in his Mercury Van over to a little office called 'Alcohol Evaluation'—connected to the courtroom & jail, where I get interviewed by a woman with a huge nose & tiny nostrils. She asks me questions like: 'How often do I drink? How much do I drink when I drink? When do I drink? Do I drink before noon? Do I drink to make myself feel better? Do I gain confidence when I drink? Do I argue with my wife about my drinking? Do I black out? Do I lose my memory? Have I ever passed out?' etc., etc., etc. So I just say 'no' to everything & she fills out some forms & I walk out the door & hand the forms to my lawyer 'Hal' who puts them in his brief-case & we walk out into the pouring rain toward the courthouse. There's a couple of pathetic photographers from local papers who make feeble attempts to grab a picture of me but I've got my raincoat hood pulled tight around my head & my shades on (Hell, man I've dodged Italian paparazzi with Brad Pitt! This is nothing—This is Normal fucking Illinois!)

Hal escorts me up to the courtroom & sits me down in the back. It looks like a bad T.V. set with fake oak paneling, American flags, eagles, the great seal of Illinois & all that shit. There's a very bored looking cop slouched in an aluminum chair, a bored looking stenographer, the prosecuting attorney who looks about twelve years old in a black suit & acne, a couple of other bored-looking stooges in suits. The whole place reeks of boredom & bureaucracy. What a way to spend one's life! I'm suddenly glad to be a drunken playwright/actor ass-hole with no connection to the world of law & order. It all looks like living death. And the weird thing is they all believe they're on the right side of the fence. I suddenly think of Lenny Bruce. Poor Lenny! How he must have suffered.

They call my name. I walk up in front of the judge—my attorney to my left & the prosecutor to my right. They swear me in. The judge reads me my rights. Then the judge asks me what I was doing getting so drunk—(my breathalyzer test was twice the State limit) in Normal, Illinois in the middle of the night when I don't even live here & I was just passing through? So I make up this story—(which is part true—the Irish say: 'Never let the truth get in the way of a good story.') about how I met 2 guys in Normal who were helicopter pilots in the original 'Blackhawk Down' incident in Somalia (true) & how I started drinking with them & swapping stories—since I was in the movie & they were in the actual real-life catastrophe. All true except I had met them a year before this drinking situation ever happened—but I figured the military aspect of it would appeal to their gung-ho enthusiasm for sobriety & it worked. No conviction on the D.U.I.—which means it won't show up on my future license record—but I do have to comply with 100 hours of public service—to be done by Sept. 25. So, I can handle that I guess. My Kentucky license will be suspended for 30 days but I'll wait it out in New York or Dublin where I won't need a car. Long-story-short—I won't be caught dead drinking & driving again. Which is a good thing, I think. God knows how dangerous it could have been—if I ran someone down in the street.

I'm sitting here in my kitchen having a 'Negra Modelo' & writing this. I don't know anymore. I used to think I could maybe give up booze altogether. But I may have been fooling myself. Little did I know that aging & alcohol are sympathetic. I must admit that I like getting drunk. I like the feeling that comes over me. The numbness. The moving into a different state. All that stuff. In fact I could make a case for wine being a low-end substitute for smack. It goes straight to your blood. Now I'm justifying alcoholism! This is really getting bad.

Just finished your long saga of Scarlett's terrible trials. I hope she's having some relief & peace now. Hard to believe what life can dole out. I don't know if Karma's the right explanation for the suffering endured but then I'm probably not smarter than hundreds of years of Tantric & Tibetan culture. Wouldn't it be nice to have the certainty of knowledge handed down through generations of elders & people of true wisdom? I guess that why we were all attracted to the Work in some way. Hope things have settled down some for you there in Deming. What a nightmare. [. . .]

I've got one more day here at the farm then back to N.Y. and on to Dublin for the opening of the new play. I think my daughter, Hannah, is coming over to Ireland to spend a few days. I'll try to call you on the road, back up North. Give my love to Scarlett & a big kiss on the forehead for being so brave.

Down the road,
Sam

Spring 2009

[TYPED]

Sam

    Read this astounding fragment account of Tolstoy's last days. He's in his 80's and decides to run away from his wife and children—from everyone. I couldn't help [but] think of you & Kentucky (even though you dread a lonely ending). But I also thought of me—though when I die I doubt I'll have anyone to leave. I've always felt alone and probably you have too. Another tie that binds us?

yr pal
John

May 7, 2009—Kentucky

[HANDWRITTEN]

Dear John, (supposedly this is the way letters started from unfaithful wives to their G.I. husbands overseas during the War when they wanted to confess their infidelity & how they'd found a new man)

Anyway, just got back to the farm in KY. after 6 weeks of doing my 'Public Service' at NYU (penance for the D.U.I. in Illinois) & then Jessica had that awful fall & I've had to nurse her back to somewhat normalcy—although her right arm is still in bad shape.[1] Opened my P.O. Box & 6 weeks of mail came pouring out including your letters.

Sometimes your letters remind me of Eloise at the Plaza—you know. . . . "I'd grab a slab of freshly baked ginger bread & whipped cream & a large glass of milk & go roller skating down thru the hallways with my turtle on a leash & push all the 'up' buttons on the elevators." That is, when you're speaking about your unfathomable past—unfathomable to me at least—you growing up in Jersey City & me in Duarte. What could be more opposite backgrounds. I never even knew there was such a thing as a maid until I saw one on t.v.—I think it was in the movie *Bringing Up Baby*—or was that a butler? I don't know. Anyway, it's charming but utterly foreign. Thank God you managed to escape!

Sorry to hear of Scarlett's on-going travails but glad to hear her English wit holds out. Your stoned adventures at the Mexican Deli continue to amaze me—like some kind of indentured servitude. How do you do it & maintain such good-naturedness? I'd probably have thrown some ugly violent fit by now & hurled all the chickens into the frozen food section. It's too bad you can't find some way to turn all that into a weird land-mark novel of some kind. It would be the wackiest book out there. I know you're entirely without ambition but why don't you try making all that experience into a book? It would be great & totally unique. There's nothing else like that out there. Believe me. I'm sounding like an agent now or some promoter. I can't think of anything I'd rather read than a daily account of your Deli sagas. Really.

1. In a fall at her home in Duluth, Lange suffered a broken collarbone.

Read the tragic Tolstoy 'flight.' He waited too long to make a decision like that. You don't wait until you're eighty some years old to get the hell out of a bad situation. Of course, I guess you have to consider it was a whole different time & culture then & splitting from your wife & kids must have been an absolute taboo in that society. I don't know. It just shows you what havoc & suffering the intellectual mind bound by ideologies & philosophies can cause. First thing he does at 4: A.M. when he escapes the house, trying to tip-toe out so as not to awaken his crazy-ass wife, is walk straight into a tree & knock his hat off. There he is, poor bastard, crawling around in the dark, in the mud, searching for his hat. Then he has to drag along his doctor friend because he's too old & feeble to harness the horses & pack his bags—so the solitude he's seeking is no solitude at all. I found it profoundly sad & pathetic. That wife of his must have been a real nightmare. But it does bring up the age-old question—how does one prepare for death? Is there any preparation? I don't know if you've read the eye-witness account of the death of Socrates who was sentenced to drink a cup of poison hemlock. He gathers his friends & family around & first thing he does is send all the women away because they're all weeping & moaning & he can't tolerate this show of emotion. Then he drinks the cup of poison & walks around so the hemlock will better circulate through his bloodstream. Then he lies down & begins to feel the numbness take over his feet then creep slowly up through his legs. Then he calls one of his friends to his side & tells him he owes a farmer down the road a couple of bucks for a rooster he'd bought & forgot to pay him. He asks his friend to make good on his debt. And then he dies. Simple as that. What do the Buddhists say? 'Leave no trace.' That's a hard one, I think. I come back to the words of Lord Pentland in one of those extraordinary lunch breaks we used to have at the 'House' where everyone seemed to be in silent slow-motion awaiting the words of the master. And then his soft English voice would come (lilting) sailing across the tables to us about what does it mean to die like a dog? We always assume this is a negative thing but perhaps it's more noble than that. To go off in solitude & lie down by yourself & die alone, without bothering other people about it—without making a fuss. And then I think of Don Hoyt,[2] found alone in a tangle of brush in the hills of Santa Cruz or wherever & I wonder if maybe he might have had these words in mind. Does it matter how we die? I guess you probably don't want to be

2. Former president of the Gurdjieff Foundation of California.

screaming & thrashing & puking & bleeding if you can help it. But I think of my Dad, mowed down by a car & dying in an ambulance. His last words were: "My name is Sam." My favorite poet—Machado, said his favorite lines (by another poet) were:

> *"Our lives are rivers*
> *flowing on to the sea,*
> *the sea of dying"*[3]

I could go on & on about death. One of my favorite subjects—so long as you can keep it at arm's length. Right now I'm in my garden again watching the Bluejays hop along the wall, pecking fresh seed that I've laid out. Spring is struggling to break thru.

'Mother's Day'—5/10
(weird when your Mom's dead)

This morning I was up early (sixish) & went out on my back porch—chill morning air but great promise of warmth & sunshine heading in from the east—bright blue sky & a few fluffy clouds. I noticed one of the many Peonies I'd planted (ask Scarlett about the Peonies—they're very English) had a full white bud that was just beginning to open. I walked over to it, coffee cup in hand (this is a gesture I'll never forget of my father's—constantly ambling around the yard with a cigarette & a cup of coffee) & on closer examination the entire outside of the bud was covered in a fragile dew like tiny glass bubbles & the very head of the bud was crawling with little ants. I went back up on my porch & planted myself in my cedar Adirondack chair & took in the smells of lilac & Iris, opened one of my latest books—*Memories, Dreams & Reflections* by C. G. Jung & the next thing I knew the sun was high in the sky & the white Peonie bud had opened into full bloom & my coffee was cold. Later, I was on the phone to Jessica (up in Minnesota) wishing her happy 'Mother's Day' & explaining the miracle of the blooming Peonie & she told me the ants had caused it to open. Evidently they chew away a delicate membrane of some kind, protecting the bud & cause it to be exposed to the sun. She was very jealous of my Peonies blooming a month before hers—me being in

---

3. Translation of lines by the Spanish poet Jorge Manrique (c. 1440–1479): "Nuestras vidas son los ríos / que van a dar en la mar, / que es el morir."

'Zone 6' & her in 'Zone 3' & even told me that now that she was aware of this drastic climate difference she might come down to Kentucky with me in May—just for the Peonies. That would be nice.

My accountant calls me & tells me I have no money. "What're we going to do?" Old Marty Licker, all bent over with terrible arthritis of the spine. Like Uncle Scrooge or something. I don't know, Marty—I don't know what we're going to do. There's no movies out there. Nobody has any money to make movies anymore & the ones they do end up making aren't anything like the movies I used to make. I don't recognize any of the stars, any of the names. They're all teen-agers. I'm a has-been, Marty. My days are over. I'm an old fart sitting in my 200 year old brick cabin on a farm in Kentucky, by the fire reading obscure literature & making up stories & plays. Movies have passed me by. Come & gone. Now I just want to be left alone in peace & poverty. "But how are we going to pay the bills, Sam?" I don't know, Marty. Before I met you I had no money & then I got some money & now I don't have any money anymore. So I don't know. I don't know how any of this happened. It's all just like the weather. It comes & it goes. "But that doesn't do me any good, Sam. I'm the one who's paying the bills here." Yeah, but you're paying the bills with my money. And now it's gone. So it's me who should be complaining. But I don't know what to do about it. I could go get a job I guess but the kind of jobs I qualify for wouldn't pay anywhere near enough money to pay the bills. I could go back to washing dishes in restaurants, busing tables, washing UPS trucks in Times Square, working as a guard for the Burns Detective Agency, typing for some big business operation but they don't need typists anymore! The Days of Typists are long gone! So get off my back, Marty! Throw me in Debtor's Prison, just like the Dickens characters. Let me live out my days in stone walls sipping soup. I don't know, Marty. I just don't know.

I like this—jumping from one random subject to another. Stringing things together. Maybe things make more sense that way.

Reading all kinds of things. Now that my own book is pretty near completion—(this is my last round with it before I hand it over to the devouring monster of publication) I can't seem to settle on any literature.[4] I'm reading a book on 'Merlin'; one called *The Diary of Samuel Pepys* (circa 1600's, England); stories by Felisberto Hernández, *Deliverance* (finally a masterpiece), the stories of George V. Higgins (on your recommendation), *Watt* by Beckett &

4. *Day Out of Days* was published by Knopf in January 2010.

323

lately *The Fragrance of Guava* by Marquez who has all kinds of smart things to say about writing & Latin American culture. But I'm not magnetized by any of it. I guess I'm in one of those in-between periods after you finish a long piece of writing that has completely consumed you. This new book has gone on seemingly forever—digging through notebooks that go back to the 70's when we were all living that extraordinary life in Marin County & Jesse was just a wee toddler. It's all heart-breaking to me now. The way things have just come & gone. I truly don't know what to do with myself. Writing has really been my life & when I'm not doing it I feel worse than useless.

Hate to end on a down note but I must come to a close so I can get this off to you in time before the country Post Office shuts its gates.

My love & best wishes to Scarlett. Hope she's not in pain.

Much fond regards,
Yr amigo,
Sam

August 9, 2009

[TYPED]

Sam

[. . .] In just a few days it will be Scarlett's 76 birthday so it's fitting that I should say a few words here. She was 34 when we met. I first saw her in someone else's apartment in New York. There was a crowd of us. I don't know what I was doing or who the others were. It had the quality of a dream. We were standing around talking when a woman barged into the room and asked for painkillers. Attractive woman. Nice ass. English accent. Red hair. Liked the way she dressed, brown suede jacket and tight jeans.

The second time I saw her I was with a girl who said, "Let's stop by this woman's apartment. I want to say hello." Imagine my surprise. Same English woman. The woman came to the door. There were smells of cooking inside and the sound of children playing. There was a bare lightbulb hanging in the kitchen. She opened the door and stood in the doorway. We didn't go in. We were introduced again. After that I left the country. See how fate works. They meet—twice, briefly and then the woman goes off to Yucatan in a van and the man sails for Africa and that—you would think, would be the end of that. The woman goes to Yucatan and then a year later to Mexico City and from Mexico City to Los Angeles. The man goes to Tangiers and from Tangiers to Spain and after a year in Spain to Connecticut. Finally they both return to

"a cozy flat
in what is known
as old Manhattan."[1]

The third time I met her she dropped by a friend's house at 3 in the morning and I walked her home.[2] The rest is history.

1. From the song "Manhattan" (1925) by Richard Rodgers and Lorenz Hart: "I've a cozy little flat / In what is known as old Manhattan."
2. Dark's note: in 1967.

It's no wonder a person has so much difficulty being present. There is no present. We're living in our own past. The present is so fleeting it's hardly worth mentioning. There's "time"—and then

there's "The Big Time." But the big time never seemed attractive to me.
That's why I was always attracted to Kerouac's books (even though Kerouac
sought the big time). His books promoted the wandering life, aimlessness,
the hobo life, Mexico City, drugs, hitchhiking, lonely railroad rooms with
just a bed and a calendar—I have no idea why that seemed so attractive to me
and not a lucrative business opportunity or an extensive education. This is
the kind of thing that fired me up as a teenager sitting in my bedroom waiting
to go to highschool listening to my parents chatting over cocktails in the
livingroom. This is the kind of thing that led me astray. [. . .]

I've always tended to romanticize the authentic man; Mr Shultz the
butcher, Mr Watson the superintendant, Carl at the fender shop, McAdams
the coach, Pierre the chef and so on. When I was young I thought I'd like
to be an Authentic Man. I wanted to believe in something. I wanted to be a
"real" person. God knows I tried. But I can see now that it was all in vain.

yr pal
John

August 19, 2009

[TYPED]

Sam,

Was it really you who climbed through the bathroom window and chased me out of my bath? Was it really me who ran through the house in a towel while the women knitted in the living room thinking we were fools. Only a certain kind of person would marry me and only a certain kind of person would marry you. All the rest would find us intolerable. [. . .]

Scarlett says things now like—what are you going to do with the stuffed animals when I'm gone? And I say, I'm going to keep them where they are. This is where they live. And she's pleased and puts her hand against the lion and rearranges the baby giraffe. I'm afraid if I had to describe my life up to this point I'd have to say it was a digression. But from what I don't know. Isn't that how the Bible begins? We digressed or transgressed or crossdressed. And God caught us just like my first wife's father caught us before we were married early one morning when we were laying in bed in her basement apartment on 115th st just off Broadway. Ah, New York. The more I see of the country the more grateful I am that I had New York. I felt at home there and I've been a wanderer ever since.

The doctor came into the room smiling, looking at Scarlett with a big warm smile on his face. I started to explain why we were there. She was down to 84 pounds and losing weight. What was going on? What could we do? He just kept nodding his head and smiling. "She's dying" he said.

"She's fading away?" I said.

"I wouldn't put it that kindly," he said. "She's dying. She has some tough genetics. She's 76. She's survived all these illnesses and all these operations and now her body is slowly running down. It's not a sudden running down like something overnight. This is her final slow decline. It could be a matter of 3 months or 6 months and who knows, a miracle might occur and she might last out the year. But there is nothing more natural to life than death and there's nothing like death to help one live fully in the moment." And all this while Scarlett was sitting there mumbling to herself, "84 pounds. How wonderful. I always wanted to weigh 84 pounds." And she almost sounded as if for the first time in her life she was satisfied with her weight.

The final stage is frightening if for no other reason than because it's a mysterious and unknown room one is about to enter, all alone, inside your body, in the middle of the night, on your back, with your eyes open, watching all the fears, the fantasies, the day dreams, cat naps and brain storms.

Scarlett very alert today. Sharp as a tack. She took the you're-dying thing surprisingly well and then I suddenly remembered back in 1967 when I met her how immediately awed I was by her English accent, the fact that she was seven years older than me, her flaming red hair, her pretty face and wonderful figure and her amazing take on the world, which I had never encountered before.

John

August 20, 2009

[TYPED]

Sam

You once told me that Castaneda told you that a woman asked him how she could live a spiritual life and Castaneda told her to sit for a half hour every day and concentrate on the fact that her husband and her children were going to die on no particular day at no particular time.

I was thinking about that yesterday and it suddenly hit me in an absolutely new way that Scarlett was definitely going to die—intellectually we know this but this was a moment in which the whole of me knew it. It was real—as though it had already happened, and it really shook me up. And for the first time I had real doubts about being able to handle it. [. . .]

Scarlett seems well enough although she is very, very thin and losing weight even though she's eating. They're going to run tests on her. They're worried about her stomach. I've been trying to fatten her up which is a balancing act because she's supposed to get a great deal of protein, which she hates, in the meat so I have to give it to her in liquid form but then she's not supposed to drink over a certain amount of fluid a day. However we've minimized her falling by making sure she stays put until I get home to help her around. At 76, and with all the things that are wrong with her body—she's right where one would expect her to be and I'm just glad I'm healthy enough to be able to work and look after her at this stage of the game but I tell you—there are times—many times—when I flag, when I don't feel equal to the task, when I feel scared.

Talk to you soon.

yr pal,
john

September 15, 2009—Kentucky

[HANDWRITTEN]

Dear Johnny—

    I've always avoided using the diminutive form of your name because it reminds me of being called "Stevie" when I was a boy & how much I despised being called "Stevie" because it immediately gave me the impression of being small, cute, impotent, & inconsequential, so I changed it to the much more manly & mysterious "Sam," although the same essential feelings of inferiority & weakness continue to run rampant through my every thought & action & I realize now (only too late) have become the very fabric of my moral & spiritual framework. (I enjoy writing in this rather pompous formality if for no other reason than it helps me line my thoughts out—my thinking—which tends to be haphazard and un-linked at best.)

    Me & Jessica have just returned from yet another whirlwind tour of Mexico which turned out to be quite wonderful & quiet—this time of year when there are no American or European tourists, being all afraid of 'Swine-Flu' or 'Hurricane Season' or 'Drug Wars' or any number of malevolent forces at work in the Daily News. Now I'm back down in Kentucky for awhile &, of course, found your letter all of which touched me in a way that's impossible to explain but deeply connected not just to our brief history together over the decades but to something much longer & probably linked to the reason we've become such indelible friends. I have a little black notebook (one of many) in which I've collected many of my favorite quotes from the likes of Joyce, Cendrars, Beckett, Borges, Machado, Vallejo etc. & I came across one in your letters about being beyond—"beyond fantasy, beyond hope, beyond art—" etc.—which I found very apt & I've added it to all the rest—hope you don't mind—I know how you hate being thought of as part of the literary marketplace. Your photo stills taken from the 8 mm movie clips are incredible or maybe it's just the re-visiting of those times—riding around on the ranch & being so absorbed by the 'Work' & a sense of starting a 'new' life out in California after 3 years in stagnant London. I think too, what those stills have is a very haunting sense of time gone by—as seen through a keyhole into a past we never knew was passing. It's amazing how there was that sense between us back then—we always talked about it—how time was passing & we couldn't quite connect with the present or our 'place' in it & now it actually is happening that time has caught up with us & we are rapidly running into our last days—weeks—months—years—being devoured by life rather than merrily rolling down the road on our Harleys or having breakfast with Lord Pentland. Still, I guess, it's good to 'keep your chin up' as the English might say. Scarlett's got to be one of the greatest examples of courage I've come across in this life.

Here's a funny example of how life turns & twists. I'm down in Kentucky & Jessica is in L.A. for the Emmy Awards (she's up for Best Actress in *Grey Gardens*). I've long ago copped out of Hollywood award show-dressing-up-in-the-tux—Sitting patiently for hours in red velvet seats with a shit-eating grin on yr face while faggot photographers snap yr picture over & over—I'm never any good at it & become a real pain-in-the-ass to be around so we've agreed that she go to these events on her own & I'll stay home. So, here I am down here in the country all by myself & it's Sunday nite so I decide to go into town to get a bite to eat but it turns out everything's closed on Sunday. So I drive all the way into the next town—about 15 miles—where I know there's a little Mexican cafe that's always open. I go in & sit in a booth & behind the little bar there's a t.v. & they're showing the Emmy Awards in L.A. but without the sound on. There's two or 3 other t.v.'s on showing College football games & NASCAR racing—all with the sound on but not the emmys. Anyway, I order some tamales & an iced tea & I look up at the t.v. & there's Jessica, looking gorgeous in a green cocktail dress & her hair all done up & she just won the Best Actress Award & she's going up to the stage to accept it. She starts giving her acceptance speech but the sound is off so I just watch her toss her hair with her beaming smile & holding the emmy award over her head & thanking everyone involved as the camera pans to various actors & big-wigs in the business & I'm thinking how wild & wonderful my life has become & here come my tamales steaming on the plate & my iced-tea & I'm trying to see over the waiter's shoulder at this woman I've had this long on-going torrid love affair with for more than 25 years & I can't hear a word she's saying. [. . .]

Yr Amigo,
Sam
Best to Scarlett & Love

Fall 2009

[TYPED]

Sam

[. . .] Many writers write out of a need to express the most wounded parts of themselves. Many writers tell amazing pirate stories with characters like Long John Silver. And how about Squire Trelawney who was the theme of my Doctorate. John Watson, Squire Trelawney, Friday and Sancho Panza. All secondary men. I know because I've been a secondary man all my life. People have tried to push me into the hero role but it's just not for me. I'm a born secondary man. [. . .]

I wonder what yr plans are now. I love listening to yr schedule it's so different from mine and sounds so much more exhausting. It's always . . . "First I'm driving down to New Orleans to catch the Derby and then I may drive to Texas to see this friend of mine who raises Australian racing hounds. Then I went to get a little fishing in up in Colorado before I hook up with the family in Minnesota for Jessie's birthday and then on the 15th I'm flying to London"—etc..

Now you've got to admit for someone who does nothing but go to work in a supermarket every day, your life has a fascinating aspect to it. You've become familiar with so many places and as you know, places have their own magic—just think of the experience of finding yourself walking down a road in Duarte or me walking down a street in Jersey City. Those are places like no others. On top of which everything has changed. You've changed and I've changed and only Proust could recapture the past.

With all the medical things that are going on and all that's wrong with her, Scarlett is looking as good as she looked in Healdsburg or even Mill Valley. We always have a good time together, just like you and me—and you're the only two people I can say that about. [. . .]

I don't know if this happens to you but every once in a while I'll wake up to the fact that this is exactly the kind of life I used to dream about living when I was a kid; the redhead with the English accent, my own little house, a good job, an old car, a big dog, a million books and a couple of guns down by the Mexican border at the beginning of the 21st century.

yr pal
John

November 28, 2009—Kentucky

[HANDWRITTEN]

Dear Old John,

Just got finished bawling my eyes out after reading the deaths of Lee and Grant—you sent me. Thanks for that. Good thing I was on the farm alone so no one could witness my wailings & carrying on to the trees, the sky, the wind etc.—a full out King Lear breakdown. Felt very good after. Cleaned out. Maybe that's how it is. Felt very good after dying. No problem. It's life that's a bitch.

As usual, I arrive here to a whole bushel of your letters & wind up spending the next morning on my porch with coffee, reading them. I try now, to arrange them in chronological order but can't always make out the El Paso postal date—faded by intense sun or just careless stamping. There was one absolute epic out of the bunch—even more testimony to the possibility of your 'deli diaries,' which I think would make an (important) immense book. But I'm reminded of one of Mr. Beckett's greatest quotes: "Of course, you don't do it in order to get published. You do it in order to breathe."[1] The stuff about meteors colliding with earth & the border drug wars in Juarez also fascinating, frightening & true. Now, I'm wondering if it might be possible to give up yet another great chunk of fear about dying, after all these years. Lee & Grant both died at the age of 63 & I catch myself thinking aha!—I've outlived them both! What a dope.

Thanksgiving passed with all the usual frenzied cooking then devouring of the bird & all the fancy side dishes then the washing up; the screaming kids, the tense terse conversations with relatives you don't know & only see at Thanksgiving & Xmas & then the great let-down & lonesome walk at nite thru Washington Square Park with the usual dealers & junkies & people still singing folk songs as tho it were 1965.

Tomorrow I'm off to Nashville to shoot a t.v. pilot about a dysfunctional country-music family that goes bankrupt & slightly berserk.[2] Should be funny. My friend T-Bone Burnett (from 'Rolling Thunder,' Dylan days) is doing the music & the writing is better than most t.v.

1. "Getting published isn't the important thing. You write in order to be able to breathe" (in Charles Juliet's *Conversations with Samuel Beckett and Bram van Velde* [1995]).
2. *Tough Trade*; the series was not picked up by Epix TV.

I've outlined them both! What a dope.
Thanksgiving past with the usual frenzied cookin
ruining of the bird & all the fancy side dishes
e washing up; the screaming kids, the tens
ersations with relatives you don't know for
hanksgiving & Xmas & then the great let-do
ome work at nite thru Washington Square to
e usual dealers & junkies & people still singi
gs as tho it were 1965.
omorrow I'm off to Nashville to shoot a t.v.
bout a disfunctional country-music fam
oes bankrupt & slightly berserk.
be funny. My friend H-Bone Burnet
Rolling Thunder, Dylan days) is doing th
& the writing is better than most t.v. fa
y. it's down to trying to make a living
movies are on the rocks — no work—
s t.v. — I don't know. Still writing
but it's petered-out drastically.
some but no real enthusiasm for it! On
t: "Where would I go, if I could go, who would I be, if I
ould be, what would I say, if I had a voice, who says th
saying it's me? ..... It's the same old stranger, as
ever, ..."

Fond Regards
from the wilderness,
Sam

fare. Anyway, it's down to trying to make a living now & movies are on the rocks—no work—so I guess t.v.—I don't know. Still writing some but it's petered-out dramatically. Reading some but no real enthusiasm for it. Only Beckett: "Where would I go, if I could go, who would I be, if I could be, what would I say, if I had a voice, who says this, saying it's me? . . . It's the same old stranger, as ever . . ."[3]

Fond Regards
from the wilderness,
Sam

3. From the fourth of Beckett's
   Texts for Nothing.

[HANDWRITTEN]

Sam

Just got back from Las Cruces—doctor's appointment for Scarlett after which another trip to Barnes & Noble so this is now what I'm reading—jumping from book to book. At any rate this seems to be my taste these days.

In the doctor's office I came across your piece in the *New Yorker* and Scarlett and I both read it (I swiped the magazine).[1] Need I say that I liked it very much. Of course I already knew about the dead guy on the plane and the seemingly endless tension between you and Jessica about how naughty you've been. You summed up in the piece what I was thinking while I was reading it— ". . . remembering the days we were seldom out of each other's sight and had no reason to doubt we'd be forever in love." because I remember and still love your letters from the road when you first took off together. In any case I thought it was a beautifully written piece. Scarlett says our styles are similar but I don't see it. I'm pretty ragged compared to you. Hell—I wish I had the desire to write about anything at this point. (I love it when you write about yourself, denying your guilt.)

Scarlett remains stable and in fact has gained some weight—up from 85 pounds to 98. Well—it's like AA—one day at a time.

Scarlett sends her love. Talk to you by & by.

yr pal
John

1. "Land of the Living,"
   September 21, 2009.

January 30, 2010

[TYPED]

Sam

[. . .] It's all so interesting. I'm reminded of death, but not as The Grim Reaper but of simply adhering to the limits of the life of the various body parts. A man gets so old he can't hear or walk or control his bladder. There are all sorts of deaths. Is it, do you think, really necessary to suffer? Can suffering be eliminated or is it rather a matter of experiencing a different relationship with suffering similar to a sore toe or a stiff neck?

Maybe I'm thinking of death tonight because Scarlett has taken a turn for the worse these last few days. And maybe what I'm really thinking about is suffering and of changing my relationship to it so that I won't mind the pain. [. . .]

A few days later. It's been storming here. Scarlett has gotten worse and I've had to quit my job because she's so weak she can't get herself out of bed to go to the bathroom or get dressed. She hasn't been eating and her chest is congested although she seems to be coughing less. We're supposed to go for X-Rays tomorrow. We were at the doctor's yesterday and he agreed that the first thing she needs is to get some calories into her. I bought a lot of high protein nutrition drinks and am trying to get her to drink them. She's also in pain around her waist. She's skin and bone—frightening to see, and on top of all this she has to go to the dreaded dialysis every other day which takes so much out of her she can't speak and of course doesn't want to eat. But I know she's getting better care here than she would at a hospital. Any T.V. romantic notions about hospitals I might have had once were dispelled last year with that bout of hospitals in Las Cruces and Arizona. I've got all her medication and her oxygen here and now that I'm not working I can be with her all the time. Of course added to all this I've got these dogs to contend with. Had I known all this was going to happen I never would have picked up this wild puppy but this is what I've got to work with. It's good O-Lan and Kathleen saw her when they did (they were here two weeks ago.) This transition took place quite suddenly. I really thought she was on her way out this time but perhaps I can get her stronger again tho how long can this go on? How much can her body take, strong as her will may be? This is the stuff that all of us will have to face in one form or another either for ourselves or for someone we love. At our age we've already seen plenty of dying, yr folks, Bill, Joe etc. and no one really tells you how to be with it. I'm just playing it all by ear day by day, bathing her and dressing her and feeding her. I don't know what will happen from one moment to the next but of course this was always the case, wasn't it? At least when she was so low last year we could point to the operations as the cause and figure it just needed time to climb back up. But this seems more like the body finally failing, pure and simple. Anyway, I'm doing the very best I can which admittedly isn't much.

john

Scarlett died on February 7, 2010.

Scarlett outside
our photo gallery

February 18, 2010

[HANDWRITTEN]

Dear John,

Another amazing time—one after another although this one seems particularly jolting & unsettling with the death of Scarlett & all the surrounding lostness you must be going through.

Just talked to you last nite after yr return from the bowling alley & the Mexican women. You sounded at least glad to be back in the land of familiarity—with yr dogs, house & job, etc. I suppose things level out eventually—but I'm not sure that's so desirable either.

I'm back in Ky.—surrounded by a blanket of snow—fire in the fireplace, coffee—sitting at the breakfast table in the kitchen, going thru yr letters. Just read the one about writing like a 20 yr old—the mind of the younger man, how Dylan probably couldn't write lines like: "Mom's in the basement, mixing up the medicine" anymore.[1] I think yr right about 'writing with a different mind'—but what mind? That's the reason I return to Beckett again & again. It seems he found his mind as he grew older & knew how tenuous it was & followed its rickety steps into old age & knew for sure it was not the same 'mind' he was dealing with back when he wrote *Fair to Middling Women* or "First Love." The stigma of 'greatness' is also very haunting. I keep thinking I'm past that but it rears its head now & then. How to simply write for oneself—like Salinger was talking about:—'There's a great peace in not being published.' For now I'm in-between things again. Just finished tumultuous activity in N.Y.C.;—two plays opening off Broadway, the new book; completing my community service hours for the D.U.I. in Illinois more than a year ago.[2] That was a hard row-to-hoe; twice a week showing up at an alcohol counseling office in mid-town (46th St. just off Broadway); signing in, giving a urine sample, sitting in a blank room on swivel chairs

1. The actual line (interestingly enough) from "Subterranean Homesick Blues" is "Johnny's in the basement."

2. The plays were *Ages of the Moon*, presented by the Atlantic Theater Company at the Linda Gross Theater, and *Lie of the Mind*, presented by the New Group at the Acorn Theatre.

with 6 to 12 raving addicts—some on heroin, Methadone, crack, pills, pot, alcohol—you name it & overseen by one poor haggard clinician who seemed maybe one shy step removed from being an addict himself. Here's an example of the way one of these so-called 'meetings' would take place: A fat blonde junkie woman named Jennifer would come in with cookie crumbs spilling off her chest; pour herself a paper cup full of weak coffee, add synthetic creamer & maybe ½ a pound of sugar—find a chair big enough to support her heaving bulk—plop down in it & spill the coffee all over her silver tennis shoes then spend the next fifteen minutes cleaning it up with paper towels. As this 'so-called meeting' continues a short stout black man with popping paranoid eyes starts a monologue about his sordid past as a crackhead in Harlem & how he danced out a 4 Story window stark naked after fucking a hooker for hours & smoking a pipefull of Crack. He landed in a snow bank below & went unconscious—when he came to he was in Bellevue wrapped up in a straight jacket. As his monologue gains energy & confidence to the point of a kind of fanatical megalomania where he starts screaming to the room at large "I mean I was completely fucked up! I was to the point of eating out of dumpsters! I was sleeping in alleys under black plastic & cardboard! Now look at this here! Look at this!" He suddenly stands & starts pulling wads of money out of his pockets—$20 bills wrapped in rubber bands. He's now throwing the money into the room. "Look at this! This is me now! I got money! I got all this money now! Look here!" Everyone just sits there flabbergasted. The clinician twitches & snaps his clip board on his knee, trying to act calm & in control of the situation. The crackhead raves on as Jennifer has now taken to fiddling with her silver scarf (to match her tennis shoes) & a meth-head from the Dominican Republic has fallen asleep with his head lolling backwards, his mouth wide open & snoring loudly. Once the raving Crackhead has gathered up all his bills from the floor, stuffed them back in his pockets & sat back down, a forty-something year old white guy who looks like he could have been a college football star but now is overweight in baggy pants & a huge Carhartt jacket begins an unbelievable tale of woe. Unbelievable, in the sense of how could this stuff have happened to any living being? His own mother had him sent to prison, accusing him of assault & violent alcohol abuse. Meanwhile, Jennifer the Junkie is now chewing on her silver scarf & the black woman next to her starts weeping because the Court has taken away her 4 year old son & she can't stop using Cocaine & Pot long enough to reclaim him. This goes on for one hour then a 5 minute break & I go into an 'Anger Management' Group where we talk about the Niagara Falls metaphor for another hour. The Niagara Falls metaphor goes like this: the emotions are the river. You are in a boat with one paddle. As you see the river gaining momentum & ultimately crashing over the falls (i.e. your gathering anger) are you going to start paddling desperately for the shore or will you just give in & let the boat go over the precipice. This brings in the concept of choice versus no choice. Bear in mind some of the folks in these groups are so violent they've actually done time in prison for it. One claims to have taken a pot-shot at his father at the age of six. Exaggeration runs rampant. Anyway, I'm done with all that & never again will I be caught drunk behind the wheel of a moving vehicle.

I certainly hope you're able to have some peace with this horrible turn of events. John, I think about you and your predicament all the time & hope you come to terms with it in a way that allows you to go on to something brand new. Maybe, 19 year old pussy isn't that bad an idea come to think of it.

Hope to hear from you soon.

Yr everlasting Pal
Sam

February 27, 2010

[TYPED]

Sam

 I want to thank you for calling after Scarlett died, for the long crazy letter
about the alcohol counseling group, which was fantastic and for even agree-
ing to fly across the country to meet me. Yr a good lad—actually the best
friend I ever had though I've always thought of you more as a brother. Looking back, you and Scarlett were the two biggest influences on my life. (She
was the good one.) I love the way we have our favorite authors who have
influenced us the most and to whom we keep going back—you with your
Beckett and me with my Kerouac, which must say something about us but
I'm not sure what. [. . .]

 I hope this Scarlett material doesn't seem too excessive to you but here
are a few pages from what I've put together so far. Of course it's only natural
to want to keep her memory alive but it's more than that. I want to see how
close I can come to show how unique and sweet she was. It's a tribute. Here
was a woman who loved me unconditionally. First my mother adopts me
and loves me unconditionally. Then I grow up and meet Scarlett who loves
me unconditionally, without condition, that is, I don't have to behave in any
particular way. I'm sure any other woman I'd meet would be eventually jealous or critical or demanding or disapproving. Scarlett hitched her wagon to
my star, such as it was, and would have gone down the toughest road with
me, would have lived in a car, slept on the floor—it wouldn't have mattered to
her as long as we were together. That's some pretty good luck for me seeing
that she was smarter and hipper and generally more present than I was. She
had an "old soul" someone once pointed out. The great thing is I told her
how much I loved her every day of our 43 years together and tried to demon-
strate it too. In fact demonstrating it became a way of life; a lipstick, a bar of
milk chocolate, a pair of slippers, 12 science fiction books, a jar of imported
English marmalade, a carton of assorted pens and little kisses all over her
face. That's what made her happy. So nothing was left undone. And if all
that's not enough her last words were "I love you." I wonder what mine will
be. I'd love my last words to be "I love you," but what if I'm found dying in
the gutter by a fat, drunken leper? [. . .]

This night the winds are blowing. But later they will have stopped, unless there's something someone's not telling. I'm in pretty good spirits most of the time but very strange to think that Scarlett's been burnt down to nothing but ashes and bones. [. . .]

John

July 1, 2010

[HANDWRITTEN]

Dear John—

First day of July—Woke up this morning early & had absolutely no idea where I was. I waited for the usual panic to set in but it didn't come. I stared at the patterns of white & dark on the ceiling trying to figure out what motel it might be—what country I was in. It seemed like it could be Mexico but it didn't sound like Mexico outside—the birds—the wind. I stared at the walls & finally it came to me—I was back in Kentucky. I love this place but it's never felt exactly like home. I don't exactly know what 'home' would feel like. Like you, I suppose, although you seem to have created a little home for yourself down there. [. . .]

Again, I'm in between things—projects—writing—women—travel. I want to get a new dog but I don't know what kind. How 'bout an Airedale? Too British maybe. I'm still affected by images—how might I appear to others from the outside—like—me, with an Airedale? What would people think? Paul Bowles had an Airedale—but he was gay, wasn't he? Would people think I was gay with an Airedale? They might. There he is again with that Airedale. Well, you know, he went off & started living all by himself & first thing you know he wound up with an Airedale. You know what that means don't you? I like them because they don't shed. That's what they all say.

Patti went off to Europe on tour with her band—Italy, Germany, France etc . . . She left me a message at the Airport saying she'd call me when she reached Berlin. She won't. She always says she'll call but she won't. <— (Eeyore)

Went to the ceremony they had in Texas for my friend Preston, who died of pancreatic cancer—just like Bill Hart died.[1] Lots of people in straw cowboy hats out in the blazing sun—even the preacher wore a straw hat—it was so hot. When the women stood up at the end of it, sweat poured down their legs & the backs of their dresses were so wet it looked like they'd all gone swimming. Afterward, everyone stood around eating BarBQ sandwiches. I drove on to Nashville 750 miles straight from Ft. Worth—felt like 400. Looks like I'll be working on that t.v. thing come fall in Nashville. I need a job. [. . .]

Yr amigo
Sam

1. Preston Carter, Jr., a member of the Texas Horse Racing Hall of Fame, owned a cutting horse ranch in Weatherford, Texas.

July 13, 2010

[TYPED]

Sam

[. . .] What ever happened with you and Jessica? How did you go from such extreme passion to this? You may not want to talk about it and it's none of my business but there must have been something under the passion when it had burned away. Did one of you change? With my first wife Jane it lasted four years and what happened was we took LSD together and she realized she didn't want to be married. She wanted to move back with her mother and get her Masters degree in psychology etc. and with me she could see we were just going to be bumming around with no ambition and she'd end up with a failure. It was all very straight forward. She simply wanted a different kind of life. But we remained friends. Then when I met Scarlett, she was everything I ever dreamed of and she wanted the same kind of life I wanted. People grow apart sometimes but if they fight as well it makes things difficult. I always assumed you two wanted different things the way Jane and I wanted different things.

I loved your musings about getting an Airedale and the image it might create. I had an Airedale when I was in high school. The first time I remember being aware of your image-concern was when you assured a visitor (up in Nova Scotia) that Nana wasn't your dog—just some weird little animal belonging to friends of yours. It's amazing that that's stayed in my mind all these years. It was the first time I realized a person might identify with the breed dog he owned. Of course now I see it everywhere—guys buying Dobermans or Pit bulls for that reason.

Gad! I started this letter too late and now I have to feed the dogs and rush off to work. So I'll end here.

John

July 16, 2010

John,

[. . .] It occurred to me yesterday, strolling around my 150 acres here—it just came to me, you know how it goes—that I believe it's true that all great writing has come out of solitude & terrible suffering. Look at: Mr. Beckett, Joyce, Kafka, Goethe, Melville, Genet, Rimbaud, Villon, O'Neill, Flannery O'Connor, Emily Dickinson, Juan Rulfo, Pavese, Machado, Cervantes, Dante, etc. Loners & sufferers all. Not to put myself in the same category at all but, by way of comparison; I know that my best stuff, whether it be plays, stories, screenplays, whatever—has come out of those same two basic ingredients: solitude & suffering. But then I asked myself (myself asking myself)—if I had a choice to continue on that track (not that we do have a choice—it's the old magic-fairy thing again offering you two alternatives) or, on the other hand, to spend the rest of my life in great happiness with a young woman who delights in my company & I in hers—would I forfeit the art & the agony? the answer is yes!!! Yes, yes, yes!!!!

Which brings me to another association I had yesterday about the great little film you made back in the 70's with Scarlett, based on a Joyce piece in which that fabulous soliloquy ends with Molly rising into ecstatic orgasm with Yes! Yes! Yes! Where is that film? You must have it tucked away somewhere in yr. archives. I think it was made in Super 8. That's something that should definitely be preserved, don't you think?

Anyway, here's to great courage in aloneness & the promise of eternal love—at the same time. Why not?

Yr Amigo
Sam

July 26, 2010

John,

Finally got my Airedale, so far don't feel the slightest inclination toward gayness but who knows—life is full of surprises. She's a beautiful dog & I wanted to call her 'Gracie' after my great aunt who ½ way raised me thru elementary school. She was my mother's mother's sister—from Wales & the widow of a man from Liverpool named Charlie Upton who became a lumber baron in So. California. He died & left her with a bunch of money & a big Chrysler sedan with plaid upholstery & those fancy ropes you could hang onto, attached to the back of the front seats. Aunt Gracie would drive me out to the Mojave desert in that car for the Date Festival where everyone dressed up like Arabs & rode camels down the main street. I must've been 5 or so—in fact that picture of me riding the dead bucking horse is from one of those trips so it was probably Aunt Grace who took the photos.[1] Anyway, 'Gracie' is what I wanted to call this dog but she's 3 years old (I didn't want to go thru the puppy housebreaking routine) & the guy who owned her called her 'Chili' for 3 years so she doesn't even recognize the sound 'Gracie' as having anything to do with her identity. It might be a long process or I might just give in to keeping 'Chili' although it doesn't really fit her. It's been a long time since I had a dog of my own & I love the feeling of having this kind of company. She's very smart & attentive but will cool down & sleep in the back of the car for miles on end. Very athletic & loves long walks thru the fields early in the morning. The things I've been missing!

[. . .] Anyway, I'll bring the letters I have & we'll find some time to work on them at Denny's—or wherever.[2] [. . .]

Mañana mas,
Sam

---

1. The photograph was used for the cover of *Day Out of Days*.
2. Letters for this book project.

July 28, 2010

[HANDWRITTEN]

Dear John,

   Sat down yesterday to go through the stack of letters I saved back of yours & at least put them in some kind of chronological order but wasn't ready for the deep sorrow in re-visiting our past lives. I guess it's that feeling of life just slipping through your fingers like so much sand—no regrets really—how else were we going to live it? I've never really felt very courageous about it all—in fact terror is closer to my real response toward the world & people in general. In the words of Master Beckett:

> *'world world world*
> *& the face grave*
> *cloud against the evening'*[1]

To find oneself alone at this stage of life is very interesting & a little disturbing. [. . .]

Yr amigo,
Sam

---

1. From Beckett's poem "Enueg II."

July 29, 2010

[HANDWRITTEN ON JACK KEROUAC POSTCARD]

John—

Now, it's turned into some crazy-ass treasure hunt—letters turning up everywhere old luggage, mildewed envelopes—folded up in books, closets, laundry rooms—incredible. Water-stained pictures—old crumbling, cardboard boxes, rusty paper clips. Ancient artifacts. Life just churning away relentlessly. Moving pictures of the Dead when they were Living—my uncles, aunts, My Mother, friends—River Phoenix who O.D.'d at Johnny Depp's club in L.A.—Tim who died of lung cancer, Richard Harris who died from alcohol.[1] I wonder what we'll die of. Here's to the book of letters. It may be our last HURRAH!

Sam

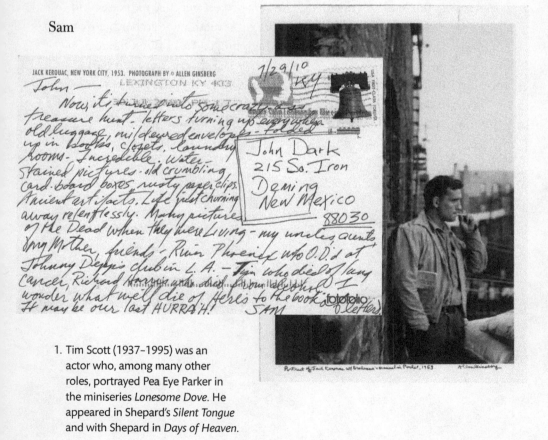

JACK KEROUAC, NEW YORK CITY, 1953. PHOTOGRAPH BY © ALLEN GINSBERG

1. Tim Scott (1937–1995) was an actor who, among many other roles, portrayed Pea Eye Parker in the miniseries *Lonesome Dove*. He appeared in Shepard's *Silent Tongue* and with Shepard in *Days of Heaven*.

July 30, 2010

Sam

Ah yes, we shall dazzle them at Denny's. I love that you have these definite ideas about almost everything—food, money, women, prose. I wish I had definite ideas. We'll go in style. We'd like a phone brought to the table and see that we're not disturbed. (These days a phone isn't even a mark of distinction. Every asshole has a phone.) We'll work on the North side by the light of the highway that runs from Hollywood to Jacksonville.

And in the first place, think of the value something like, this will be to all yr kids. A final message from the grave which should throw everyone into a tailspin.

Anyway I'm glad you decided to do this project because in the second place it's clear that you and I should work on something together before one of us croaks, kicks the bucket, takes the big plunge. And I think the reason we never did it before is because I was always less than inspired, mired in peanutbutter, generally disinterested, restless and not at all serious when we could have been out in the street on pogo sticks or seeing if our bikes would roll all the way from the Book Depot to the house without using the pedals. [. . .]

John

August 6, 2010

[TYPED]

Sam

[. . .] It's impossible now to write a letter without knowing that someone I don't know will be reading it. I want to say "Turn around, I want to tell Sam something." It's like when we were young men living in the house in Mill Valley and we used to lock Jesse (now 40) out of the basement room where we were talking about women, smoking cigars and getting stoned. Remember how he'd bang on the door? "Hey, can I come in? What are you doing in there?" He must have been about seven years old.

SAM: Go away.
JESSE: Whaddya doing in there?
SAM: None of your business.
JESSE: Can I come in?
JOHN: You can come in in a minute.
JESSE: What are you doing?
JOHN: Wrapping presents.
SAM: That's right. And if you want to get one you'll stop banging on
       that door.

What's weird is first we're writing letters and then (and we never could have imagined such a thing) we're writing letters about writing letters. The University wants letters? They've finally smartened up down there. Well, I'll give them letters they won't forget. There will be sleepless nights, I assure you. I may write a letter to you about writing a film treatment about writing letters. [. . .]

Not only is the Universe expanding but all our friends are drifting further away as though with the years the gravity between us is weakening or the velocity of their lives is increasing. Now, with Scarlett gone it becomes easier for me to see if I actually have a life without anyone applauding it. [. . .]

yr pal
John

August 12, 2010

[HANDWRITTEN]

Sam

It's Scarlett's birthday today (tomorrow)—the first birthday in 43 years we haven't celebrated together—so here I am in Denny's having a hot fudge sundae in her honor. Boy, would she be pissed not to be here. [. . .]

yr pal
John

August 15, 2010

Dear John,

[. . .] Working on another book but can't quite get the shape of it—always a problem. I'd love to hook onto a form for this—the form out front rather than trying to shuffle thru tons of notebooks—collaging away as I usually do. I know the tone I want though—Women & Death—I even thought of 'Death & the Bitches' as a title but sounds maybe too Miles Davis. Talk about Miles—I was listening to that landmark album he did in '59 or '60—*Kind of Blue* with Cannonball Adderly & it just blew me back into the 60's again. That incredible muted trumpet moaning & probing through space—same with *Sketches of Spain*—now both of those albums are icons of the time, but back then I remember listening to them as partners in some kind of lonely emotional wandering I was going on.

Re-reading Cabeza de Vaca's account of his treks thru Florida into the Southwest before any Europeans had ever encountered the continent. Incredible descriptions of linking arms with his men to keep from getting blown away in a hurricane. Also reading *Dirt Music* by Tim Winton—very strong Aussie writer—great language guy—kind of crashing around like Harry Crews but maybe more focused.

Took Gracie for a walk in the back fields & she jumped a skunk. Couldn't call her off the thing so now, of course, she stinks & I'll have to keep her in the barn a few days. Sun has come up gigantic red & fierce. Another August scorched—very little rain but the dew is thick this morning. Skunks like to lay around in the long grass soaking up the moisture.

8/16

Next morning—6 a.m.—walked early while it's still cool. Beautiful & still. Mares grazing thru the fog. Geese going over. Just a hint of Fall in the air. I don't know where it comes from—that slight sense of a season turning—surprisingly makes me miss the North country & that crisp cold snap in the air. Gracie still slightly skunky but overjoyed to be out of her kennel & plunging thru the long grass. She sticks right close at my knee but when we hit the big fields out back she's gone hunting. I love to see that in a dog where suddenly it's all about the scent, head low to the ground & the human contact can take a hike. She loves hunting field mice & does that high leap & pounce thru the grass like a fox or coyote.

Feel good this morning—more back to myself—no thoughts about women—no yearning anyway. Hope everything's good with you & that God is in his kitchen.

Adios for now,
Sam

August 20, 2010

[TYPED]

Sam

[. . .] Thanks for yr last letter (which you probably don't remember) about the peaceful life down there on yr ol' Kentucky home. So let me get this straight. There we were in New York sitting on a stoop in our twenties and then you went off to England and I went off to Yucatan and we both had wives and then there we were in California and now here we are without wives with you in Kentucky and me in New Mexico. how did all that happen? [. . .]

I'm looking forward to both yr visits, yours and Jesse and Maura, which is what you'll be experiencing too. You and Jesse and Maura in New Mexico and you and me in New Mexico. Isn't it odd we should be coming together to work on a project which by its nature took 40 years to materialize and just at that moment, Jesse should appear as he did when he was a kid wondering what we were doing in the basement, and we both get to see him but in separate places but both in New Mexico where Mathew and yr Dad died? Well, that's what I'll be experiencing too. And then it'll be over. Never to come again for any of us at this time, at this age, in this place. I find that exhilarating, like brassily trying to grab the merry-go-ring. There's so much material to dig. We in fact have become The Two Prospectors.

this may be optimistic but
more later
John

August 21, 2010—Kentucky.

[HANDWRITTEN]

Dear John—

Yes—I indeed found the bound book of conversations deep in the dark vaults of moldy old cardboard boxes. [. . .] Photo of us on the porch in Nova Scotia in another attitude of conversation when we were much younger & thought we'd never die or if we thought we might, it was so far off in the future it was merely some abstract idea that we could negotiate our way out of thru correct understanding of Zen books or Gurdjieff philosophy or the Diamond Sutra or something. Now—here it is upon us with all its ghastly talons out & drooling at the mouth; the list of the dead grows deeper & deeper: Jim Gammon, Preston Carter, Sally Sommers, Scarlett, Bill Hart, Dennis Hopper, etc.—Oblivion, Oblivion, Oblivion—[1]

Just returned from Lexington this morning in a misty rain [. . .] As things developed thru the night of more & more liquor consumed the ex-E.R. doctor surreptitiously calls me aside in a corner of the porch & in hushed tones offers to sell me quantities of Viagra at ½ price. I tell him my problem has never been getting hard—it's not knowing when I've had enough.

So this morning—rushing back in the rain to the farm to let my poor dog out—who's been just sitting in the barn/kennel for more than 12 hours now. She's very glad to see me & get her breakfast. We go for a long walk in the tall wet grass after my cup of Mexican coffee & her kibble. She's a great dog the way she sticks right with me until we get out into the wilder part of the farm & she suddenly takes off like a rocket for the underbrush, nose to the ground, on the trail of something furry that humans can't smell.

Just a touch of fall in the days now—clear skies & an afternoon breeze. Funny how we crave the next season—just like we look forward to a future we can't see. [. . .]

Yr cohort,
Sam

1. James Gammon (1940–2010), a noted American character actor, appeared in Shepard's *Buried Child* and *The Late Henry Moss*. He is best known for his role as the manager Lou Brown in the film *Major League*. Sally Sommers was a member of Scarlett and O-Lan's Keystone Workshop, a theatre group.

August 23, 2010

John—

[. . .] Some scarey part of me actually believes it's possible to burn bridges & start completely new. My favorite line of Bertolt Brecht: "A man can make a fresh start with his last breath."[1] Maybe it's some hang-over impulse from my Puritan Father's heritage—this American notion that you just leave a place when you're not welcome & start from scratch. Create a whole new country & damn the torpedoes!—damn the Indians!—Damn the buffalo!—damn the environment! Fuck 'em all—God says we're entitled to this place!!

Yesterday, I'm in the barn & I get a call from my old friend Bob M. who's just finished his last round of chemo—for some Leukemia condition he's got.[2] This is where you walk into a room with flowered wall paper & recliner chairs in a semi-circle, magazines, t.v. etc. & they hook you up to a 5 hour drip of intravenous poison that swims thru yr whole blood & nervous system. Similar, I suppose, to what Scarlett went thru with her blood procedure dialysis—Ghastly stuff. Bob was raised farming & exposed to chemicals & pesticides his whole life—breathing fly spray for horses that's misted into all the stalls thru out the summer. When you walk into one of these barns that's been rigged with fly spray, you feel it immediately in yr chest, eyes, nose, mouth—you are being drenched in poison! What's going on with human beings where they don't realize this stuff is killing us? Anyway, Bob is on his way out & he knows it—knows his days are numbered. But he still likes to get out on a horse now & then & just ride thru the woods with another guy, Spaulding, who has a sorrel mule that can out-trot any horse. So I load up my little mare & haul over to Paris, Ky.—to meet them. Beautiful day—2500 acre farm—rolling hills—wild turkey—bass boats on the river. My cell phone goes off while I'm driving—forgot to turn it off—I answer & it's Hannah in Ireland. She's just finished the thesis at the University in Galway & wants to send me a copy. I have a scholar for a daughter. She's working on her doctorate in Irish Studies—wants to

1. A translation of lines from Brecht's "Alles Wandelt Sich" ("Everything Changes"): "Everything changes. You can make / A fresh start with your final breath."
2. Bob M. not identified by Shepard.

teach college. She'll probably return to Minnesota & settle in there. She loves the mid-West & being close to her Mom. As our trail-ride goes on into the afternoon, it gets very hot & Bob starts to suffer some. His face is bright red & dripping so we suggest he dismount with a bottle of water & wait under a shade tree while we take his horse back to the barn—then I'll come get him with my truck. On the ride back to his farm he's much better—cooled down some but he keeps staring out the window at the bucolic countryside. He speaks without turning to me: "Sam, I just can't believe it—all those years I was strong as an ox. Never sick a day in my life & now I can't hardly mount up. I never used to even think about it back then. I just lived, that's all. I just lived." He snorts a little at the window glass in disgust at his own fate.

Up at 6 a.m. next morning—pitch black—dog is growling & prowling around clicking her nails on the pine floor. Something's outside so I let her out into the dark—probably Raccoons eating her leftover dog food. I try to go back to bed but can't sleep. Think about maybe going down to Nashville for a few days. [. . .] Don't know what I'll do. Get up again & make coffee. Study Bolaño—Cabeza de Vaca—*The Masks of God*[3]—watch the mind leap around making all its wild & wooly assumptions.

Mas tarde,
Sam

3. Joseph Campbell's four-volume
   work on world myth and religion.

August 25, 2010

Dear John,

One thing I realize I love about the 'letter' as a form is that it's conversation;—always available. You can just sit down any old morning & have a conversation whether the person's there or not. You can talk about anything & you don't have to wait politely for the other person to finish the train of thought. You can have long gaps between passages—days can go by & you might return & pick it up again. And the great difference in all other forms of writing is that it is dependent to a large extent on the other person. It's not just a solo act. You're writing in response to or in relationship to someone else—over time. I think that's the key—over time. We're very lucky, I figure, to have continued the desire to talk to each other by mail for something like 40 years. But then again, what else were we going to do? It is probably the strongest through-line I've maintained in this life. Everything else seems to be broken—except, of course, my other writing which has been with me constantly since about 1963. I'll never forget the elation of finishing my first one-act play. I felt I'd really made something for the first time. Like the way you make a chair or a tale. Something was in the world now that hadn't been there before.

I think I'd like to return now to a play—after all this plunging into short fiction. I've started something called: 'Man Kills Every Dog in Town'—based on a headline in a small-town Texas newspaper I'd read years ago. It's the kind of situation, characters, predicament that could ramble all over the place—scenes, music etc.—just turn it loose on itself & see what happens. Nowadays it's more a question of just sitting down daily & spending time at the typewriter. [...]

Another beautiful morning here. Dew on the pasture. Horses grazing. It's a 'Kentucky Bluegrass' postcard. Just a hint of fall in the air, the humidity has lifted & it's like somebody just pulled a big heavy blanket off yr shoulders.

Hope this finds you in fine fettle or fettil or whatever it is.

Yr Amigo,
Sam

August 26, 2010

Sam

[. . .] I was like you—used to be I couldn't wait to get out of the house. My old man was always in the other room and the livingroom furniture was from another century, the couch had tassels and there were ash trays and candy dishes all over the place. There was a fireplace with phony logs and a red light behind them. There was a swinging door between the kitchen and the diningroom. My mother rang a silver dinner bell to call the maid.

I couldn't wait to see American towns from the front seat of a car at four in the morning and descend into a valley of lights. Even with various drives across the U.S. that "dream" was never fully realized until I traveled with Sharon; fifty joints, a bottle of Vodka between my knees and a blonde in boots riding shotgun.

I wanted to sleep with my head on a duffel bag in the waiting room of Western depots. I wanted to wander down small town streets like Deming in the evening and watch people digging into their Turkey dinners. These days I just want to fry up some beans and sit in the greenhouse reading about the Nile.

yr pal
John

Postmarked August 27, 2010.

Sam

[. . .] We're so different sometimes I realize that on some level I don't know you at all. What's it like to always be wanting to go away, to actually want to go fishing and gambling and riding and roping and reading in public and writing insane plays and playing polo and drinking in bars and chasing loose women? And what do you make of a guy who never wants to leave his house, wants to be left alone with his dogs and spends all his time laying in his bathtub? That's why I think this will be a great book if we can get it together. If there is a book. And if we actually can get it together.

I go by many names but my friends call me

Yan Chim Kee

September 10, 2010—Kentucky

[HANDWRITTEN]

John—

   Suddenly it's Fall. Another exquisite morning—Waking up now around 5 a.m.—sun just cracking through trees—coffee—feed the dog—two baby fox go scurrying across the hill pasture toward the pond—saw their Daddy a few days ago on the driveway—big bushy tail—just staring at me—Deer on the banks of the pond—cattle down below—Feed my mares carrots—Train rolling down the Midway. I think constantly of my kids now. Haven't seen the young ones for 6 months. That's a long time. Maybe by Thanksgiving— that's when Hannah graduates from Galway. Of course, Jessica will be there too—haven't seen her since March 5. In 4 days I'll be back on the road head- ing toward Santa Fe [. . .] —remember breakfast there with Jessie & Shura back in early eighties when Shura was just a baby. Aah, nostalgia & granola! Lots of water under the bridge. It will be good to get back together with Jesse & Maura. I love them—the way they are together. I envy them—their sweet- ness—the joy they get from each other. [. . .]

Mas tarde,
Sam

January 27, 2011

[TYPED]

[. . .] Here at home Scarlett's pictures are everywhere. You can't imagine how much I miss talking to her and hugging her and bringing her gifts. She was sharp as a tack. Remember the way she was at the hospital with you in New York. I should be bringing burnt offerings as a sign of my gratitude. You realize that if I hadn't met her—none of this would have happened.

[. . .] We have a nice tempo going you and I even after all these years. I don't talk to many intelligent people so it's a pleasure to hang out and talk with you and even the most disturbing things seem slightly funny. I always feel we're confiding instead of discussing. However emotionally, you're going to need a complete overhaul. Of course I'm not one to talk but I would have to say that although our positions have exchanged places many times over the past years, this time you are definitely the crazy one. I'll be talking to you soon.

yr pal
John

January 30, 2011

[HANDWRITTEN ON SANTA FE INSTITUTE STATIONERY]¹

Dear John—

[. . .] Having the weirdest dreams I've ever had lately—total strangers showing up—lots of murder & intrigue. This morning two men in a truck with caged chickens in the back come to my door & place small white linen bags on my shoulders filled with some sort of powder or dust—as though measuring my weight or worth or something—some preparation of death. And then one of the men throws himself down in the dirt right in front of me & starts rolling around & agonizing as though suddenly seized by epilepsy. He may be dying, I don't know. I feel no panic or urgency to help him. I'm just a witness. Don't know quite what to make of it all.

Been poring thru the letters one by one; reading them carefully— [. . .] Many impressions & emotions along the way. [. . .] had to stop when I became overwhelmed with grief about the broken relationship aspect of much of it. No way of getting around it. Then the Dylan song came up— "Everything Is Broken"—maybe we'll use it in the film.[2]

Sounds like you're well ensconced in your lair & whirling away. Very difficult for me now to try returning to my other work (the plays) when the letters seem to have a hold on me.

I'm off to Kentucky Wed. then up to see my kids for a bit. I'll keep in touch. Meanwhile there's plenty on our plates. For that we must be grateful!

Regards &
best wishes,
Sam

---

1. In 2010, Shepard was named a Miller Scholar at the Santa Fe Institute, a multidisciplinary research community of scholars.

2. A documentary film titled *Shepard and Dark* (2012) about Sam and Johnny's relationship and the making of this book, directed by Treva Wurmfeld.

John —

    Here are all these letters of your... I've just realized that I have co... the end of this obsession of long ... of it. I'm no longer interested in po... the past — re-making the past — go... the past — reminiscing about the pa... visiting the past. I need to move o... my stuff & leave this behind. It may ... emotional territory I'm going t... has prompted this — in the same ... ...aring Jessica. But in any case ... phase of things is over & done wi... ...t. Finished.

    As far as I'm concerned you can con... my way you want. ~~you can write e... letters of, of course, all your letters~~. ...range them in any order — with ot... ~~you can throw in additional dialogue~~... ...one — be my guest. Take it away, Johnny, ... luck!

                   Sam

March 18, 2011

John

Here are all the letters of yours back. I've just realized that I have come to the end of this obsession & long to be free of it. I'm no longer interested in poring over the past—re-making the past—goofing on the past—reminiscing about the past or re-writing the past. I need to move on to my own stuff & leave this behind. It may be some emotional territory I'm going thru that has prompted this—in the same way as leaving Jessica but in any case this whole phase of things is over & done with, for me. Finished.

As far as I'm concerned you can continue in any way you want. You can arrange them in any order—with or without dates—I don't care—be my guest. Take it away, Johnny & good luck!

Sam

List of Illustrations

Index

See also Characters, pages 1–2, and illustrations list, pages 372–373. Page numbers in *italics* indicate photos.

Walken, Christopher, 111n1

Walker Payne (dir. Williams), 274n1

Walter Benjamin at the Dairy Queen (Mc-
Murtry), 207, 210n2

Warchus, Matthew, 205n1

Warden, Jack, 112

The War in Heaven (Shepard), 129n1

Waterloo, Iowa, 85–89

Waterston, Sam, 111n1

Watt (Beckett), 323

Waugh, Ric Roman, 294n1

Wayne, John, 189, 267

Webb, William Prescott, 130

Weber, Bruce, x, 269

"Webster," 161

Weld, Tuesday, 79

Wenders, Wim, 79, 113, 241, 265, 271

West Village, New York, 266, 270

When the World Was Green (Shepard),
129n1

White, Susanna Fuller, 276–277

Whitefish, Montana, 212

The Wild Bunch (Peckinpah), 267

Wild Child (Truffaut), 47–48

Wilder, Gene, 54

Williams, Matt, 274n1

Williams, Tennessee, 270

Winchester, Simon, 206n2

Wings of Desire (Winders), 113

Winter Project (Allen), 111n1

Winton, Tim, 355

Wire to Wire (Holmes), 157

Wisconsin, 137n2, 140, 143–144,
178–179, 247

Wittliff, Bill, 33, 88n3

Wood, Phil, 102

"The Work," x–xi, 115, 195; Dark on, 37,
164, 308; Dark's first encounter with,
245, 296; Dark's interest in waning, 42,
115, 138, 195; and death of Lord Pentland, 109–110; Mary and, 101–102,
107; position of women in, 5; Shepard
compared to aging, 156; Shepard early
reactions to, 5; Shepard on anxiety and,
171; Shepard on attaining emptiness,
271; Shepard on cycles of, 96–97;
Shepard on guilt and tension, 80;
Shepard on life inside, 69, 87; Shepard
on "not thinking" of, 192; Shepard's
memory of, 231, 245, 305–306, 318

Wrenshall, Minnesota, 67, 111

Wurlizter, Rudy, 290

Wurmfeld, Treva, 367n2

Wyoming, 168–170

Yates, Reena, 227

Yeats, W. B., 201, 285

Yucatan, Mexico, 143, 219, 325, 357

Zabriskie Point (Antonioni), x

Zen Mind (Suzuki), 137n1

Printed in the USA
CPSIA information can be obtained
at www.ICGtesting.com
LVHW041409080923
756208LV00007B/77